Exceptional States

The publisher gratefully acknowledges the generous support of the Sue Tsao Endowment Fund in Chinese Studies of the University of California Press Foundation.

Exceptional States

CHINESE IMMIGRANTS AND TAIWANESE
SOVEREIGNTY

Sara L. Friedman

UNIVERSITY OF CALIFORNIA PRESS

University of California Press, one of the most distinguished university presses in the United States, enriches lives around the world by advancing scholarship in the humanities, social sciences, and natural sciences. Its activities are supported by the UC Press Foundation and by philanthropic contributions from individuals and institutions. For more information, visit www.ucpress.edu.

University of California Press
Oakland, California

Library of Congress Cataloging-in-Publication Data

Friedman, Sara, author.
  Exceptional states : Chinese immigrants and Taiwanese sovereignty / Sara L. Friedman.—1st edition.
     pages cm
  Includes bibliographical references and index.
  ISBN 978-0-520-28622-1 (cloth)—ISBN 978-0-520-28623-8 (pbk.r)—ISBN 978-0-520-96156-2 (e-book)
    1. Women immigrants—Taiwan—Social conditions.   2. Chinese—Taiwan—Social conditions.   3. Foreign spouses—Taiwan—Social conditions.   4. Intercountry marriage—Political aspects—Taiwan.
  5. Self-determination, National—Taiwan.   6. Citizenship—Taiwan.
  7. Taiwan—Foreign relations—China.   8. China—Foreign relations—Taiwan.   I. Title.
  HQ1777.F75   2015
  362.83′98120951249—dc23
                                                            2015019120

24   23   22   21   20   19   18   17   16   15
10   9   8   7   6   5   4   3   2   1

for Maddie

CONTENTS

List of Illustrations ix

Preface xi

Acknowledgments xvii

Note on Romanization and Naming xxiii

Introduction: Sovereignty Effects 1

PART ONE
BORDER CROSSINGS

1 · Documenting Sovereignty 27

2 · Real or Sham? Evaluating Marital Authenticity 51

PART TWO
IMMIGRATION REGIMES

3 · Exceptional Legal Subjects 81

4 · Risky Encounters 112

PART THREE
BELONGING

5 · Gender Talk 143

6 · Home and Belonging 170

Epilogue 193
Notes 197
References 219
Index 231

ILLUSTRATIONS

MAPS

1. Map of Taiwan. *xxiv*
2. Map of Hong Kong, Macau, and Southern China. *40*

FIGURES

1. Storefront sign in Chiayi County, "Mainland Little Sister Communist Bandit Cakes." *8*
2. Registered marriages in Taiwan, 1998–2013. *9*
3. Documents issued to Chinese spouses. *39*
4. Protester carrying a sign with the slogan "Protect Basic Human Rights, Eradicate the Financial Requirement." *96*
5. "UN for Taiwan" banner promoting Taiwan's entry into the United Nations. *98*
6. "Bride" shackled by oppressive restrictions, aspiring to the goal of acquiring a national ID. *99*
7. Shackled "bride" strangled by an imperial official with riot police in the background. *101*
8. Main auditorium of Chiayi policy-education forum. *120*

PREFACE

This book has two origin stories. The first began in the late 1980s and early 1990s when I spent several years living on both sides of the Taiwan Strait, just as China and Taiwan were reestablishing relations after some four decades of military and ideological conflict. As a curious but somewhat naive recent college graduate, I quickly grew attuned to the differences and similarities between the two societies without fully understanding their roots or current significance. A few years later when I embarked on research as a graduate student in anthropology, I took up residence in a fishing village located directly across from Taiwan on China's Fujian coast. There I observed firsthand the various permutations of the burgeoning cross-Strait relationship: family members reunited after forty years of forced separation; renewed economic ties that provided local fishermen with jobs on Taiwanese fishing boats; village households gathered around television sets, avidly watching Taiwanese programs transmitted through improvised antennas; and the military exercises and missile tests conducted by China in 1996 with the goal of deterring Taiwanese voters from electing a president who had proclaimed Taiwan's status as an independent nation-state.

But what also piqued my interest at the time were the marriages that were beginning to take place between village women and Taiwanese men. I was puzzled at first when local women asked me to find Taiwanese husbands for them or their daughters, requests that I initially interpreted as playful fun. But I soon learned that two women from the village had recently married Taiwanese men, and I realized that the requests I faced might in fact be serious. As I listened to villagers debate the merits of cross-Strait marriage, I wondered what life was like for the women who had migrated to Taiwan through marriage. Did Taiwanese society feel comfortable to them or strange? How did they manage their new domestic relations despite what appeared to be regular returns to the village? Were they wedded to a future on one side of the Strait or the other?

Had I pursued research on cross-Strait marriage from this perspective, I would have focused on the everyday life of these couples: how they forged intimacy across borders, how they adjusted to what seemed at times to be substantial cultural and social differences, and how they understood their marital motivations and family needs. Interesting as these questions were (and they still interest me, as evidenced by their repeated appearances in this book), I soon discovered that cross-Strait marriages were significant in other ways that gradually came to occupy my attention. From my narrow vantage point in coastal Fujian during the years leading up to the new millennium, I had little inkling that cross-Strait marriage migration was poised to become a popular trend that would involve diverse segments of the populations on both sides of the Strait. Only when I returned to Taiwan in the summer of 2002 did I discover the heated debates then gripping the island about the status of Chinese spouses in these marriages and their rights as residents and future citizens of Taiwan. Those debates and the public protests that followed alerted me to the contested place of Chinese spouses in a newly democratic Taiwan engaged in a delicate balancing act between its own desires for sovereign recognition and China's refusal to countenance any challenges to its stance that Taiwan was merely a renegade province destined ultimately to return to the mainland's embrace.

Here, then, began the second origin story for this project. Based on the research I conducted in Fujian, I ultimately wrote a book (Friedman 2006) that asked how marriage and intimate life more generally became important elements of the Chinese state's efforts to build a new socialist society after 1949 and why so many of those initiatives only bore fruit once market reforms were introduced in the 1980s. I sought to understand how state power worked through the pathways of intimate life and, in turn, how intimate relationships and practices transformed state goals by deflecting them altogether or channeling them in new directions. Influenced by this interest in the intimate face of state power, I began to see cross-Strait marriages as key to Taiwan's larger sovereignty challenges. But initially I wondered how to take a topic such as sovereignty, which I understood as the domain of political science or perhaps history, and make it an anthropological problem. How could I study sovereignty struggles using the tools and insights of ethnography, with its careful attention to everyday life, self-presentation, and the insights gained through observing people and events as they unfold on the ground? I took inspiration from the small but insightful body of anthropological work on sovereignty by authors such as Aihwa Ong (2006), Yael Navaro-Yashin (2012), and Danilyn Rutherford (2012), but I found myself having to craft my own strategies for pursuing the topic.

Studying sovereignty ethnographically required an entry point from which I could both train a careful eye on the nuances and unpredictable outcomes of everyday encounters and bureaucratic practices and look broadly to policy-making debates, activist campaigns, and public maneuvering by government officials. I needed access to moments when immigrants crossed borders both literal and figurative, when state actors and immigrants engaged directly with one another, and when Taiwanese from various walks of life grappled with the vexed role of Chinese spouses in their midst. These challenges ultimately took me to places I could not have predicted when I embarked on this project.

Wives and husbands from China provided my initial entry point, and I began with the methods that one might expect in a study of cross-border marriage: interviews, often repeated over the years, with nearly 170 Chinese spouses and, in some cases, their family members, as well as regular participation in their daily lives. I socialized with them during classes, leisure outings, shared meals, and visits to their homes and mine. I returned with some to their natal communities in China, and I also met with cross-Strait couples that resided for the most part in China. This component of the research took place in sites familiar to many urban ethnographers: in homes, coffee shops, restaurants, parks, and shopping malls, on public transportation, or while standing on street corners or in elevators.

But I had to look elsewhere to understand how sovereignty was produced at the intersections of intimate life and state power. And here I turned to places and moments in which the impact of cross-Strait marriage migration on the future of the Taiwanese polity came to the fore, sometimes explicitly and other times as an unspoken backdrop. I accompanied Chinese spouses as they interacted with Taiwan's immigration regime—completing paperwork, moving across borders, seeking redress for a difficult situation, or challenging policy restrictions during public forums attended by local- and national-level civil servants. I sought out bureaucrats and officials across the immigration and policy-making bureaucracies and participated in meetings marked by varying degrees of formality, both one-on-one and those including immigration activists, NGO representatives, social workers, and Chinese spouses. This research took me to featureless government offices, cramped meeting rooms and ostentatious conference halls, immigrant detention centers, and service centers across the island where immigrants processed documents and applications. It also led me to Taiwan's physical borders, such as the control zone of the main international airport, where border officers interviewed Chinese spouses arriving for the first time and inspected their travel documents as they passed through immigration. Reflecting on these encounters, bureaucrats expressed deep investments in producing certain kinds of outcomes from their interactions with Chinese spouses, often musing aloud about how their exchanges offered potential opportunities for asserting Taiwan's fragile sovereignty claims. I gradually came to realize that these desired outcomes were part of a broader field of sovereignty effects generated by the mundane bureaucratic practices employed by state actors to manage this contested immigrant group.

To grasp the ever-changing tenor of public discourse about immigration and national identity, I looked for settings where Chinese spouses interacted with Taiwanese from different walks of life. Some of these involved everyday encounters with service workers, family members, or coworkers, but I quickly found that I gained greater insights from venues and interactions that featured conflict, agitation, and even organized struggle. Courtrooms, the offices of lawyers and social workers, meetings of feminist and immigrant rights groups, press conferences, public demonstrations—all of these offered valuable insights into both the kinds of intimate contestation faced by Chinese spouses (domestic violence, divorce, child custody battles) and the larger debates in which those contests were embedded: what kinds of families created the foundation for a robust Taiwanese nation, and how could that nation best assert Taiwan's sovereign standing in the world?

Certainly not all meetings or events proved to be useful, and as bureaucrats droned on about policy details or activists debated the fine points of different campaign strategies, I sometimes wondered whether I should be directing my energies elsewhere. But more often than not, there would be a particular moment, either in the midst of a meeting or as I wrote about it afterward, when I suddenly realized what was at stake in the details of policies and strategy decisions: how cross-Strait marriages were not merely part of but in many ways the linchpin of Taiwan's larger political struggles. To recognize and fully appreciate these moments, I had to understand the relevant laws and policies being debated and the consequences of different policy orientations, becoming in turn a kind of anthropologist-immigration expert. That hard work paid off in the end, for it taught me not only how the details fit together but also how they pointed to logics and potential ripple effects well beyond their immediate scope.

Through these various research strategies, I came to see the different kinds of encounters I observed and participated in as important venues where sovereignty was debated, asserted, and challenged. Some of these sovereignty claims seemed to resonate with interlocutors, while others fell on deaf ears. But instead of measuring relative success or failure, I sought to understand the substance of sovereignty struggles and the various forums and encounters with Chinese spouses through which sovereignty—both actual and aspirational—made its presence known. This was the path I had pictured only dimly when I began the project. This book is its culmination, although by no means the end to the story.

ACKNOWLEDGMENTS

The research for this book spanned a decade from 2003 to 2013 and incurred debts of gratitude to many different organizations and individuals. For their generous funding support for a year of research in Taiwan and China in 2007–8 and a three-month follow-up trip in summer 2009, I thank the National Science Foundation (BCS-0612679), the Wenner-Gren Foundation for Anthropological Research, and the Chiang Ching-kuo Foundation for International Scholarly Exchange. During that time, I was a visiting scholar at the Institute of Ethnology at Academia Sinica in Taiwan, and I am grateful to the Institute and its director Dr. Huang Shu-min for their invaluable assistance with my project. I also thank Indiana University and the Taiwan Economic and Cultural Affairs Office in Chicago for supporting shorter research trips in 2003, 2005, 2010, 2011, and 2013.

I have struggled over the years with how best to express my gratitude to the many Chinese and Taiwanese women and men who introduced me to their lives and families, generously took time out of busy schedules to speak with me about their experiences, and provided valuable insights into the transformative effects of marriage across contested political borders. Many have become good friends over the years, and on each return to Taiwan, I eagerly looked forward to catching up and learning how their lives had changed since my last visit. To protect their identities, I do not name them here, and in places I have changed or eliminated critical identifying information. Despite this anonymity, I hope they will recognize themselves in these pages and know that I took what they told me to heart.

Many Taiwanese officials and bureaucrats gave generously of their time to meet with me over the years, often on multiple occasions. They tolerated naive questions and patiently explained the detailed nuances of laws and policies.

Most important, they offered astute insights into how they managed their tasks and obligations as representatives of a not quite sovereign state, ever cognizant of their marginal status and the potential political significance of even the most mundane of acts. I am very grateful to the many individuals from the Mainland Affairs Council, the Ministry of the Interior, the National Immigration Agency, the Veterans Affairs Council, the Straits Exchange Foundation, and the Taipei City government who agreed to interview requests. Sensitive to the constraints they face speaking publicly about the issues discussed in this book, I have chosen not to use their real names except in the case of recognizable elected or appointed officials.

For their sustained interest in my research over the years, I would like to thank the various Taiwanese NGOs that generously included me in their activities, providing valuable research opportunities as well as introductions to immigrants and government officials. CARES (*Zhonghua Jiuzhu Zonghui*), a Taipei-based service organization, allowed me to observe courses and information sessions for Chinese spouses across Taiwan, to participate in meetings between immigrants and government representatives, to frequent their drop-in center on a regular basis, and to join in outings to sites outside the capital. I greatly appreciate the support of Ge Yu-chin, Zhang Zhengdong, Lin Ying-zhen, and Ding Yu-ching.

The leadership of the Cross-Strait Marriage Promotion Association (*Zhonghua Liang An Hunyin Xietiao Cujinhui*), especially Huang Jiangnan, agreed to requests for interviews and invited me to observe many of the planning sessions and street protests organized by or participated in by Association members. The various member representatives of the Alliance for Human Rights Legislation for Immigrants and Migrants (*Yimin Yizhu Renquan Xiufa Lianmeng*), a coalition of NGOs devoted to labor rights, women's rights, and im/migrant rights, kindly allowed me to join meetings, strategy sessions, listserv discussions, press conferences, and public demonstrations. Through my participation in the Alliance, I was able to observe negotiations between Alliance representatives and government officials where the Alliance pressed for specific policy revisions on matters related to foreign and Chinese spouses. I am especially indebted to Chen Hsueh-hui, Hsia Hsiao-chuan, Bruce Yuan-hao Liao, Tseng Chao-yuan, Wang Juanping, and Wu Jia-zhen. My work with the Alliance and the Marriage Promotion Association provided valuable introductions to Chinese spouses more inclined to agitate publicly for immigrant rights as well as those who had sought assistance from these organizations because of major crises they faced in Taiwan.

I have had the great fortune to benefit from the guidance and encouragement offered by many colleagues in Taiwan over the years. I express my deep thanks to Antonia Chao, Chen Chao-ju, Chen Yi, Chen Yichien, Lai Fang-yu, Lan Pei-chia, Liu Shao-hua, Teri Silvio, and Wang Hai-ling. My research assistants have collaborated with me on all facets of this project, always with good cheer and keen insight. I am grateful to Chang Fan-ju, Chen Hung-ying, Lin Jia-he, Wang Hsiang-ning, and Wang Zih-huei for their help with fieldwork in Taiwan. In Bloomington, Chang Yun, Li Ke, Wang Hsiang-ning, and Zheng Yanqiu ably collected news stories and transcribed interviews.

Friends new and old have made my years in Taiwan all the more meaningful and enjoyable. For their generosity and willingness to share both laughter and tears, I especially thank Chen Yichien, Fan Meiyuan, Lin Shu-yi, Teri Silvio, and Tiao Manpeng. The Chiang household became our home away from home, and I am immensely grateful to the entire family for welcoming us into their midst with such warmth and love. Tai Rui-lin and Li Yan filled our recent trips with wonderful fun and adventure.

I began writing this book while a residential fellow at the Woodrow Wilson International Center for Scholars in Washington, DC. I thank the Center for providing the luxury of time to think and write in a quiet space of my own, and I appreciate the valuable support and feedback I received from Denise Brennan, Shel Garon, Bob Hathaway, Pardis Mahdavi, Sonya Michel, and Karsten Paerregaard. Numerous individuals took time out of busy schedules to comment on chapters at various stages in the writing process. Purnima Bose, Lessie Jo Frazier, and Brenda Weber read multiple chapters (and multiple versions of those chapters!), and I am deeply grateful for their astute suggestions and unflagging encouragement. Denise Brennan, Julie Chu, Debbie Davis, Elizabeth Dunn, Shane Greene, Jennifer Hubbert, Tamara Loos, Pardis Mahdavi, Richa Nagar, Teri Silvio, and Li Zhang provided helpful comments and interventions at various points in the writing process. I owe a great debt to Ilana Gershon, who enjoys a rare gift of insight that enables her to see through the thicket of verbiage to expose the heart of an argument and to communicate it all with grace, clarity, and encouragement. This book is much improved as a result of her tireless feedback.

Over the years I have presented portions of the project to audiences at venues large and small. Although they are too numerous to name individually,

I would like to express my appreciation to the Departments of Anthropology at the University of Michigan, the University of Chicago, and Yale University for their engaging, probing questions. Participants in the "Rethinking Intimate Labor through Inter-Asian Migrations" workshop at the Rockefeller Bellagio Center, in the "Mobile Horizons" workshops sponsored by the Institute of East Asian Studies at University of California–Berkeley, and in the "Reproduction Migration" workshop of the Inter-Asian Connections II conference were valuable interlocutors as I developed my ideas. An early version of chapter 5 appeared as "Mobilizing Gender in Cross-Strait Marriages: Patrilineal Tensions, Care Work Expectations, and a Dependency Model of Marital Immigration," in *Mobile Horizons: Dynamics across the Taiwan Strait*, edited by Wen-hsin Yeh (Berkeley: Institute of East Asian Studies Publications Series, University of California, 2013). Portions of chapter 2 appeared in "Determining 'Truth' at the Border: Immigration Interviews, Chinese Marital Migrants, and Taiwan's Sovereignty Dilemmas" (*Citizenship Studies* 14 (2): 167–83, 2010); and parts of chapter 3 appeared in "Marital Immigration and Graduated Citizenship: Post-Naturalization Restrictions on Mainland Chinese Spouses in Taiwan" (*Pacific Affairs* 83 (1): 73–93, 2010).

Steve Stanzek's careful editorial eye has, I sincerely hope, made this book a more enjoyable read. Nicole Constable and the other reviewers for University of California Press offered excellent suggestions and criticisms that helped immensely as I revised the manuscript. My editor, Reed Malcolm, has been a pleasure to work with, and I greatly appreciated his calm counsel at a critical moment in the writing process. Stacy Eisenstark skillfully shepherded the book through to publication. Bill Nelson ably drew the maps and figure 2. I thank Chen Chieh-jen for graciously granting permission to use a still image from his video art production, *Empire's Borders I*, for the book cover.

In Bloomington, I have had the good fortune to enjoy the support of a wonderful circle of friends who have always been willing to listen to ideas, guide me back on track, and sustain me with excellent food and conversation. For all that and more, I thank Purnima Bose, Melanie Castillo-Cullather, Sam De Sollar, Kon Dierks, Melissa Dinverno, Michael Foster, Shane Greene, Stephanie Kane, Sarah Knott, Rebecca Lave, Alejandro Mejias-Lopez, Christy Ochoa, Radhika Parameswaran, Michiko Suzuki, and Brenda Weber. My "rise-n-shine" compatriots—Purnima Bose, Melanie Castillo-Cullather, Julie Irons, Lisa Kaufman, and Enrico Lunghi—have provided running companionship and a general sense of fun, keeping me sane, healthy, and happy during the many years it has taken to complete this project. My family members near and far regularly remind me of the communities that nurture us in ways both big and small. For their love and support, I am deeply indebted to Bill and Ellin Friedman, Ruth Drosdek, Betsy Judson, Jen Friedman, Janet Paskin, Stuart Friedman, Cindy Krieger, and, perhaps most important, all the munchkins of the next generation.

Above all, I am grateful to Gardner and Maddie for accompanying me on this journey and gamely exploring its many divergent paths. It is an understatement to say that the experience would have been much less meaningful without them. Indeed, it is hard to imagine how I would have come this far without their love and unfailing willingness to embark on new adventures without knowing exactly where they might take us.

NOTE ON ROMANIZATION AND NAMING

Throughout this book, I generally romanize Mandarin Chinese words, names, and expressions using the *pinyin* system. Where relevant, however, I adopt Taiwanese romanization conventions for place names and personal names. For instance, I refer to Jilong, Taiwan's northern port city, as Keelung in accordance with the city's official romanized spelling. I adopt personal naming practices in Taiwan that insert a hyphen between the two characters of a first name. Therefore, I refer to a Taiwanese individual as Wang Hai-ling, but a mainland Chinese as Wang Hailing. Because romanization practices in Taiwan do not consistently observe the standards of one particular system, I do my best to follow typical conventions when rendering Taiwanese names in Mandarin. For both Taiwanese and mainland Chinese, I follow local naming practices and put the surname first, followed by the personal name.

I employ pseudonyms throughout the book to protect individual identities. The only exceptions are cases where I refer to elected politicians (legislators, presidential candidates, and presidents) and identifiable appointed officials. In the few instances where the chosen romanization of a politician's real name might be confusing to a Mandarin speaker, I have added the *pinyin* version in parentheses.

Finally, when referring to Taiwanese bureaucrats and officials, I use the English titles "Mr." and "Ms." to reflect the more formal quality of our interactions. For all other Taiwanese and Chinese discussed in the book, I use some combination of their surname and personal name.

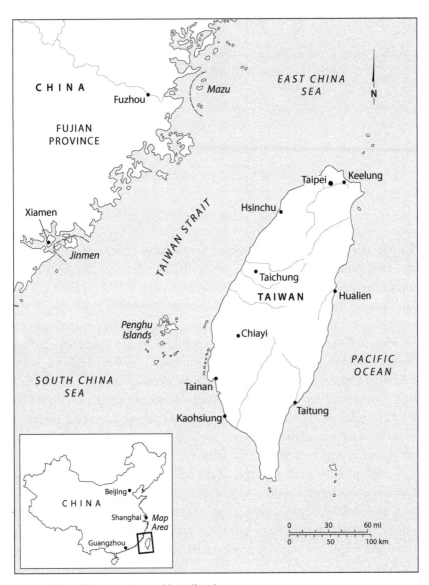

MAP I. Map of Taiwan. Prepared by Bill Nelson.

Introduction

EMPIRE'S BORDERS I

Black-and-white shots of security cameras emerge silently on the screen, the camera eyes trained ominously on the viewer. An empty institutional room then comes into view, its white walls interrupted only by a row of dark reflective windows. Subtitles at the bottom of the screen identify the space as the American Institute in Taiwan (AIT), the unofficial consular office of the United States. The next scene shows eight young Taiwanese women standing in front of each window with their backs to the viewer. The camera angle shifts to reveal their expressionless faces as one by one they speak to the reflective window in an emotionless monotone, narrating their encounters with AIT interviewers who denied their applications for a nonimmigrant visa to the United States. Unable to comprehend the logic behind their rejections, the women speak of thwarted efforts to reunite with sick and dying family members or to pursue dreams of travel and study abroad.

The second part of the video cuts to shots of arrival signs at Taiwan's Taoyuan Airport marked with arrows directing travelers toward immigration processing. Again, the space is empty, until a group of women appear standing silently behind the signs, facing away from immigration with their luggage carts in front of them as if they are being sent back to their point of origin. One woman begins to read in an impassive voice from notes jotted on the back of an official-looking form. The camera zooms in on her attractive but expressionless face as she identifies herself as the mainland Chinese wife of a Taiwanese man and describes her experience of being interviewed by border officers in this very airport when she first arrived in Taiwan. The other women in the group, all Chinese wives, speak in voices similarly devoid of emotion, creating a stark contrast between their lifeless delivery and the moving content of their narratives: being refused entry to Taiwan following a border interview, living with constant fear of abuse or deportation after entry, and being denied citizenship after eight long years in Taiwan. Only when they speak do viewers clearly recognize the women's non-Taiwanese origins, encoded in mainland-accented Mandarin and regional dialects that attest to their diverse ages, backgrounds, and home communities in China.

The short video ends with two screens of text. The first describes a recent agreement the Taiwan government has signed with the United States that would make Taiwan a candidate for visa-exempt status should the government meet the technical requirements of the US antiterror campaign. The second details the legislative progress of revised employment and inheritance policies for Chinese spouses in Taiwan and the Taiwanese government's refusal to eliminate border interviews or reduce Chinese spouses' eight-year-long wait for naturalized citizenship. The texts reaffirm the message of the video's first two segments by situating Taiwan at the borders of two powerful empires: the United States and China.

TAIWANESE ARTIST CHEN CHIEH-JEN'S video production, *Empire's Borders I* (2008–9), powerfully conveys the challenges that beset Taiwanese sovereignty. In so doing, it introduces a main point of this book: that we find sovereign claims and practices in what are otherwise rather mundane and, at times, unlikely places. Created in response to Chen's own humiliating treatment by an AIT interviewer when he applied for a visa to participate in the New Orleans Biennial, the video uses personal narratives to evoke the heartlessness of bureaucratic decisions and to expose the Faustian bargains made by the Taiwanese government in its search for international recognition as a sovereign power. *Empire's Borders I* portrays marital status as the linchpin in the sovereign decisions of both the United States and Taiwan by pairing the visa travails of young, single Taiwanese women seeking to enter the United States with the intense state regulation faced by Chinese wives in Taiwan.[1] The Taiwanese women are denied US visas because their unmarried status raises suspicions about their weak connection to Taiwan and presumed "illegal" intentions to overstay in the United States, even to seek citizenship by marrying an American. Similarly, the Chinese women face intrusive state evaluations precisely because their cross-Strait marriage bestows rights to residency and ultimately citizenship in Taiwan.

This book addresses Taiwan's struggles as a merely de facto state to produce sovereign recognition, contested and fragile though that sovereignty may be, through its engagement with the largest group of permanent immigrants in the country: the Chinese wives and husbands of its citizens. Since relations between Taiwan and China resumed in 1987, regulating cross-Strait marriages has become an important means for the Taiwanese government to enact policies and engage in bureaucratic practices that assert national sovereignty by displaying the government's conformity to international standards of border control and population management. Throughout the book, I analyze the logics and detailed features of these regulatory practices to explain how they weave intimate relationships into the fabric of sovereign claims, simultaneously producing and reaffirming a persistent exceptionalism that marks both Chinese spouses and the Taiwanese nation-state. What is it like to live in this exceptional state, I ask? And how does the plight of Chinese spouses mirror the challenges faced by the Taiwanese polity as a whole?

As legal immigration routes have shrunk around the world in recent decades, cross-border marriage has become one of the most prominent channels available to those who seek entry and permanent residence in countries other than their own, especially in the global north. Family reunification applications have skyrocketed in the European Union, for instance, as other possibilities for legal immigration have gradually disappeared. Although advanced capitalist nations in East Asia—such as Taiwan, South Korea, and Japan—have opened their doors to certain categories of temporary migrant workers, they have limited eligibility for permanent immigration almost exclusively to family reunification claims, with marriage to a citizen occupying a privileged status. Therefore, regardless of whether cross-border marriages emerge out of other recognized immigration trajectories (as in Europe and North America) or whether they are defined from the beginning as the privileged route to permanent legal status, the end result is quite similar: an intense state gaze fixated on the perceived quality and authenticity of transnational marriages. This gaze draws state actors into the intimate lives of citizens and immigrants in these unions as bureaucrats evaluate couples' motives, assess their life decisions and economic worthiness, and judge the authenticity of their marriages.

Empire's Borders I shows how the Taiwan government has developed a robust set of laws and bureaucratic regulations directed specifically at Chinese spouses and oriented toward the larger aim of asserting its status as a sovereign power. Although marriages between Chinese and Taiwanese represent the burgeoning of intimate and economic ties in the wake of renewed political relations across the Taiwan Strait, these deepening interpersonal bonds have done little to resolve tensions that linger between the two countries. The Chinese government repeatedly asserts that Taiwan is not an independent country but a renegade province that will eventually return to the PRC's national domain. Despite China's concerted efforts to block recognition of Taiwan's sovereign statehood, however, Taiwan continues to function as an independent nation-state with its own elected government, military, currency, and forms of national identification (such as a passport). Yet it enjoys de jure recognition from only the Vatican and a mere twenty-one small states in Africa, Oceania, and Central America.

Chinese spouses stand in for this contested relationship between Taiwan and China, their very presence a constant reminder of the delicate political maneuvering necessary to maintain peaceful relations across the Taiwan Strait. Their status as an exceptional immigrant group, however, does not simply derive from perceptions of irreconcilable difference: in fact, it is precisely the similarity of mainland Chinese to Taiwanese that makes Chinese spouses both the source of acute Taiwanese anxiety and the target of government intervention. The lack of clarity about whether Chinese spouses are or are not "like us" has triggered a proliferation of laws and policies that perpetuate this ambiguity by affirming the need to treat Chinese spouses differently from all other marital immigrants in Taiwan. Identified neither as foreigners nor as natives, Chinese spouses play an iconic role in Taiwanese society that uncomfortably sutures their personal struggles for familial and national inclusion to Taiwan's search for sovereign recognition.

To convey the complexities of this mutually dependent relationship between Chinese spouses and Taiwanese state actors, I approach sovereignty and citizenship as contested practices that often fail to produce meaningful experiences of inclusion and belonging. Rights-based definitions of citizenship and juridical understandings of sovereignty can only take us so far in capturing processes of inclusion and exclusion that operate across scales of experience (encompassing immigrants and state actors) and that derive from assessments of similarity as opposed to difference. Throughout the book, I underscore the substantive practices of citizenship and sovereignty enacted on the ground and the deep emotional investments they inspire in order to understand how cross-Strait marriages have become critical to the process of asserting Taiwanese sovereignty. In so doing, I also draw attention to how the sovereignty effects thus produced are themselves marked by the ambiguity that characterizes Chinese spouses' own marginal status in Taiwan: neither foreigner nor native, neither renegade province nor fully sovereign nation-state.

GAMBLING ON MARRIAGE

The diverse experiences of the women whose accounts we hear in *Empire's Borders I* attest to the wide variation in the types of people marrying across the Taiwan Strait and in the outcomes of their marital decisions. Despite significant differences in age, education, origin, and previous marital experiences, many Chinese spouses described their cross-Strait marriage to me as a gamble, a bet on intimacy that enabled some to develop (*fazhan*) but entangled others in disappointment, poverty, or abuse. There were various routes into a cross-Strait marriage and multiple paths for couples to embark on after taking the marriage gamble, most of which were winding or even circuitous, far from the linear progression mapped out by Taiwan's immigration policies. Some couples married in China and then moved immediately to Taiwan; others married and remained in China, making only short visits to Taiwan; and still others alternated their place of residence, cycling back and forth in search of job opportunities or to accommodate family needs. Marriages, too, unfolded in unpredictable directions: for all the couples who resided in conventional nuclear or multigenerational households, there were an equal number who lived apart for months or years on end or whose marriages ended in divorce or widowhood—outcomes that, for many, led to subsequent cross-Strait marriages.

The first time I watched *Empire's Borders I*, I noticed how the Chinese wives portrayed on the screen mirrored the kinds of Chinese women I encountered during my research. The older women in the video were part of a marriage trend common in the early years of post-1987 cross-Strait rapprochement, when elderly veterans in Taiwan returned to the mainland in search of wives to provide companionship and care as they aged, partnering largely with divorced or widowed middle-aged women.[2] These "caretaking marriages" empowered Taiwanese immigration bureaucrats to assess Chinese wives' commitment to a gendered paradigm of care in order to legitimize their claims to citizenship. Rendered suspicious by age (some wives were thirty or forty years younger than their husbands) and popular assumptions that veterans' wives only sought access to Taiwan's more lucrative job market (to support their family members back home), Chinese women in caretaking marriages triggered the expansion of an extensive bureaucratic regime designed to investigate their marriage motives and commitment to spousal care.[3]

Younger cross-Strait couples also came under this regulatory regime, even though some marriages more closely resembled modern ideals of love matches or traditional couplings that paired a male breadwinner with a female homemaker. As growing numbers of Taiwanese traveled to China for work, study, or pleasure, they met potential spouses through chance encounters or casual introductions from friends, family, and coworkers. Others found partners online through social networking websites such as QQ, while some Taiwanese men utilized the services of commercial matchmaking agencies. Courtships mediated by a matchmaker might last only a few days, but others extended over months of phone calls, letters and emails, Skype chats, and brief visits.[4]

By far the most common pairings matched Taiwanese men with Chinese women (over 90 percent), but the characteristics and aspirations of each party diversified over the 1990s and into the new millennium.[5] Some Chinese spouses hailed from urban areas, while others were part of the waves of migration from rural villages in China's interior to the booming coast. Primary, middle, and high school graduates mixed with young professionals who boasted university or even graduate degrees, and divorcees populated the ranks of Chinese spouses along with the never married. Some Taiwanese husbands conformed to stereotypes that portrayed them as undesirable partners for local women: they might be poor, working class, or disabled; never married but middle-aged; or burdened with children from a previous marriage or other family members to support. By looking for a wife from China, these men might be able to benefit from the perceived economic advantages of life in Taiwan while avoiding the language barriers and ethnoracial differences that came with marrying a woman from Vietnam, Indonesia, or the Philippines, popular destinations for those seeking a foreign wife. Other Taiwanese spouses, however, were well-educated professionals who happened to meet their partner in China or during residence or travel in a third country. In these cases, couples typically emphasized the power of fate and attraction over pragmatic considerations when explaining their marital decisions.

Regardless of Chinese spouses' own background or that of their citizen partner, when they relocated to Taiwan, they confronted the same set of immigration regulations and similar societal anxieties about their impact on Taiwan's population and national identity. Most, however, knew little about Taiwan or the policies they would face prior to actually gambling on marriage and moving across the Strait, other than knowing that they must first marry their partner outside of Taiwan before they could begin the immigration process. In search of disparate goals—an emotionally fulfilling relationship, economic advancement and professional success, new life opportunities— Chinese spouses arrived in Taiwan to find that these diverse motivations were often reduced to stock portrayals that emphasized their indelible mainland origins, desire for easy wealth, and suspect political commitments.[6] Many were shocked when they encountered assumptions from Taiwanese family members or neighbors that they came from impoverished backgrounds or had been steeped in socialist values, especially those who were born during China's market-reform era after the decline of Maoist socialism. Women bristled when hailed with belittling appellations such as "mainland bride" (*dalu xinniang*) or worse, "mainland little sister" (*dalu mei*), with its derogatory connotations of sexual promiscuity, desire for easy wealth, and communist infiltration (see figure 1). In place of this discriminatory terminology, I generally use the gender-neutral terms "spouse" (*pei'ou*) and "marital immigrant" (*hunyin yimin*) to refer to Chinese wives and husbands. "Spouse," in particular, is the term that Chinese and foreign spouses (*waiji pei'ou*) find most acceptable (Hsia 2005), and it is now the norm in most government, scholarly, and media discourse in Taiwan. Both terms, moreover, recognize the small but significant number of Chinese men in cross-Strait unions, some of whom establish households in Taiwan, where they must reconcile their own standards of masculinity with the disempowering effects of immigration policies.

By the end of the first decade of the new millennium, more than 300,000 Chinese marital immigrants had entered Taiwan, a number that Taiwanese bureaucrats liked to point out was nearly the population of Taiwan's fourth largest city, Keelung. More striking than this cumulative figure, however, was the proportion of cross-Strait unions among all marriages in Taiwan. Compared to declining marriage rates among citizens, unions with mainland Chinese increased over the 1990s and spiked in the early 2000s. By 1999, 10 percent of all annual registered marriages in Taiwan included a

FIGURE 1. Storefront sign in Chiayi County, "Mainland Little Sister Communist Bandit Cakes." Photo by author.

mainland Chinese spouse, and by 2003, a staggering 20 percent fit that profile (while 32 percent of all marriages that year involved a non-Taiwanese partner). Although unions with mainland Chinese have declined since this high point, in part due to heightened regulatory measures in Taiwan such as the border interview system discussed in chapter 2, to this day some 12,000 to 14,000 cross-Strait couples register their marriages in Taiwan each year, constituting on average 9 percent of all annual marriages (see figure 2).[7]

These numbers have exacerbated anxieties across Taiwanese society about the potential impact Chinese spouses will have on both the country's national integrity and the political commitments of the next generation of Taiwanese citizens. When Chinese spouses gamble on a cross-Strait marriage and relocate to Taiwan, therefore, they find themselves caught up in a drama that weaves Cold War legacies and Taiwan's contemporary sovereignty challenges together with changing expectations about marriage and family formation on both sides of the Strait (Davis and Friedman 2014). Their own fragile status as exceptional immigrants and their subsequent efforts to forge a sense of belonging in their new home situate their personal struggles at the center of this drama. By following their migration trajectories, I show how sovereignty is both asserted and potentially undone through the Taiwanese government's engagement with this vital yet highly contentious community.

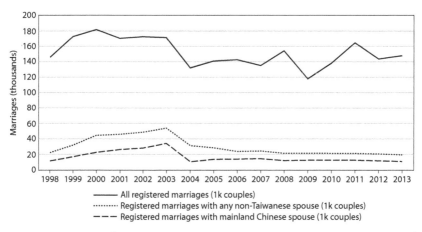

FIGURE 2. Registered marriages in Taiwan, 1998–2013. Source: Taiwan Department of Household Registration, Ministry of the Interior, "Statistics on Marriages between Nationals and Foreigners."

EXCEPTIONAL SUBJECTS

In *Empire's Borders I*, the first Chinese speaker ends her narrative with two probing questions: "Why is it only mainland spouses who suffer endless scrutiny in Taiwan? Can't we just be treated the same as other people?" Her questions point to the use of separate legal regimes to regulate the Chinese and foreign spouses of Taiwanese citizens. The latter group is composed primarily of women from Southeast Asian countries who, together with foreign migrant workers (*waiji laogong*) and all other categories of foreigners, fall under Taiwan's Immigration Law (*ruchuguo ji yiminfa*). Mainland Chinese, by contrast, are barred from entering Taiwan as temporary labor migrants, leaving marriage migration as their main path to entry as well as to permanent residence and citizenship. The laws and policies designed to manage the two groups of marital immigrants, however, bestow different configurations of rights, wait times to naturalization, and citizenship classes—in most cases treating Chinese spouses more stringently than their foreign counterparts.

Under the Immigration Law, foreign spouses receive residency and unconditional work rights upon first arrival and become eligible for naturalization after four years of residence in Taiwan.[8] Chinese spouses, by contrast, waited at least twice as long for citizenship, obtained residency initially through a quota process and then after two years of marriage or birth of a child, and faced a delay in acquiring legal work rights that stretched from two to six years, depending on individual and familial circumstances—inequities that were only partially remedied by policy reforms in 2009. Despite Chinese spouses' desire for the rights and recognition bestowed through legal residency and citizenship status, however, many recognize that these achievements may not provide the security and sense of belonging that they desire in their new home. One of the Chinese speakers in *Empire's Borders I* affirms this point when she concludes that although she has become a Taiwanese citizen, "people still look at me differently"—her juridical inclusion diminished by her mainland origins and the threat to Taiwanese national integrity such origins portend.

Chinese spouses' ambiguous status in Taiwan derives from a system of legal classification that positions them on the margins of normative identity categories organized around foreigner/native and diaspora/homeland distinctions. This exceptional legal regime originated with a founding piece of legislation, the Act Governing Relations between the People of the Taiwan Area and the Mainland Area (*Taiwan diqu yu dalu diqu renmin guanxi tiaoli*, hereafter the Act), implemented on September 18, 1992 by a legislature newly reconfigured by democratic reforms that followed after nearly four decades of martial law in Taiwan. The Act consigned all post-1987 mainland Chinese arrivals to a legal category that collapsed distinctions between population and territory: people of the mainland area (*dalu diqu renmin*).

This anomalous legal classification emerged from the outcome of China's civil war, which ended in 1949 with victory for Mao Zedong and the Communists who established the People's Republic of China (PRC) on the mainland and defeat for Chiang Kaishek's Nationalist regime, which fled to Taiwan, where they reestablished the Republic of China (ROC). The Act's use of the spatial language of "area" was a direct reference to the postwar ROC Constitution, which had created two classes of Chinese based on politically differentiated, territorial criteria: those of the "free area," which included Taiwan and the scattered smaller islands under post-1949 ROC control, and those of the "mainland area," who presumably were not free because they lived under Communist rule. The ROC Constitution identified residents of both areas as ROC "nationals" (*guomin*), their integration the product of a descent-based or jus sanguinis model of the nation. The potential consequences of this shared identity became more pronounced with the granting of substantive citizenship rights to Taiwanese under post–martial law democratization and the resumption of cross-Strait ties in the late 1980s (Rigger 2002). What would happen if eligible PRC citizens sought to claim their rights as ROC nationals and enter Taiwan?

The Constitution remained silent on this issue, but the ROC Nationality Law (*guoji fa*) affirmed that nationals were not automatically citizens. The status of citizen with its attendant rights and responsibilities was granted only to those nationals who had established official household residence in Taiwan (*she you huji*). And the ability to establish official household residence was tightly controlled, limited primarily to nationals whose immediate relatives were themselves ROC citizens. In short, the ethnoracial, descent-based model of the Chinese nation was shrunk in scale to meet the political needs of the ROC polity on Taiwan. The only major exceptions to this narrow jus sanguinis basis for incorporation were claims based on marriage to a citizen.[9]

Although the Act applied to all mainland Chinese in Taiwan, it had the most powerful impact on Chinese spouses who, as marital immigrants, were the primary group of Chinese citizens who enjoyed rights to long-term residence in Taiwan and future citizenship.[10] By defining Chinese spouses as "people of the mainland area," the Act constituted them as subjects who were "cognizable by law" (Yngvesson and Coutin 2006, 178) but for whom that legal status would always be at once insufficient and too encompassing. This new legal category integrated Chinese spouses into the political community, although always with an anomalous, even "degraded" status, a sign of persistent suspicion about their commitment to mobilizing their family roles in the service of the Taiwanese nation (Disch 2003; see also Das and Poole 2004). This anomalous category has, in turn, spawned an expanding set of regulatory policies both recognized and exceptional, substantiating Taiwan's claims to sovereign status, while also underscoring the merely approximate qualities of that sovereignty.

At first glance, the immigration sequence applied to Chinese spouses was future-oriented, always looking ahead to the next stage with its more expansive rights and recognition. By granting benefits and greater security to Chinese spouses who bore Taiwanese children, moreover, the system enacted a form of "reproductive futurism" that identified Taiwan's desired political future with its citizen children (Edelman 2004).[11] But by defining Chinese spouses as people of the mainland area, this immigration regime also reaffirmed Chinese spouses' atavistic association with their mainland roots and Maoist legacies of deprivation and socialist indoctrination. As a result, Chinese spouses were presumed to need more time than other marital immigrants to acclimate to Taiwanese society and comprehend the workings of a constitutional democracy—hence the Act required an eight-year wait time to citizenship as opposed to the four years expected of foreign spouses.

The first version of the Act implemented in 1992 laid out a framework for Chinese spouses' immigration trajectory as temporary visa holders, then legal residents, and ultimately candidates for citizenship.[12] The many years spent as a temporary visa holder and the short stays in Taiwan such visas granted, however, imposed numerous hardships on cross-Strait couples. Chinese women who married during this first decade of cross-Strait rapprochement narrated harrowing accounts of years spent traversing the Strait prior to acquiring residency status, journeying over long distances with babies and small children, and battling the bureaucracy in both countries to process the needed paperwork. One woman described herself as a "person constantly in flight" (*kong zhong feiren*) to convey her experience of perpetual movement and the powerful sense of unrootedness it created. Her story, like those told to me by others who wed in this period, emphasized how the temporality of migration produced experiences of marriage, parenting, and domesticity that were continuously in motion, unmoored from secure foundations, provoking a persistent state of anxiety about the future (Shah 2011).

Toward the end of the 1990s and in the early years of the new millennium, the government began to grant some exceptions to the short-term visas that created this insecure temporary status. In 2004, President Chen Shui-bian's government overhauled the entire visa and residency system by dividing the eight-year wait time to citizenship into four discrete stages, the first of which no longer required Chinese spouses to leave the country every six months.[13] Yet by increasing the number of immigration stages and instituting an interview system to police Chinese spouses' progress through those stages, these reforms expanded the state's regulatory reach and created new opportunities for bureaucrats to intervene in Chinese spouses' lives, enhancing the potential sovereignty effects produced by this mainland-directed immigration regime.

The 2004 reforms introduced complex calculations of time that moved Chinese spouses at faster and slower paces through the immigration process. These temporal equations assigned abstract values to time that enabled it to translate "certain kinds of attributes, actions, and relationships" into "rights-bearing political statuses" (Cohen 2010, 465; 2011). Durational time, which measured the length of a marriage and the time spent at each immigration stage, represented the qualities of societal integration (*rongru shehui*), a Chinese spouse's commitment to a Taiwanese family, and her understanding of the principles and workings of a constitutional democracy (Friedman 2010b). But durational time had to be supplemented by physical presence in Taiwan: for the time spent at each residency stage to "count" and qualify a spouse to progress to the next stage, she was required to reside in Taiwan for a minimum of 183 days in a given year. Depending on individual circumstances, therefore, an immigrant's combination of durational time and physical presence might produce an eight-year wait time to citizenship, or it might not, and quotas might extend the wait by months or a year even for those who met all other temporal requirements.[14] Time, in other words, was integrated into the immigration process to counteract concerns about a Chinese spouse's political allegiances and fledgling identification with Taiwan, drawing out the process of acquiring Taiwanese citizenship in order to cultivate and evaluate Chinese spouses' commitment to Taiwanese families and the nation.

In 2009, the Nationalist-led government under President Ma Ying-jeou revised some features of this immigration sequence, granting Chinese spouses residency status and work rights upon first arrival and shortening their time to citizenship by two years. Yet Chinese spouses still encountered numerous obstacles to inclusion in Taiwan that set them apart from other foreign spouses, from difficulties verifying their identity, school records, and marriage certificates, to obstacles recognizing their postsecondary degrees or entering the civil service. To this day, opposition legislators have blocked efforts to equalize the citizenship time frame imposed on the two groups, retaining a two-year difference with foreign spouses that underscores the persistent exceptionalism of mainland Chinese in Taiwan.

The Chinese women and men whose experiences I recount in the chapters to follow have marital and immigration histories that traverse the three broad immigration regimes described above: 1992 to 2004, 2004 to 2009, and post-2009. The specific orientations of these regimes reflect national-level political shifts defined by the Taiwan independence platform of DPP President Chen Shui-bian's leadership (2000–2008) and the transition to Nationalist President Ma Ying-jeou's more China-friendly administration from 2008 onward.[15] Although attuned to the variations produced by these different immigration regimes, I emphasize throughout how the temporal orientations of immigration policies defer Chinese spouses' desired inclusion in the nation and remind them, at regular intervals, of their suspect status. Their delayed access to work rights prior to 2009 made them dependent on their citizen partner and undermined their own efforts to build a new life in Taiwan. For some, the extended wait time to citizenship disrupted the assumed linearity of marital immigration as a path to citizenship by increasing the likelihood of marital dissolution through divorce or widowhood, an outcome that typically disqualified Chinese spouses for citizenship unless they met a narrowly defined set of criteria. This deterrent effect spurs common depictions of cross-Strait marriage as a gamble, one whose ultimate outcome remains uncertain across numerous dimensions, from spousal harmony to the acquisition of secure, if not fully equal, legal status.

SOVEREIGNTY EFFECTS

Widespread fears of "waning sovereignty" (Brown 2010) in an age of globalization and neoliberal restructuring have encouraged many states to shore up national borders through enhanced physical infrastructure (literally "walling in" the nation) and increasingly restrictive regulatory regimes. These desperate, and often futile, attempts to stem cross-border migration reflect the contradictory nature of sovereignty in the contemporary world. New regimes of global governance, transnational markets, and capital flows are seen to erode sovereign power, prompting in turn heightened efforts to control human mobility and secure the borders of the national domain. Despite the uncertainty produced by fears of sovereignty on the wane, however, established states have multiple means of affirming their sovereign status, including the mutual recognition provided by other countries and the assurances of noninterference in national affairs that such recognition promises. De facto states typically lack this kind of sovereign recognition, and therefore they must adopt different strategies to declare their standing on the world stage. In place of grand declarations of statehood or the flexing of military muscle, de facto states assert sovereignty through the repetition of mundane bureaucratic acts, such as the regulatory practices that enact a state's power to control movement across borders or to police access to naturalized citizenship. Producing documents, stamping papers, monitoring border flows, investigating the intimate relationships that legitimate immigration—all of these acts proclaim sovereignty in the face of international denial or indifference (Navaro-Yashin 2012). Their repetition offers the promise that by acting as a sovereign, a de facto state may, in time, be recognized as such by the international community.

By regulating Chinese spouses, Taiwan produces sovereignty effects that generate the appearance of sovereign statehood. But what does sovereignty ultimately mean in this context? The Chinese government refuses to rule out the use of military force to achieve its proclaimed aim of reuniting Taiwan with the mainland, a position held over from China's civil war and the decades of Cold War–inflected conflict that followed. Since the ROC lost its United Nations seat to the PRC in 1971, moreover, the Chinese government has actively sought to obstruct any international action that might acknowledge Taiwanese sovereignty, repeatedly blocking Taiwan's attempts to gain official membership in international bodies such as the United Nations and the World Health Organization, and insisting that other states formally recognize only one government (a position known as the "one China" principle).[16]

Taiwan's de facto sovereignty poses several challenges for our existing models of sovereign recognition. Much recent scholarship on sovereignty follows a juridical tradition outlined by Carl Schmitt (1985) that privileges the ability of a state or ruler to assert sovereignty through the decision to make an exception to the existing legal armature of statehood (such as suspending the Constitution), thereby deciding which subjects will be excluded from the protections of the law (see also Bodin 1992). Following Schmitt and others, philosopher Giorgio Agamben (1998, 2005) identifies the core of sovereignty as a foundational marginality that is simultaneously outside the law and constitutive of it, a state of exception defined in spatial and human terms, the Nazi concentration camp his example par excellence. For Agamben, biopolitical decisions create a state of exception at the threshold of life and death, and these decisions serve as the foundation of sovereign power at the same time that they enact that very power. Agamben's emphasis on violence as the heart of sovereignty, however, limits our ability to understand exceptionalism that is framed in terms other than life and death or to grasp how sovereign claims are substantiated through laws and governmental practices enacted by de facto polities profoundly insecure about those very claims.

Although Agamben alerts us to the significant role of exceptionalism in sovereignty's constitution, he does little to help us understand the actual practices that instantiate sovereign claims or the lived experiences of the exceptional subjects who are so vital to sovereignty itself. Scholars studying immigration and citizenship in various parts of the world have challenged Agamben's portrayal of a universal subject of exception, arguing instead that contextual specificities matter deeply when analyzing how inclusion and exclusion are forged through particular bodies and their relationships to different states (Partridge 2012; Ticktin 2006; Willen 2010). Precisely because otherness is not generic, these authors contend, the practices and discourses that mobilize otherness in the service of sovereign claims will differ significantly in accordance with specific histories and patterns of geopolitical, economic, and social inequality (see also Fernando 2013; Surkis 2010).

As exceptional states such as Taiwan engage in the material practices that constitute sovereignty, they remain closely attuned to the possibility of recognition by both international and domestic interlocutors. And although this recognition is deemed imperative for these states' very existence, it is, as the actors involved frequently acknowledge, far from guaranteed (Dunn and Cons 2013; Navaro-Yashin 2012). In this fraught field, Taiwanese bureaucrats and immigration officers encounter an array of objects and categories as they perform bureaucratic-cum-sovereign acts: identity and travel documents both unique to cross-Strait mobility and internationally recognized, authenticating devices such as official stamps imprinted on those documents, "law-like" statuses created by legislators to make Chinese immigrants legible in Taiwan, and formalized standards for evaluating Chinese spouses' grounds for entry to and standing in the country. A state that does not enact such material practices invites the impression of failed or inactive sovereignty. But nowhere does this risk of failure loom larger than in cases where sovereignty itself is contested or even denied (Dunn and Cons 2013; Navaro-Yashin 2012; Rutherford 2012).

On numerous occasions, Taiwanese immigration officials and bureaucrats emphasized how important it was for them to engage in regulatory acts and create institutional structures that realized the country's sovereign aspirations, ever cognizant of the impact these actions might have on China and other members of the international community. For many, the most powerful sign of state sovereignty was the formalization of Taiwan's immigration bureaucracy under the National Immigration Agency (NIA) on January 2, 2007. A senior border officer who worked at Taiwan's main international airport expressed this sentiment explicitly as we chatted one March evening in 2008 during a lull in travelers arriving from China: "Only with the establishment of the NIA could we proclaim that Taiwan is a sovereign, independent nation-state (*zhuquan duli de guojia*)," he argued, emphasizing how bureaucratic normalization created a recognizably sovereign status for Taiwan. For this official, robust governing institutions strengthened the country's efforts to resolve persistent anxieties about its national standing. He was not suggesting that these practices or institutions were unique to Taiwan, but that for administrators of an unrecognized state, their very presence affirmed both juridical power and regulatory capacities taken for granted by recognized sovereigns (Navaro-Yashin 2012).

Not all bureaucratic practices contributed equally to generating sovereign recognition, however, as the senior officer reminded me. As we continued our conversation in the airport control zone, he added, "Only when the Entry/Exit Immigration Police Department was upgraded to the level of an agency could [we] effectively manage our duties with respect to mainland Chinese" (interview, March 20, 2008). Ostensibly addressed to the hierarchical ranking of departments as opposed to agencies, the officer's statement underscored how cross-Strait migration literally invested certain kinds of governing practices with a productive power that exceeded their intended scope. From his perspective, it was not just any kind of immigrant who was more effectively managed by the NIA but specifically those from China. In other words, mainland Chinese—among whom Chinese spouses figured most prominently—also served as *vehicles* through which Taiwanese state actors sought to resolve the country's sovereignty dilemmas.

The officer's comments attest to the powerful lure of state actors' engagements with Chinese spouses and the multiple investments engendered by such encounters. Following a recent shift in bureaucratic studies, I turn in this book from a Weberian emphasis on modern rationality and ossified procedure to examine how bureaucracies produce and regulate sentiments, including those of civil servants (Das 2004; Graham 2002; Navaro-Yashin 2006, 2007; Stoler 2004). The anxieties about a secure future experienced by individual Chinese spouses find their parallel in bureaucrats' own concerns about Taiwan's lack of sovereign recognition. In their public encounters with immigrants, bureaucrats appeal to the rational logic of legal precedent, democratic governance, and national security to shore up their status as the face of the Taiwanese state, but they often do so as part of responding to Chinese spouses' demands and, on occasion, seeking to resolve their dilemmas—especially those produced by the very same immigration regime bureaucrats have helped to create. These encounters reveal how the two groups view each other as the necessary audience for their respective claims and the possible solution to their plights. Sympathies that flow across the immigrant-bureaucrat divide foster a sense of shared fate as people enmeshed in a struggle for recognition—sympathies that are as necessary for the "public efficacy" of bureaucratic-sovereign practices

(Mazzarella 2010, 298) as they are for Chinese spouses' efforts to bend inflexible policies to meet their own needs.[17]

Chinese spouses experience the fragility of belonging that plagues the Taiwanese people and nation: the contingent quality of their national membership reflects the ever-present possibility of being undone that also lingers over those who feel secure in their citizenship and national belonging (Salter 2008). Taiwanese bureaucrats seek to assuage these anxieties by asserting the country's sovereign standing through controlling movement across borders, bestowing legal standing on some immigrants but not others, and policing paths to naturalized citizenship, all the while struggling to address the fallout from these regulatory practices for marital immigrants themselves. This sovereign power is all the more potent because it is produced through engagement with immigrants deemed most similar to the native population, thereby emboldening state actors to craft a robust immigration regime that draws ever finer lines of inclusion and exclusion within and between populations. Yet because much of this sovereignty work hinges on categories, documents, and practices that merely resemble those used to manage foreigners, it ultimately promises to produce a form of "as if" sovereignty, a mere approximation of sovereign recognition granted to established states. Chinese spouses' presence in the country is such a thorny issue for Taiwanese state actors precisely because they acknowledge that Chinese immigrants are vehicles for much-desired sovereignty effects but that even those effects may fail to create the full scope of sovereign recognition to which they aspire.

THE THREAT OF SIMILARITY

Over the postmillennium decade during which I conducted the research for this book, I struggled to reconcile the status of mainland Chinese in Taiwan with that of marital immigrants elsewhere in the region or in other parts of the world. The concerns about racialized difference and colonial legacies so salient in many of those cases seemed to have little relevance in the context of my research. Although some questions were applicable to Taiwan, such as how cross-border marriages introduced undesirable forms of alterity into the national population, the terms through which alterity was defined and the historical contexts of immigration flows differed significantly from what scholars of cross-border marriage had found in Japan (Faier 2009; Suzuki 2000), South Korea (Freeman 2011; Kim 2007), or France (Cole 2014; Neveu

Kringelbach 2013), for instance. Mainland Chinese did not represent ethnoracial, religious, or cultural differences devalued by the civilizational hierarchies of European or Japanese imperialism, nor could they be integrated as bearers of authentic, traditional Chinese culture, as South Koreans initially imagined ethnic Korean wives from China to be (Freeman 2011). Instead, the dilemmas of cross-Strait migration centered on the threat of perceived similarities that Chinese spouses shared with Taiwanese citizens.

Assessing the first decade of renewed cross-Strait ties, Shu-mei Shih (1998, 295) used the phrase "threat of similarity" to describe how Chinese women were portrayed in the Taiwan media. Shih characterized this perceived threat as an absence of difference: Chinese women lacked "the *difference* necessary to maintain and police the boundaries of national identity" (1998, 294–95). As a consequence, she concluded, media portrayals showed how Taiwan's de facto independence might be threatened by a silent invasion of mainland women whose very presence could help China achieve its goal of reuniting Taiwan with the mainland without the need for military force.

Shih's analysis skillfully pointed out the unsettling features of Chinese women's similarity to Taiwanese citizens, but her article left open the question of how this threat was experienced in everyday interactions or integrated as part of the policy regime that developed over the 1990s and into the new millennium. Although Chinese spouses look like Taiwanese and even, as some claim, share similar "blood," very few actually are taken to be Taiwanese. Their similarity stops at the perceived "ocular component" of ethnoracial origins (Sturm 2013, 593): once Chinese spouses interact with Taiwanese, their mainland roots become more obvious, encoded through a bodily habitus expressed in their movements, dress, and speech. Their differences are identified through gendered styles of interpersonal interaction—for instance, Chinese women are viewed by Taiwanese as direct, forceful speakers attuned to their own interests—and Taiwanese interpret these gendered traits as signs of different socialization experiences under a socialist regime. This imagined history of formative influences fosters stereotypes of Chinese women as calculating materialists with suspect commitments to both their marriage and Taiwan's political integrity. The problem lies in fears that these differences are being "smuggled in," so to speak, under the cover of similarity, making them all the more threatening because Chinese spouses potentially introduce them into the heart of families that reproduce the Taiwanese nation.

Ultimately at stake for Taiwanese policy makers, legislators, and bureaucrats, then, is not so much Chinese spouses' ability to pass as Taiwanese but the risk that they might render unclear the very boundaries of similarity and difference. To mitigate this anxiety, policy makers have diversified existing legal categories and created more fine-grained distinctions among types of citizens and immigrants. If fully including Chinese spouses in the Taiwanese nation requires first reversing their invisibility (a kind of assimilation through marking), then this process must simultaneously make visible the two key groups destabilized by the threat of similarity: "true foreigners" (i.e., racialized others such as Southeast Asian spouses [Wang and Bélanger 2008]) and, more important, what Balibar (1991, 60–61) terms "true nationals"—in this case, the Taiwanese. Chinese spouses resemble other interstitial figures such as transnational adoptees and deportees in that they are precisely the type of immigrants who "anchor (but also possibly unsettle) . . . the 'native citizen'" (Yngvesson and Coutin 2006, 178). They enact the "as-if-ness" of national membership by drawing attention to the simultaneous taken-for-granted qualities and exclusionism that shore up national belonging (2006, 187). This "as if" feature destabilizes the presumed foundations of the national community at the same time that it undermines the sovereignty effects produced by the very regulatory regime designed to manage the threat of similarity.

Taiwanese immigration policies integrate the threat of similarity into calculations of foreignness that distinguish mainland Chinese immigrants from all other groups. Chinese spouses' similarities to native citizens do not make them more reassuring to a society uneasy about persistent tensions with China and the growing numbers of Chinese immigrants and visitors in their midst: instead, spouses' more visible resemblance to Taiwanese hinders their efforts to claim belonging in Taiwan because of fears that those similarities may obscure important differences in political outlook and marital motivations. The modifier "as if," therefore, captures both the "not quite" quality of their resemblance and its unsettling effects on presumably distinguishable categories of citizen and foreigner—evoking statuses for which there are no obvious labels and emotional states that are difficult to reconcile with legacies of Cold War ideological conflict and the violent histories of war.

The threat of similarity attributed to Chinese spouses pivots on deep-rooted tensions in Taiwan about what makes the Taiwanese nation different from the Chinese nation and, subsequently, how that disputed nation can serve as the basis for sovereignty claims (Chang 2000; Chun 1996; Wachman 1994). In their contemporary form, these conflicts date to the Nationalists' defeat at the end of the civil war and the subsequent flight to Taiwan of some two million Nationalist soldiers and civilians from the mainland. This sudden population influx created an explosive political mix with native Taiwanese communities that were only beginning to adjust to the end of Japanese colonial rule (1895–1945).[18] Four decades of martial law kept these tensions forcibly in check, but they reemerged in the post-1987 era in the form of debates about what constituted the Taiwanese nation and what political future would best advance the interests of that nation.[19] Chinese spouses entered the domestic scene at precisely this fraught moment, introducing what were perceived as threatening political values and uncertain national commitments into a contested field of national identity.

The Taiwanese government has developed an intrusive set of disciplinary practices to contain widespread anxieties about Chinese spouses' national allegiances: quotas to slow Chinese spouses' progress through the immigration sequence, port-of-entry interviews, fingerprinting at the border, home inspections by immigration officers, registration with local police, and even police harassment in public spaces.[20] These exclusionary interventions have been paired with productive practices designed to cultivate new traits in Chinese spouses and alleviate concerns about hidden forms of difference. Border interviews and state-funded acculturation and training courses impart messages about proper domesticity and gendered behaviors with the goal of teaching Chinese women and men how to successfully perform their desired roles as parents, spouses, workers, and future citizens. Productive interventions aim to neutralize anxieties about Chinese spouses' suspect political allegiances by educating them in Taiwanese familial roles and social norms, all in the hope of transforming them into committed family members dedicated to the larger good of the nation.

But once Chinese spouses enter Taiwan and embark on the path to residency and citizenship, they find that their legal immigration status rarely defuses the deep unease they inspire among many Taiwanese, nor does it foster their own more substantive sense of belonging to local society.[21] On the one hand, even those who had become Taiwanese citizens recognized that the kind of citizenship available to them denied them certain rights enjoyed by native-born Taiwanese and naturalized foreigners: for instance, to join the civil service or receive recognition of their postsecondary degrees. Although legal citizenship provides important protections, it is by no means a unitary status that automatically conveys "full" citizenship rights and recognition.[22] Instead, the presumed homogeneity of legal status may be undone by characteristics, values, and fears attributed to especially contentious immigrant groups (Cohen 2009).

On the other hand, Chinese spouses' similarities with Taiwanese—encoded formally in their constitutional status as nationals and enacted through claims to shared "blood" and cultural heritage—frustrate their desire for substantive inclusion by challenging the foundations of a distinctly Taiwanese citizenship. By embodying the threshold between similarity and difference, Chinese spouses call into question the presumed naturalness of this Taiwanese citizenship, even as their presence repeatedly provokes the need to draw a line somewhere. In other words, mainland Chinese are not just any kind of immigrant other but precisely the "immanent" other necessary to constitute the citizen as a privileged category (Canaday 2009; Disch 2003; Isin 2002).[23] If Taiwanese citizenship literally requires this immanent other as its condition of possibility, then the differentiated, second-class citizenship granted to Chinese spouses is more than a permanent feature of democratic citizenship (Cohen 2009): it is actually necessary for Taiwanese to assert their own national identity and sovereign standing.

These contradictions create what I call "the insufficiencies of legal status"; they underscore both the limitations of a strictly juridical approach to understanding citizenship and the inability of legal citizenship to counteract the suspect nature of Chinese spouses' mainland origins (see also Dauvergne 2009; Greenhouse 2002; Heyman 2002; Newendorp 2008; Ong 1999, 2003). Chinese spouses who become Taiwanese citizens are regularly reminded of their differentiated standing, both through formal obstacles to full inclusion and through the myriad, small yet cumulative ways they are singled out as not quite belonging. Over the course of the book, I recount the tortuous trials of one young woman, Deng Lifang, who despite her burning desire to acquire the legal imprimatur of citizenship in Taiwan, nonetheless recognized that even with this formal recognition, she would remain merely "a mainland person with a Taiwan national identification card (*you Taiwan shenfenzheng de dalu ren*)." The categorical weight of the designation "person of the mainland area" makes it virtually impossible for Chinese spouses to shed their mainland origins, regardless of their legal status (Friedman 2010b).

In sum, even when legally resident in Taiwanese territory, Chinese spouses must regularly negotiate the insufficiencies of their juridical status and the repeated experience of crossing national borders that such insufficiencies produce. These border crossings are reenacted in every evaluation of their marital intentions, in contexts official and informal, both before and after they acquire Taiwanese citizenship.[24] The persistent state gaze that follows Chinese spouses points to the sovereignty stakes of these regulatory practices, for by demanding repeated performances of border crossings, Taiwanese state actors reaffirm their right as representatives of a sovereign power to decide who crosses the country's borders, in what capacities, and with what present and future rights. As a consequence, Chinese spouses are left wondering whether the taint of their mainland origins will ever fade sufficiently to permit national incorporation in Taiwan.

MAPPING THE BOOK

The chapters to follow capture a particular moment in the mid- to late-2000s that simultaneously looked back to the uncertain first decade of cross-Strait opening and gestured forward to a future marked by greater social and economic integration but persistent political uncertainty. How Chinese spouses lived through this critical period and the significance of their experiences for Taiwan's own sovereignty battles constitute the threads that run through the book.

Part I begins at the border where immigrants and Taiwanese bureaucrats meet for the first time, examining the travel and identity documents used to manage the anomalous cross-Strait relationship (chapter 1) and the border interviews that produce standards of marital authenticity through policing the fuzzy distinction between "real" and "sham" marriages (chapter 2). These two chapters shift between the perspectives of bureaucrats and immigrants as each group responds to the anomalies of Chinese spouses' legal status and Taiwan's own not quite sovereign standing. In so doing, they underscore the many ways that border encounters produce effects that travel with Chinese spouses, extending the space of the border into their interactions with family members and state actors.

Part II addresses the consequences of asserting fragile claims to national sovereignty through crafting and contesting immigration laws and policies that are based on anomalous legal categories. Chapter 3 introduces the immigration regime that constituted mainland Chinese as exceptional legal subjects, and it examines the effects of this atypical regime on official sovereignty claims and activist campaigns to support immigrant rights. Chapter 4 turns to public encounters between immigrants and bureaucrats during policy-education forums and acculturation classes, analyzing these encounters as moments when bureaucrats asserted state sovereignty through affirming the robust impartiality of Taiwan's immigration regime and audiences countered such assertions with demands for policy flexibility and national inclusion—all without, however, denying the government's power to regulate them as outsiders to the polity. As in Part I, these chapters incorporate the voices and experiences of bureaucrats and immigrants, adding perspectives from NGO workers and activists to the mix.

Part III analyzes how Chinese spouses strive to create marital and familial harmony and forge their own sense of belonging across the Strait despite their anomalous legal status. Chapter 5 assesses the gendered foundations of Taiwan's immigration policies, in turn asking how Chinese spouses' gender roles and behaviors become a means to talk about and potentially minimize their perceived threats to Taiwanese family life and national cohesion. Chapter 6 probes the costs of cross-Strait mobility by showing how Chinese spouses' formal status as legal immigrants and Taiwanese citizens produces new anxieties, an even greater sense of insecurity, and powerful feelings of not belonging anywhere. These two chapters interrogate the diverse stakes of enacting sovereignty through anomalous legal regimes and regulatory practices—the struggles of marital immigrants to forge belonging on the edges of family and nation an uncanny reflection of Taiwanese state actors' endeavors to carve out a recognized status in the international community.

Read together, the three parts ask what tensions arise when similarity becomes the starting point from which states craft legal and regulatory remedies to de facto sovereignty. The chapters map the various fields of contention in such sovereignty struggles, pausing periodically to point out unintended consequences and possible solutions that emerge in the process. The epilogue returns to the unresolved conflicts that continue to permeate relations between Taiwan and China. It asks what these conflicts might teach us about the potential of shared intimacies to generate new paradigms for resolving old animosities and imagining alternative futures.

PART ONE

———

Border Crossings

ONE

Documenting Sovereignty

June 25, 2009

Mr. Zhu and I sat in his cramped office in the multistory building that housed the headquarters of the National Immigration Agency (NIA), located in an older section of Taiwan's capital, Taipei. Mr. Zhu was a seasoned middle-aged bureaucrat who appeared to have made an effortless transition from police official to immigration officer, his slight paunch and fleshy jowls a sign of his current desk job heading the NIA section responsible for issuing temporary visas. Feeling frustrated by Mr. Zhu's unenthusiastic responses to my questions about how the NIA managed the growing numbers of Taiwanese and Chinese moving across the Taiwan Strait, I asked him to describe his own experiences of crossing the border into China. Mr. Zhu hesitated, a bit unsettled by my sudden change of topic, then leaned back in his chair and tapped his fingertips together in a contemplative pose, a cynical smile spreading across his broad face. When passing through immigration, he explained, PRC border officers stamp the Taiwan compatriot pass issued to him by the Chinese government. They might look at his ROC passport to confirm his identity (and he always brings it with him, he emphasized), but they would never stamp it. Similarly, he continued, although some Chinese citizens entering Taiwan will carry a PRC passport, they must have an entry permit issued by the Taiwanese government to cross the border. "Taiwan authorities will not stamp the PRC passport," Mr. Zhu noted. "They will only stamp the entry permit." Mr. Zhu chuckled and paused before speaking again, this time his voice quivering with excitement: "We want very much to stamp [the PRC passport; *women shi hen xiang qu gai ah*]! But at present, we still don't know what subtle effect this stamp might have on cross-Strait relations."

THE UNEXPECTED BURST OF EMOTION in Mr. Zhu's voice as he conveyed his investment in stamping a PRC passport surprised me at the time, but I gradually came to understand his response as emblematic of the frustrations and desires generated by the seemingly endless deferral of Taiwan's sovereign recognition. Mr. Zhu expressed a strong desire to imprint a Taiwan stamp on a PRC-issued travel document, only to temper that desire by acknowledging that such a simple act comes weighted with significant import for relations across the Strait. His portrayal of his own border crossings shows how the very act of stamping an identity document affirms the sovereign status of the stamping authority, while it also recognizes the legitimacy of the government that issued the document in the first place (Wang 2004).[1] Moreover, in his expressed desire to stamp a PRC passport, Mr. Zhu recognized that everyday bureaucratic acts were, in fact, anything but mundane: they were powerful political claims and bids for recognition as a sovereign authority.

Mr. Zhu was by no means the only NIA official attuned to the power of stamps. Not long after our conversation, I traveled to Taiwan's main international airport to meet with Mr. Lu, then second in command of the NIA Border Affairs Corps, to discuss recent changes to the process for interviewing the Chinese spouses of Taiwanese citizens. In the midst of this conversation, Mr. Lu, too, quickly raised the topic of stamping a PRC travel document:

> Of course, I've always thought that the immigration stamp (*zhangchuo*) is a symbol of sovereignty. Each country is the same. How do we make a breakthrough here, how do we issue that stamp in their [Chinese citizens'] passports? That is very difficult right now. . . . I need to stamp a "Taiwan" here in your passport, a "Republic of China" right here. The symbolic and practical meaning of that [act] must be stronger than the interview. This is what I firmly believe, I don't know if it is right or wrong.

Like Mr. Zhu, Mr. Lu described the stamping of a PRC passport as a powerful assertion of Taiwanese sovereignty. For him, the physical presence of the stamped words "Taiwan" or "Republic of China," inked permanently onto a PRC-issued document, evoked both symbolic and practical effects.[2] As official stamps indexically "trace a network of relations on the page" (Hetherington 2011, 194), they enact those relations in a specific form, in this case through the desired framework of sovereign recognition. Although Mr. Lu's "need" to imprint those characters in a Chinese passport reaffirmed his commitment to Taiwanese sovereignty, he was too savvy an official to rashly proclaim his desire to act on this impulse. Instead, he softened his "firm belief" with a final disclaimer: "I don't know if it is right or wrong."

In this chapter, I analyze how identity and travel documents function both as contested symbols of state sovereignty and as sites of emotional investment for those who bear or handle them. Taiwanese bureaucrats and Chinese immigrants alike express anxieties and desires about personal and sovereign status through these very documents. The fragility of Taiwan's standing as a nation-state preoccupies Taiwanese civil servants who confront both the lure of sovereign recognition in their encounters with Chinese travelers and its refusal, as seen in their inability to engage in the mundane yet highly symbolic act of stamping a PRC passport. Chinese spouses are frequent interlocutors in these bureaucratic encounters, and they also express an ambivalent relationship to the atypical documents that facilitate their cross-Strait journeys and chart their protracted progress as immigrants, seeing their documents as material signs of their exceptional immigration and citizenship standing in Taiwan. These interactions between people and documents produce an array of emotional states—desire, anxiety, humiliation, and pride—that reflect both the material qualities of the documents themselves and what I call documents' "circulation effects"—what they can and cannot do as signifiers of individual and national identity and as facilitators of cross-border mobility.

Much of the literature on identity documents and travel papers approaches such documents as elements in a larger state classificatory project—a project through which states recognize and make legible their own populations, while simultaneously excluding outsiders from the citizen body (Caplan and Torpey 2001; Scott 1998; Torpey 2000). These classifications of individuals and groups, however, are rarely seamless or uncontested.[3] By turning our attention to the materiality of identity documents—what Matthew Hull (2012) terms their "visibility"—we can better understand how documents engage in a form of signifying work that extends through and beyond documentary encounters: in other words, documents serve as "vehicles of imagination" (2012, 260) that generate new social and political possibilities even as they foreclose others (Riles 2006).

In the absence of a recognized state-to-state relationship between China and Taiwan, the documents used to facilitate cross-Strait flows of Taiwanese and Chinese merely borrow the trappings of international border crossings. These documents, which resemble passports and visas but are neither, manage border crossings by keeping the status of that border intentionally ambiguous. As a consequence, the migratory circumstances of Chinese spouses fit uneasily with dominant modes of classifying territories, borders, and the people who move within and among them. Although Taiwan classifies

Chinese marital immigrants in ways that mimic internationally recognized sovereign practices for managing migration, it does so without openly challenging China's stance that Taiwan is not an independent nation-state and thus that travel from China to Taiwan does not involve crossing a foreign border.

Through their daily engagement with the atypical documents that facilitate this cross-border movement, both Taiwanese bureaucrats and Chinese spouses participate in the production of sovereignty effects that merely approximate international standards of border control and population regulation. NIA officials themselves acknowledge that the use of travel passes and entry permits, as opposed to passports and visas, reaffirms the "strange relationship" between Taiwan and mainland China and undermines Taiwan's aspirations for a recognized state-to-state relationship. Although this ambiguity keeps potential political tensions across the Strait in check, it simultaneously frustrates those who seek to assert Taiwan's sovereign control over its borders.

The critical role of documents in this process of claiming and undermining sovereignty raises the question of how effectively documents constitute both identity and belonging for individuals and states alike (Yngvesson and Coutin 2006, 185). Although "paper selves" are ephemeral, enacted in moments of border-crossing and bureaucratic encounters, they also create the possibility of official recognition and its potential to facilitate claims to belonging. Document-mediated circuits rest on identification processes both compelled (required by state actors) and claimed (asserted by immigrants themselves). By analyzing the materiality of documents and the affective investments they inspire among these groups, I aim to deepen our understanding of the contested relationship between trajectories of identification and their implicit promises of sovereign recognition and national inclusion—promises, nonetheless, that often go unrealized.

A PRO/CONFUSION OF DOCUMENTS

The number and types of people moving between China and Taiwan have expanded exponentially since cross-Strait ties resumed in 1987. Until quite recently, Taiwanese accounted for most of the travel across the Strait: businessmen seeking new investment opportunities in the mainland, employees sent by their companies on multiyear expatriate packages, students studying abroad, veterans and other Mainlanders who fled to Taiwan with the Nationalists returning to visit surviving family members, and a steady stream of tourists. Estimates suggest that millions of Taiwanese now travel regularly to the mainland each year, and more than one million Taiwanese reside for extended periods of time in China, with enclaves clustered around the core sites of Taiwanese investment (Dongguan in Guangdong Province and Kunshan in the Shanghai-Nanjing economic corridor) and major coastal cities such as Beijing, Shanghai, and Xiamen.[4]

Before July 2008, the Taiwanese government permitted very few mainland Chinese to visit the country. Most of those granted entry qualified for reasons of family reunification: visiting an elderly or sick relative, attending a relative's funeral, or reuniting with a parent, sibling, or spouse, with the spousal category vastly outnumbering the rest. The travel procedures were cumbersome and time-consuming. Even as formal cultural and educational exchanges expanded, most individual Chinese without direct kin ties to Taiwanese assumed it would be very difficult, if not impossible, for them to receive travel approval from either their own government or that in Taiwan.

This situation changed dramatically in the summer of 2008 following Taiwan's election of Nationalist President Ma Ying-jeou, whose administration granted permission for Chinese tour groups from designated mainland cities to visit the island. Since then, the number of source cities has expanded rapidly, and individual travel to Taiwan is now possible for residents of China's major urban centers. Institutions of higher education in Taiwan have also opened their doors to Chinese students (some undergraduate, but most at the graduate level), and Taiwan has begun to cultivate a medical tourism industry. As a result, in recent years there has been a rapid expansion in the number of Chinese traveling to Taiwan and in their reasons for travel.[5] Although Chinese spouses still dominate the category of long-term residents, short-term visitors from China have become a recognizable presence in Taiwan, and one encounters them at tourist sites and transportation hubs across the island.

The multiplicity of documents employed by these travelers as they move across the Strait underscores the ambiguous status of the border between China and Taiwan and reenacts the contestations over sovereignty and national identity that dominate official cross-Strait exchanges. As Mr. Zhu explained, neither Chinese nor Taiwanese border crossers use passports to journey across the Taiwan Strait, and many Chinese spouses in Taiwan do not have a PRC passport at all.[6] If we accept, as John Torpey (2000) and Yael Navaro-Yashin (2007) contend, that passports constitute and convey "state-ness," then it should be obvious why Chinese and Taiwanese do not use passports for cross-Strait travel, for to do so would suggest that China recognizes Taiwan as an independent nation-state. The absence of passports, however, does not mean that movement between China and Taiwan does not *resemble* international travel. Chinese, Taiwanese, and foreign travelers pass through immigration and customs at airports and seaports; they are required to show state-issued documentary proof of identity at points of entry and departure; and they encounter different border officers and procedures when they depart one country and arrive at the other. Although foreign nationals use passports and visas to journey between Taiwan and China, Taiwanese and Chinese who cross these borders are required to display documents that are distinct from those used for travel to a third country.

The PRC government requires Taiwanese to enter the mainland on what is known colloquially as a "Taiwan compatriot pass" (*taibaozheng*). In turn, it issues its own departing citizens a "travel pass" (*tongxingzheng*) designated specifically for Taiwan. These documents are small booklets that resemble a passport in form and content: they have a rigid, colored cover, and the first page contains a photograph and identifying information such as a unique number, the bearer's name, date of birth, sex, place and date of issuance, and date of expiry. Inside pages contain "visas" that are valid for a fixed period of time and permit single or multiple entry and exit.

The documents' official names, printed in full on the cover, demonstrate some of the common rhetorical strategies employed by China to contain cross-Strait ties within a domestic, intranational framework.[7] First, the two countries are identified not by their formal names but as regions or areas: Taiwan and the mainland. Second, the documents are defined not as passports (*huzhao*)—using the documentary language of citizenship, sovereignty, and international travel—but as travel passes, a term that suggests heightened state control over internal mobility (Torpey 2000, 165), as seen in its use for documents that regulate movement between China and Hong Kong or Macau (both former European colonies that are now special administrative regions under PRC control). By issuing mainland Chinese "travel passes" for travel to Taiwan and by identifying the bearers of these documents as merely residents (*jumin*), not citizens, the PRC government explicitly enfolds Taiwan into its domestic space. Third, the presence of directional verbs in the full names affirms the geographical perspective of China as the issuing authority: Taiwan residents "come to" (*laiwang*) the mainland, whereas mainland residents "go to" (*wanglai*) Taiwan. These verbs position China ("the mainland") as the central actor managing cross-Strait flows, thereby denying Taiwan an independent sovereign status.

When Chinese spouses travel to Taiwan, they depart China using their travel pass; they enter Taiwan, however, on a document issued to them by Taiwan's National Immigration Agency (or, prior to January 2007, by its predecessor unit). Unlike the booklet-type documents issued by China, this "Exit and Entry Permit" (*ruchujing xukezheng*) is a single piece of paper folded in thirds to make it roughly the size of a passport, with the "title page" bearing an image of the ROC national flag and the document's official name in Chinese characters and English. One section of the permit provides instructions to the bearer about the required port-of-entry interview for Chinese spouses arriving in Taiwan for the first time and includes a space for border officers to add stamps to confirm that the bearer passed the interview and had the permit extended for an additional six months. Most of the document's information is included in the bottom third of the permit, which is laid out much like the first page of a passport, with a photograph in the upper left corner and identifying information to the right. In addition to the bearer's name, date of birth, sex, and the permit's date of issue and expiry, the document also includes information that is typically included in visas or arrival forms completed at the port of entry: spaces for purpose of entry, duration of stay, and address. The country of residency is conveyed by a line of text above the photograph that identifies the bearer as a "person of the mainland area." The purpose of entry is defined as "reunion" (*tuanju*), a category used specifically for family reunification. Finally, the address included is not the bearer's address in her place of origin, as one might find in a passport, but the official household residence of the bearer's Taiwanese guarantor.

Prior to June 2009, all Chinese spouses embarking on their first trip to Taiwan were required to transit through Hong Kong or Macau.[8] After a spouse's application for an entry permit was approved, the NIA or its predecessor unit generated two copies of the permit: an original that it mailed directly to the Hong Kong or Macau airport branch of Chung Hwa Travel Service (Taiwan's unofficial consular office) and a copy that it sent to the Chinese spouse's guarantor in Taiwan (typically the Taiwanese spouse). The guarantor then mailed the copy of the permit to China so the Chinese spouse could use it to apply for a travel pass from PRC authorities. With the travel pass and the entry permit copy, the Chinese spouse traveled by land or air to Hong Kong or Macau and, at the airport desk of Chung Hwa Travel Service, exchanged her copy for the original. Now with the original entry permit safely in hand, she could board a plane for Taiwan.

Why this elaborate system of "original" and "copy"? I assumed that it rested on the symbolic message of sovereign recognition conveyed by a Taiwan government agency directly mailing an official document to China. But when I queried Mr. Zhu about the process in the summer of 2009, he instead emphasized the potential dangers that derived from Chinese propensities to forge documents. Drawing on his many years of experience working in the immigration police bureaucracy, Mr. Zhu claimed that "in the past many people forged entry permit copies and used them to enter Hong Kong to work and earn money, not to come to Taiwan [because the Hong Kong airport had the original against which the forged copy could be checked]." Once Chinese spouses were allowed to fly directly across the Strait beginning in June 2009, however, they no longer had to transit in Hong Kong or Macau (although many still did because of cheaper airfares). As a result, the NIA had no choice but to issue the original entry permit directly to the Taiwan guarantor, who then mailed it to his spouse in China.[9] "Because of this," Mr. Zhu continued, "the risk we must take over here is even greater! There is no 'interview,' [we] haven't seen the person. Because, after all, many of them over there forge documents."

Mr. Zhu's concerns reflect deep unease about the identification capacity of documents in the hands of mainland Chinese and the potential lack of correspondence between an identity document and the individual who uses it. The distribution of original and copy was intended to protect the original from fraudulent use in a context where Taiwan was unable to independently confirm the identity of Chinese citizens and government officials assumed that Chinese would forge documents if given the opportunity. In Mr. Zhu's narrative, both the original and the copy are susceptible to forgery, but the threat of a forged original is more powerful because of the original's capacity to enable its bearer to enter Taiwan. Officials such as Mr. Zhu experience a forged original as a direct challenge to Taiwan's sovereign authority to select the individuals on whom it will bestow the right to cross its borders.[10] Mr. Zhu's framing of this potential risk positions "we over here" against "they over there" in an attempt to maintain a distance otherwise collapsed by direct flights across the Taiwan Strait and the government's issuance of original entry permits.

Chinese spouses' use of exceptional travel and identity papers further widens the gap between them and all other foreign spouses of Taiwanese citizens, for the latter enter Taiwan with foreign passports stamped with entry visas and, shortly after arrival, receive residency status conveyed through a laminated plastic card that closely resembles Taiwan's national identification card. This documentary exceptionalism continues to influence the everyday experiences of Chinese spouses as they begin life in a society where most of them lack the two most widely recognized forms of identification: either a national ID card or a foreign passport. Burdened with a multitude of documents issued by different governments, Chinese spouses are often at a loss as to which document to use where or when—their entry permit (converted to a reunion permit after passing the port-of-entry interview) or the travel pass issued by the Chinese government. Some resort to the widely recognized National Health Insurance card that they receive after their first four months of residence in Taiwan. Nor are Taiwanese bureaucrats always certain which form of identification to require, even in official encounters where a premium is placed on accurate identification. The practices that emerge around identity documents—what I term "documentary acts"—affirm Veena Das and Deborah Poole's (2004, 24) insight that state-issued identity documents "acquire a different kind of life" as they are manipulated for diverse ends by state actors, ordinary citizens, and, as the cases below suggest, immigrants themselves. These documentary acts not only undermine state projects to make populations legible but also disturb the very foundations of citizenship and sovereignty on which such projects rest.

Adjudicating Identities

Meng Hua's experience in a Taipei district courtroom in the winter of 2008 reveals some of the contradictions inherent in the process of relying on documents to produce immigrants' identities. A fifty-three-year-old woman from Jiangxi province in China's interior, Meng Hua had married for the third time in 2005 to Li Yuan-ming, an elderly veteran who originally hailed from Hunan province. From the beginning, however, Taiwanese authorities had refused to recognize their marriage because Meng had previously wed another Taiwanese man and had never legally divorced him in Taiwan.[11] Although Meng had filed for divorce in China, she had no means to initiate a divorce in Taiwan without her second husband's support, and he had disappeared. Because of this situation, Meng and Li's 2005 marriage had been declared null and void by Taiwan's immigration police, who required that Meng first legally end her previous union with a Taiwanese. After years of consultations and bungled efforts, which resulted in Meng and Li divorcing in China and then remarrying twice, Meng finally managed to divorce her second husband in Taiwan and received an entry permit as Li's legally recognized spouse.

The couple's travails did not end with Meng's 2007 arrival in Taiwan, however. Li's bad temper had fostered a habit of litigiousness, and after Meng was ostensibly mistreated at a city hospital following a hand injury, Li decided to sue the hospital. The case brought the couple's marital complexities to the attention of the public prosecutor, who claimed he was obligated by law to bring a case against Meng for bigamy (in reference to her 2005 marriage to Li when she had not yet divorced her second husband). It was on the occasion of this court hearing that I accompanied Meng and Li to the Taipei District Criminal Court on the outskirts of the city's bustling Ximending shopping area.[12]

Meng and Li were sitting on the wooden benches outside the courtroom when I arrived. Short and plump, with her long hair piled high on her head, Meng perched nervously on the edge of her seat, while the seventy-something Li contained his impatience in a stiff, erect posture honed through years of military service. The reporting clerk came bustling down the hallway and ushered us into the courtroom, asking immediately for Meng's documentation as the defendant. She first handed him her entry permit, but he shook his head and said that he needed her "passport," stating the term in English (which neither Meng nor Li spoke) and then repeating it in Chinese (*huzhao*). "Oh, my passport (*huzhao*)," Meng replied, and handed over her travel pass issued by the PRC government. The clerk accepted the travel pass without comment and entered the necessary information into his roster.

In this exchange Meng first assumed, not without reason, that the court required an identity document issued by Taiwanese authorities, but instead the clerk privileged the PRC travel pass as the document of record. Neither commented on the confusion of terms in their encounter or the ease with which the travel pass was made to stand in for a foreign passport. This confusion continued after the court session began, when one of the court recorders asked Meng whether she had a Taiwan national ID, a question to which Meng replied matter-of-factly, "No, only a passport (*huzhao*)," meaning, once again, her travel pass and not an official PRC passport, which she did not possess.

As the presiding judge initiated the hearing, she looked over both Meng's and Li's identification documents, reading their numbers aloud for the court recorder. In the midst of examining Meng's travel pass, however, she paused and then said to Meng, "This [the travel pass] is from the mainland. Didn't Taiwan give you an entry permit?" Meng quickly handed over her entry permit and the proceedings continued, with the judge fingering both documents throughout her questioning.

Even in a formal legal setting such as a courtroom, expectations for identification documents fluctuate among individuals and over the course of the hearing itself. The ease with which both Meng and the various court officials moved seamlessly between different kinds of documents issued by different authorities attests to the mediating power of documents and their ability to integrate diverse legal regimes as if they were equivalent (for instance, travel passes that stand in for passports) (Hull 2012, 253). But that presumed equivalence also raises questions about the authority of the document's issuing body and the state's capacity to produce citizenship and sovereignty by authenticating and classifying individuals under its purview. The courtroom encounter did not resolve these questions; it simply suspended them in the name of legal efficiency. By requiring that an official Taiwan government document be added to the mix, the presiding judge intimated that the PRC-issued travel pass failed to stand as a document of record for the purpose of definitive identification in Taiwan, but she did so without acknowledging the anomalous features of those very documents or how they undermined the implicit claim to sovereign authority that underlay her very demand.[13]

Navigating Documentary Circuits

Chinese spouses gradually learn to manage some of these documentary insufficiencies and confusions as they navigate a growing circle of public spaces and bureaucratic encounters in Taiwan. During a government-sponsored acculturation class for Chinese spouses that I attended throughout the fall of 2007, participants frequently shared embarrassing tales of pulling out the wrong document in the wrong place.[14] The vivacious, thirty-year-old Liao Lijing had just returned from registering for a belly-dancing class at a community college near the Chiang Kaishek Memorial one late August afternoon, and she had her classmates in stitches as she recounted how she had brought her PRC travel pass as her form of identification. "That's useless in Taiwan," one woman retorted, and another added that she had to use "the Taiwan one, the green one," referring to her reunion permit. Whether green, purple (the travel pass), or light blue (the kin-based residence permit most of these women would not acquire for nearly two more years), these were documents that Chinese spouses had to learn how to use, where to use them, and with what effect (figure 3). At best, pulling out the wrong document in the wrong place exposed one to ridicule and dismissal; at worst, it might create additional complications by drawing attention to one's mainland origins or, in China, by suggesting one was a viable target for additional fees and other forms of bureaucratic malfeasance.

At the same time, I was repeatedly impressed by how quickly many immigrants learned to use the ambiguous status of these documents to their advantage. This process required that they master extensive knowledge about what documents enabled what kinds of mobility and opportunity. Women who were experienced in managing bureaucratic obstacles in China were at an advantage, and they put their skills to good use in squeezing greater resources out of documents that had been designed with fixed routes and limited stays in mind.

Wu Yan had invited me to lunch shortly before the 2008 Chinese New Year and only two days before she herself was scheduled to depart for Macau, where she would join her parents and infant son. Both Wu Yan and her husband were in their early thirties, well-educated, with solidly established careers—she in the radio industry in China and he as a doctor of Chinese medicine in Taipei. As a consequence of these career trajectories, the couple had lived apart for much of their nearly eight-year-long marriage, and Wu Yan had turned to her parents to care for her son once he was old enough to be separated from her. Her father was now working in Macau, and her mother had taken the child there for a visit. Wu Yan would celebrate the holiday with them, and her husband would fly over from Taiwan for a few days shortly thereafter.

Given that Wu Yan still had several years before she would be eligible for Taiwanese citizenship, I was curious about how she was able to spend over a month in Macau, which, as a special administrative region of the PRC, did not permit free entry by mainland Chinese.[15] As we lunched in a noisy Japanese restaurant in one of Taipei's lively business districts, she explained that because of her father's work assignment, she was eligible to apply for a Hong Kong–Macau travel pass from the Chinese government. With the pass she

FIGURE 3. Documents issued to Chinese spouses. Photo by author.

could remain in Macau for fourteen days, after which time she simply crossed the border to Zhuhai in Guangdong Province and then reentered Macau on her travel pass for Taiwan (see Map 2). This document granted her a seven-day stay in Macau. If she wanted to extend her visit, she could return again to the mainland and apply for a visa to Singapore or another Southeast Asian country at a consulate in Guangzhou. With the visa she was able to reenter Macau using her PRC passport, as if she simply was transiting there on her journey farther south. As a transit traveler, she was allowed to stay in Macau for an additional fourteen days.[16]

Through her savvy use of multiple documents, Wu Yan was able to extend her time in Macau for over one month. Her plan displayed considerable knowledge of the mobility benefits available through her mainland travel pass as a spouse of a Taiwanese, as well as extensive familiarity with which third-country tourist visas were easily procured by PRC passport holders and what transit privileges such visa recipients enjoyed in Macau while ostensibly en route to destinations elsewhere. Although Wu Yan's documentary strategies were all technically legal, her use of a third-country visa as a means of entry into Macau (with no intention of continuing on) offered a striking resemblance to what NIA official Zhu decried as the forging of Taiwan entry permit copies by Wu's less-privileged compatriots to enter Hong Kong in search of employment. As this comparison makes clear, legitimate and illegitimate mobility strategies draw on similar forms of expertise and knowledge to overcome the restrictions imposed by seemingly unique and inflexible travel documents (see also Chu 2010).

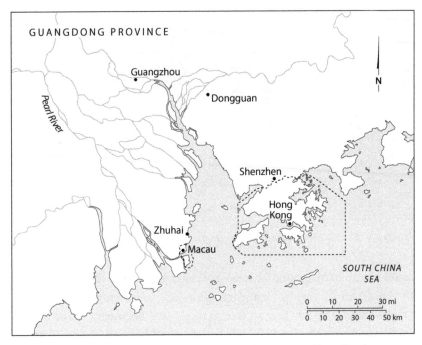

MAP 2. Map of Hong Kong, Macau, and Southern China. Prepared by Bill Nelson.

Circulation Effects

Chinese spouses from a wide range of backgrounds frequently discussed the different kinds of mobility available to them at different stages in Taiwan's lengthy immigration and naturalization process. At stake in these conversations were the "circulation effects" produced by various identity and travel documents—how well those documents constituted them as desirable travelers and how widely their documents enabled them to travel. Middle-aged women who aspired to visit adult children from previous marriages now studying or residing in Europe and North America claimed that such travel was only feasible once they had received Taiwanese citizenship because many countries in that part of the world did not freely grant tourist visas to PRC passport holders. Through the discursive circulation of knowledge and experience among immigrants, it became clear that the relationships among specific documents, the statuses they indexed, and the forms of mobility they enabled were far from fixed. Wu Yan's plan reflected an adept use of multiple travel and identity papers that was beyond the reach of many Chinese spouses in Taiwan who lacked a PRC passport or were unfamiliar with the travel benefits granted by other documents. And yet even those with more limited knowledge or fewer documentary resources were ever alert to possibilities for achieving greater mobility despite their liminal status in Taiwan.

During the government-sponsored policy education forums that I attended across Taiwan during the late 2000s, I could count on at least one audience participant to pose the question of how to manage third-country travel. NIA officials at these forums discouraged Chinese spouses from considering such travel during the initial reunion stage because most held a single-entry permit. Although they could submit the paperwork for another entry permit just before they departed Taiwan, the NIA would not issue the new permit until the original one had been collected by border officers when the Chinese spouse left the country, a policy designed to prevent one individual from holding two entry permits, one of which could be sold or given to someone else for fraudulent use. After the Chinese spouse departed Taiwan, the NIA mailed the new entry permit to her Taiwanese guarantor, who then forwarded it on to her, typically to her home in China.[17] With third-country travel, the new permit would have to be mailed to a strange destination, and NIA officials feared it might be lost in transit. The language of inconvenience and unpredictability also served as a screen, therefore, for concerns about fraudulent documents and "illegal" immigration.

The question of third-country travel also arose in discussions about the difficulties of returning to distant home communities in China. In the midst of a sleepy afternoon session of the 2007 acculturation class, a comparison of colloquial expressions used in the mainland and Taiwan quickly evolved into a debate about travel routes after Liao Lijing complained vociferously about how long it would take her to return to her home in northeastern China. The Taiwanese instructor leading the session that day interjected to ask Liao why she didn't use the faster route of transiting through South Korea, displaying her ignorance of the practical travel difficulties faced by Chinese spouses. The class awoke from their slumber at this remark, and several women chimed in to explain that Chinese spouses could not transit through Korea; they had to go through Hong Kong or Macau. Was it because they didn't have a passport, the instructor asked? Couldn't they go to a third country? No, retorted Chen Yueying adamantly, drawing on her experience as the class member with the longest history in Taiwan. She had asked on numerous occasions and each time was told that she could not travel to a third country. But another student had gone with her husband on a vacation to Malaysia, throwing a wrench in Yueying's tale. In the end it turned out that Yueying did not have a PRC passport as she first claimed, merely a travel pass. But was a PRC passport sufficient to travel elsewhere from Taiwan or to transit through a third country to return to China?

This exchange took place long before the initiation of direct flights across the Taiwan Strait, meaning that even those headed for destinations in northern China first had to fly south to Hong Kong or Macau before embarking on travel northward. Moreover, as described above, even Chinese spouses with a PRC passport did not use it on such trips because they exited Taiwan on their entry permit and entered China on their travel pass. Third-country travel required a Chinese spouse either to apply for a visa with her PRC passport in Taiwan or to return to China to apply at a consulate or embassy there. The success of a Taiwan-based application depended in part on what immigration stage a spouse had reached in Taiwan, and some countries required residency status if Chinese spouses were to apply for a visa from Taiwan. In sharing stories of successful and failed applications among themselves, most Chinese spouses concluded that applying at the reunion stage was fruitless and that one had much better chances at the residency stages.

Certainly there were instances of Chinese spouses receiving visas for travel to other countries, mostly Southeast Asian nations that were popular tourist destinations for both Chinese and Taiwanese. But the ability of a PRC passport to enable this kind of mobility depended on a number of factors, including the requirements demanded by the country of destination, the route to be taken, and the ability of the passport itself to vouch for the bearer's trustworthiness as a desirable traveler. Nearly everyone I spoke with assumed that it was virtually impossible for them to visit the United States prior to becoming a Taiwanese citizen because of strict US controls on issuing visas to PRC citizens for fear that they might overstay or seek to emigrate. Stories abounded of Chinese spouses who had been denied US visas even after they obtained Taiwanese citizenship, confirming the lingering taint of their mainland Chinese origins. But other countries were also infamous as difficult destinations. Over the spring of 2008, Jiang Meifeng regularly updated me on her efforts to accompany her Taiwanese husband and his relatives on a family vacation to Japan. Jiang was a cosmopolitan professional from Sichuan Province whose PRC passport bore the physical evidence of her many departures from and returns to China. Despite her well-stamped travel document, however, she encountered so many obstacles applying for a Japanese visa as a PRC citizen that the family finally was forced to cancel their trip.[18]

Tourist routes also affected Chinese spouses' travel mobility, especially when they sought to join Taiwan-organized tour groups that would visit several countries in a single trip. In the spring of 2008, Luo Jing's mother-in-law invited her on a tour to South Korea, but the travel agent claimed that Luo's documents posed a problem given the tour's itinerary. The group planned to continue on to Hong Kong from Korea and then to return to Taiwan. Although Luo might obtain a visa for South Korea, she did not have documents that would enable her to enter Hong Kong from a third country, and the tour did not permit her to return directly to Taiwan from South Korea. In her account of her travel difficulties, Luo never quite settled on one explanation for why her documents were insufficient, but it was clear to her that the travel agent was unwilling to handle the complications caused by the combination of her PRC passport with the atypical documentation used to manage cross-Strait travel.

More striking, however, was the questionable status of Luo Jing's PRC passport as a document that facilitated and accurately documented her cross-border journeys. Luo had applied for her passport just prior to departing for Taiwan in 2005, and because she had never traveled anywhere outside of China other than Taiwan, it contained no travel stamps to prove that she had legally departed the country. In other words, although Luo was no longer physically in China, her official travel document as a Chinese citizen did not provide evidence of a legal departure, entry elsewhere, or a return, all of which would constitute her as a desirable traveler who conformed to designated travel routes and permitted lengths of stay. Instead, her cross-Strait journey was documented by her travel pass and entry permit alone. For Chinese spouses in Taiwan, therefore, their passports do not accurately reflect their cross-border movement, precisely because the Taiwan-China border is constituted as not quite international by these merely passport-like documents. Cross-Strait mobility renders Chinese spouses out of place, located elsewhere to the routes tracked (or not) in their passports, further undermining their efforts to use valued passports for travel beyond Taiwan and China.

DOCUMENTARY AFFECT

Chinese spouses recognize the atypical features of the documents that facilitate their cross-Strait travels, and they regularly criticize the material insubstantiality of those documents as symbols of their own insecure standing in

Taiwan, emphasizing in particular the flimsiness of the single-sheet entry permit.[19] Taiwan-issued papers "transmit an affect of tentativeness" (Navaro-Yashin 2007, 86), not only in the sense of being ephemeral (easily destroyed) or bestowing limited circulation effects, but also because they affirm the uncertain sovereignty of Taiwan as the issuing body and Chinese spouses' own sense of never quite belonging in Taiwan. Chinese spouses' exceptionalism is reproduced through the ephemeral aura of the documents they carry and through the inability of those documents to constitute recognized identities and to enable desired forms of mobility—literally, across all borders, but also figuratively, in the sense of marital decisions and life circumstances in Taiwan that do not always live up to their imagined potential.

As merely "a piece of paper," the reunion permit that many of the Chinese spouses I knew received upon first arrival was frequently singled out for its lack of substance.[20] In contrast to the booklet form of the travel pass, residence permit, and passport or the laminated plastic card that connoted everyday citizenship in both Taiwan and China, this single sheet of paper was viewed by many as insubstantial and even humiliating, its flimsiness a symbol of their own tentative status in Taiwan. Even Taiwanese husbands took umbrage at paper documents and associated them with officials' discriminatory attitudes toward mainland Chinese. In 2003, I met a Taiwanese academic who had completed his PhD in Beijing and had married a Chinese woman who held a master's degree from Beijing University, China's premier academic institution. On his wife's second visit to Taiwan in 1997, border officials at the airport seized all of her documents, including her PRC passport. In his retelling of his wife's border-crossing experience, the husband described how the official had eyed her with suspicion, then tossed a pile of papers in her direction and brusquely instructed her to fill them out. Adding insult to injury was the flimsy document the official gave her in exchange for her other papers: a temporary ID that was merely, in her husband's words, "a very thin, very thin piece of paper (*hen bao hen bao de yizhang zhi*)."

Progressing from the insecurities of temporary reunion status to kin-based residency (*yiqin juliu*) was an experience marked not only by greater rights (the ability of some to work legally, for instance) but also by more substantial documents. With changes to the immigration sequence in 2004, Chinese spouses became eligible for kin-based residency following two years of marriage or the birth of a child, and they looked forward to this first residency stage as a sign of recognized standing in Taiwan. Many articulated the transition through reference to the physical form of their new identity document.

Unlike the sheet of paper that certified reunion status, kin-based residency was documented by a passport-like booklet with a light blue cover. Chinese spouses referred to their newly acquired status by underscoring the weight and substance of this document: they identified it as "the booklet" (*benzi*) or the "blue booklet" (*lanse de benzi*), and they frequently mentioned that it had multiple pages. In contrast to the insecurity experienced by holders of reunion permits, the kin-based residency booklet inspired a sense of pride and confidence among its bearers because of its material substantiality.

Chinese spouses' attachment to the kin-based residency permit also derived from assumptions about the greater circulation effects of that document as opposed to the reunion permit. Luo Jing, whose failed effort to join a tour to Korea I described above, was eager to pick up her new residency permit on the cool fall day in 2007 when I accompanied her to NIA headquarters in Taipei. She had checked the status of her application online that morning to confirm that the document was ready and had emailed me to arrange a time for us to meet at the bus stop near the apartment she shared with her husband, father-in-law, and the latter's second wife. Our bus ride took us from the upscale neighborhoods of northeastern Taipei to the mixed business and working-class streets of the older, western part of the city. We arrived at the NIA in the early afternoon and proceeded down the escalator to the cavernous hall dedicated to mainland Chinese applicants. Women and men of all ages walked back and forth across the hall, some pulling along small children, others arguing amongst themselves or looking bewilderedly at the vast number of service counters or the forms spilling from their hands. Fortunately there was no line to pick up processed applications, and Luo confidently approached the woman seated at the desk. The clerk's attitude was brusque and businesslike, and when it turned out that Luo had forgotten to bring her receipt, the woman asked in an exasperated voice whether she had any identification. Luo retrieved her National Health Insurance card from her purse and handed it to the clerk, who, appeased by the familiar card, pulled out Luo's new document from her file drawer.

As we walked away from the desk, the light blue booklet in hand, Luo Jing turned to me and asked whether now she could enter and leave Taiwan without additional paperwork. In search of a definitive answer, we returned to the desk, and Luo asked whether the booklet enabled her "to come and go freely." Before leaving the country, she needed an exit stamp (*jia qian*), the clerk replied, and she turned the pages to show Luo the stamp that came with her new document. We sat down on a bench in the large hall, and Luo leafed carefully through the booklet. The first inside page of Luo's document looked very much like a passport and included her photograph and identifying information, such as date and place of birth, reason for entry (kin-based), and her husband's name. There was a line stating that she was required to submit to fingerprinting on her first entry and a notation indicating that she had. The remaining interior pages were blank, except for the one exit stamp and another stamp with the permit's expiration date.

Although Luo had high hopes that this new document would facilitate greater mobility beyond Taiwan and China, she would soon learn that her kin-dependent status did not enable unfettered movement across borders. Not only was she required to visit the NIA for an exit stamp before returning to China, but she would find that the blue booklet did little to resolve obstacles to third-country travel (although it did finally make her eligible for visas from some countries). Luo's investment in the new document had more to do with its material qualities and perceived linkages between the booklet's substantiality and her own gradually improved status in Taiwan. But because both kin-based and extended residency (*changqi juliu*) were merely stages in a longer progression toward Taiwanese citizenship, their impact on mobility beyond cross-Strait journeys was mixed, and third-country travel remained dependent on how well Chinese spouses' PRC passports identified them as desirable travelers. Chinese spouses quickly came to learn that the widest scope of mobility could be attained only with a Taiwan identification card and passport, and they often expressed their desire for that mobility through the compact physicality of the national ID.

The Terminal One arrival hall at Taoyuan International Airport was bustling with travelers when Deng Lifang and I disembarked from a direct flight from China's coastal city of Fuzhou in April 2008, after visiting Deng's parents and younger brother and making final arrangements for the new apartment she had purchased in the small city near her home village. As we proceeded toward immigration processing, I asked Deng whether she needed to be fingerprinted, and she replied no. She had resided in Taiwan since the late 1990s and now held extended residency status, her eligibility for citizenship endlessly deferred by her husband's premature death due to suicide. Despite regular travels across the Strait to visit her family, Deng seemed unfamiliar with the admission process, and we searched around the hall for a blank entry form because she had forgotten to complete hers on the airplane. When we reached the head of the immigration line, I saw the border officer glance quickly at her documents and then gesture toward the mainland arrivals counter behind us. We left the line and approached the counter, where the officer on duty briefly looked over her documentation and instructed her to come behind the counter to be fingerprinted, after which he stamped her entry permit and we lined up once again to proceed through immigration.

Passing through this time with no delay, Deng Lifang turned to me as we walked toward baggage claim and looked yearningly at the foreign resident card I held in my hand, a laminated plastic card I had received through the sponsorship of my research institution in Taiwan. She sighed and added that she wished she, too, could use a card like mine, especially because it so closely resembled Taiwan's national ID. I was struck at the time by the poignancy of Deng's remark: despite a decade of residence in Taiwan, she still struggled to create a sense of belonging in the only place she now felt she could call home, and experiences such as being turned back from immigration to be finger-printed only reinforced her outsider status. At the time, it was not the fingerprinting per se that disturbed Deng but rather the inadequacies of her documents that failed to provide the kind of state recognition that would enable unfettered entry into Taiwan. In yearning for an ID such as mine, Deng Lifang conveyed her desire for much-delayed citizenship status through her attachment to the compact materiality of a small, laminated plastic card.[21]

DOCUMENTARY STATENESS

In his history of the passport in Western Europe and the United States, John Torpey argues that "the emergence of passport and related controls on move-ment is an essential aspect of the 'state-ness' of states" (2000, 3). Torpey builds on Max Weber's theory of state legitimacy to suggest that monopoliz-ing "the legitimate means of movement" was critical to modern state building. Adam Mckeown interprets the growing emphasis on documentation and related immigration procedures as key components of "a broader diffusion and standardization of principles about what it meant to be a sovereign state within an international system" (2008, 13).[22] Asserting sovereignty, therefore, required conforming to such documentary practices, a task all the more imperative for unrecognized or even illegal states. As Yael Navaro-Yashin ar-gues, "Documents are among the primary paraphernalia of modern states and legal systems: they are its material culture. A wannabe 'state' would have to produce documents too, in order to look and act like a state" (2007, 84).

Unrecognized states, in other words, seek to generate stateness through their very documentary practices (see also Navaro-Yashin 2003, 2012).

Both Taiwan and China display a certain degree of ambiguity and anxiety about their documentary claims to stateness, despite their very different experiences of international recognition as sovereign states. The passport, ostensibly that supreme document for producing and representing state sovereignty and citizenship status, is beset with problems for both countries, albeit in different ways. PRC passport holders encounter numerous obstacles when applying for visas, as Jiang Meifeng discovered when planning her trip to Japan. The infamous association of Fuzhounese with human smuggling and fraudulent travel documents undermines the face value of the PRC passport by subjecting all who bear it to greater scrutiny at foreign consulates in China and at points of entry elsewhere (Chu 2010; Wang 2004).

Although Chinese spouses idealize the circulation effects of Taiwanese passports and their ability to propel them beyond the narrow confines of cross-Strait travel, the Taiwanese passport, too, is limited in its ability to facilitate unfettered mobility, convey stateness, or demand sovereign recognition. Precisely because stamping a passport is widely viewed as a practice that enacts and bestows sovereignty, as Mr. Zhu and Mr. Lu claimed, some countries hesitate to stamp the Taiwan passport out of concern that such an act would connote recognition of Taiwanese sovereignty and provoke retribution from China. Instead, those countries issue Taiwanese travelers a visa on a separate piece of paper and require border officers to stamp the visa and not the passport. In addition to the hypocrisy of this practice (because the visa *is* issued in the end, and the traveler *is* allowed to enter), these separate visas may enhance suspicions about forgery and engender humiliating scrutiny at border crossings (Wang 2004, 363–64).

The Taiwan passport also suffers from misrecognition, both in terms of what country it represents and because its bearer may be mistaken for a PRC citizen. Prior to 2003, the passport cover bore only the name "Republic of China," generating confusion among foreign border officers who might not associate Taiwan with its formal name or who might mistake it for China's official name, "the *People's* Republic of China." After much domestic debate, the Chen Shui-bian government issued a new passport in 2003 that added "Taiwan" to the cover, but this addition also produced confusion at border crossings, especially when groups of Taiwanese carried both old and new passports, arousing suspicion about the documents' authenticity (Wang 2004, 361, 365–67).[23]

Moreover, the bearers of Taiwanese passports may be treated harshly at border crossings because their documents, and thus their identities, are seen as suspect, too easily adopted by mainland Chinese.[24] On numerous occasions, NIA officials and border officers complained to me that Taiwanese have exceptionally high rates of passport "loss," a phenomenon they attributed to the ease with which Taiwanese passports could be altered for fraudulent use by PRC citizens.[25] In the course of our 2009 interview, Mr. Zhu casually mentioned that Taiwan was in the midst of discussions with Canadian authorities about granting visa waivers to Taiwan citizens. The stumbling block, he contended, was concern on the part of the United States government that Chinese might use a forged Taiwanese passport to enter the United States illegally via Canada.[26] Fear of this outcome increased US pressure on Canada and delayed approval of the visa waiver until November 2010.[27]

Put simply, a Taiwan passport is evaluated internationally not only as a document that identifies its bearer as a Taiwanese citizen and asserts Taiwan's sovereign statehood, contested though that assertion may be. The Taiwan passport is also evaluated in relation to its potential for fraudulent use by mainland Chinese and this possibility compromises its association with a unique individual identity. What grants the Taiwan passport value in the realm of forged documents (the ease with which it enables "illegal" Chinese migration) is also what undermines its ability to facilitate ostensibly unique identification and legitimate cross-border mobility.[28] The ambiguity that burdens the Taiwan passport stems not only from Taiwan's own uncertain sovereign status (not illegal, but not fully sovereign) but also from Taiwan's relationship to China and how that relationship is imagined by border officials around the world and potentially manipulated by travelers.

This chapter has shown how documents often fail to perform the work they are intended to do, despite the heartfelt investments of those who generate them, evaluate their authenticity, and use them to assert identities, claim recognition, and facilitate mobility. For Chinese spouses and Taiwanese bureaucrats, identity and travel documents are fraught sources of both anxiety and aspiration, condensing individual and national desires for the security bestowed by mutual recognition and belonging. Because the documents that facilitate cross-Strait travel are approximations of internationally recognized identity and travel documents—mere "as if" passports, visas, or national ID cards—they also reproduce Taiwan's uncertain sovereignty and its not quite state-to-state relationship with China. For Chinese spouses, this documentary approximation has the added consequences of limiting their documents' circulation effects beyond the narrow realm of cross-Strait travel and widening the gap between them and all other foreign spouses of Taiwanese citizens. As Chinese spouses move between China and Taiwan and through Taiwanese society, their documents set them apart from other travelers and immigrants, while they simultaneously reenact cross-Strait contestations over Taiwanese sovereignty.

TWO

—————

Real or Sham? Evaluating Marital Authenticity

The proportion of sham marriages among Chinese spouses is as high as 70 percent. This is a big social problem; this is not discrimination.

HSIEH CHANG-TING, *DPP presidential candidate,*
March 10, 2008

My definition of sham marriage is as follows: "The male and female parties concerned lack the idea of a real marriage. Formally they have legally married by registering in the mainland or Taiwan and meet the objective conditions for a legally established marriage. But basically they lack the subjective intention to jointly create a family and lead a life together. This is what is called a sham marriage."

NATIONAL IMMIGRATION AGENCY BORDER AFFAIRS
CORPS OFFICIAL, *June 22, 2009*

DURING TAIWAN'S 2008 PRESIDENTIAL CAMPAIGN, Democratic Progressive Party candidate Hsieh Chang-ting uttered a casual remark in the midst of a meeting with scholars and activists who challenged his stance on immigration. Responding to their concerns about his refusal to expand work rights for Chinese spouses, Hsieh justified his position with the quote in the first epigraph, pointing to ostensibly high rates of sham marriage (*jia jiehun*) among cross-Strait couples. This marriage fraud, he argued, justified the government's efforts to restrict the entry of mainland spouses (Cai 2008).

Hsieh's claimed figure of a 70 percent sham marriage rate provoked a backlash from immigrant rights organizations and Chinese spouses themselves.[1] In the Internet-mediated debate that followed, however, no party questioned the existence of sham marriage itself. Instead, the arguments and statistics trafficked back and forth reinforced the government's claim that categories of "sham" and "real" marriage actually existed and that immigration bureaucrats were equipped to recognize them and make decisions accordingly.

Around the world, marriage migrants are often portrayed as desperate "mail order brides" or crafty women and men seeking financial gain, their motives flattened into simplistic rationales of material deprivation and lack of opportunity. By contrast, a rich ethnographic literature has documented more varied and complex motivations for marriage migration, including love and affection, limited opportunities to find a desirable spouse or bear children in one's home country, and aspirations of personal advancement, adventure, and economic security, among others (e.g., Cole 2014; Constable 2003a, 2003b; Faier 2009; Freeman 2011; Newendorp 2008; Schaeffer 2013). These diverse motives combine with intense state regulation to create pervasive suspicion about couples' intentions and the quality of their marriages, forcing marriage migrants to negotiate with care a terrain that links cross-border marriage to immigration and citizenship status (Kim 2010; Neveu Kringelbach 2013).

Governmental and societal anxieties about marital fraud have made authenticity the dominant metric for evaluating intimacy and intentions in cross-border unions. In the case of cross-Strait marriages, widespread Taiwanese suspicions about Chinese spouses' marital motives support a bureaucratic regime organized around the distinction between "real" and "sham" marriages, authorizing more restrictive immigration policies and engaging bureaucrats, immigrants, and citizens in the delineation of proper marital roles, with the effect of legitimizing some types of marriages and intimate behaviors at the expense of others. These efforts to identify and police marital norms among cross-Strait couples rest on the specific regulatory practices, cultural norms, and forms of knowledge that empower bureaucrats to evaluate the authenticity of intimate relationships that facilitate immigration. These authenticity paradigms measure affective labor against instrumental motives by invoking a specific model of a caring relationship that is comprehensible and credible to various state and societal actors. The linking of intimacy and authenticity, however, creates a narrow vision of domestic relations that often fails to capture the complex motivations and living arrangements of women and men who marry across the Taiwan Strait.

To evaluate marital authenticity, the Taiwan government has designed immigration policies and border practices that aim to block the entry of immigrants in sham marriages, utilizing definitions such as the one quoted in the second epigraph above, coined by a senior NIA official who had many years of experience interviewing Chinese spouses at the border. In our conversation, this official distinguished between the legality of a marriage (its objective basis) and the subjective intentions of the two parties. From his perspective, the challenge faced by the border official or immigration bureaucrat is to determine whether a couple truly intends to build a life together or whether their marriage merely utilizes the scaffolding of legal recognition to support nonmarital aims.

Border interviews presume that states have the sovereign power to regulate cross-border flows and to determine the composition of their citizenry, in this case through adjudicating the authenticity of citizens' marital relationships with noncitizens (Friedman 2010a). As an official bureaucratic encounter between a mainland Chinese and a representative of the Taiwan state, the border interview enacts Taiwanese sovereignty both by restricting who can enter the country and by schooling immigrants in the roles the state envisions for them as permanent residents and future citizens. Certainly, Taiwan is not alone in regulating the entry of foreign spouses or in monitoring their path toward naturalization, nor is it unique in evaluating the perceived quality of its citizens' transnational marriages (e.g., Constable 2003a; Neveu Kringelbach 2013; Surkis 2010). Border inspections and police and consular interviews have long been used by governments around the world to produce categories of people deemed desirable and undesirable from the perspectives of family stability, the health and uniformity of the population, and national reproduction.[2] But in many places anxieties about marital immigrants surface due to concerns that binational marriages exploit loopholes in immigration regulations, providing entry and citizenship rights to foreigners otherwise deemed unassimilable to the shared "community of value" that constitutes an imagined nation (Anderson 2013, 2–5; see also Neveu Kringelbach 2013). Taiwan's motivations for evaluating the authenticity of cross-Strait marriages are more complex: although immigration interviews seek to obstruct the fraudulent use of marriage for immigration purposes, they also make a claim about Taiwan's status as sovereign nation-state that participates in a community of like-minded polities committed to regulating border flows and defining the composition of the national population.

Taiwan began to interview mainland Chinese spouses in the early years of the twenty-first century when soaring rates of cross-border marriage sparked growing anxieties about the changing face of the country's population and the impact of migration from China. As the Entry/Exit Immigration Police Department (*ruchujing guanliju*) developed an interview system designed to evaluate cross-Strait unions and Chinese spouses' applications for residency and citizenship, it sought guidance and training from local consular representatives from the United States, Canada, and Australia. Over the years, government officials have repeatedly invoked international precedents to justify Taiwan's interview system, and in so doing, they simultaneously asserted Taiwan's conformity to sovereign practices widely adopted by other nation-states.

In late 2002 and early 2003, immigration police began to request interviews with Chinese spouses already in the country whose applications for residency or citizenship aroused suspicions about the status of their marriage. In the summer of 2003, officials at the airport conducted a two-month trial during which they interviewed all mainland Chinese entering Taiwan, not only spouses but also those coming to visit relatives, care for sick family members, or attend a funeral. In September of that year, they narrowed the scope of interviews to spouses only. Although all cross-border marriages involving a Taiwanese citizen are assessed for marital authenticity, only Chinese spouses face this specific border interview regime. Because China refuses to recognize Taiwan as a sovereign state, the Taiwanese government is unable to establish an official consular office in the mainland. Therefore, it must wait until Chinese spouses arrive at their first port of entry, typically one of Taiwan's two major airports, to conduct an interview with the couple. This regulatory regime further distinguishes Chinese spouses from all other marital immigrants who are interviewed with their citizen spouse at Taiwan's de facto consular office in their home country.

The new immigration sequence for Chinese spouses written into law and implemented in March 2004 required in-country and border interviews as part of the entry application process.[3] First, the Taiwanese spouse was interviewed in-country to investigate his social and economic standing in order to assess whether he would be able to support his wife before she acquired legal work rights, which prior to August 2009 took anywhere from two to six years. Interviewers also looked for situations that might indicate a sham marriage, such as unemployment, high debt levels, or homelessness. Most Tai-wanese spouses I encountered typically passed the interview on the first round, especially if they brought supporting documentation, but some went through as many as four or five in-country interviews before satisfying NIA demands. In these cases, NIA investigators had to walk a fine line between, on the one hand, claiming to block sham marriages or protecting the interests of a perhaps naive immigrant spouse and, on the other hand, discriminating against poor citizens by challenging their right to marry.

If the citizen-spouse passed the interview, he was eligible to apply for an entry permit for his Chinese partner. The entry permit enabled the Chinese spouse to fly to Taiwan, but it did not guarantee admission into the country until the couple passed another round of interviews at the border. The air-port interview delves most deeply into the marriage itself and compares ac-counts by the two spouses. Hence it is here that marital intentions come under rigorous scrutiny as interviewers strive to unravel neatly constructed tales and memorized narratives.

During the early years of the interview system, interviewers at both the airport and Immigration Police headquarters were drawn from multiple police agencies and rotated in on a temporary basis, receiving little if any training. Officials at the airport who participated in the establishment of the interview system emphasized that the percentage of "sham marriages" was initially very high: one quoted an off-the-cuff figure of thirteen out of a daily total of sixty one, nearly 5 percent (interview March 4, 2008), and statistics provided by the Taoyuan Airport Border Affairs Corps in 2008 indicated that 14 percent of those interviewed from September through December 2003 were deported immediately, and 17 percent were required to submit to sec-ondary interviews within thirty days of entry. Yet looking back on that pe-riod, many bureaucrats argued that a substantial number of cases slipped through precisely because interviewers were poorly trained and unable to "seize the main point" necessary to unravel a tale. The Taiwanese press regu-larly reported on interview abuses, and these often sensationalist accounts fo-cused with prurient interest on interviewers who asked detailed questions about couple's sexual relations (frequency, sexual positions) and other intimate habits because they lacked more skilled questioning techniques.

Once the NIA was established in January 2007, all interviewers were drawn from NIA ranks and received regular supervision. When I first ob-served airport interviews in 2008, NIA bureaucrats were quick to reassure me that interview training had improved over the years.[4] This regularization fostered shared agreement among interviewers about what features raised suspicions about a possible sham marriage: couples who failed to describe their courtship or shared life in any detail (or who provided contradictory details), a large age gap between spouses, a very short period between meeting for the first time and deciding to marry, or evidence of behaviors that did not conform to interviewers' expectations of conventional marital roles. But the establishment of the NIA also came at a price, for many experienced interviewers moved on to more prestigious positions in the agency's investigative division, and the total number of personnel on each team was slashed in half.[5] Hence bureaucratization, despite normalizing the interview process itself, did not necessarily produce greater efficiency or effectiveness (McKeown 2008).

The majority of Chinese spouses arriving in Taiwan for the first time land at Taoyuan International Airport's Terminal One on afternoon or evening flights from Hong Kong or Macau. After disembarking in the air-conditioned yet still humid air of the airport's older terminal, they follow the signs toward immigration, passing duty-free shops, where Taiwanese rush to make last-minute purchases of alcohol, cosmetics, or cigarettes before proceeding through body heat sensors installed in the aftermath of the 2005 SARS outbreak. Instead of lining up for immigration inspection as do other travelers, Chinese spouses look anxiously around the arrival hall until they spot the long counter marked with a sign indicating mainland arrivals processing. The counter is staffed by NIA desk clerks, mostly female, and young men completing their military service who have been assigned to a base near the airport and who perform clerical work to compensate for the reduction in airport staffing with the establishment of the NIA.[6]

Clerks working the counter receive regular faxes from the Hong Kong and Macau airport offices of Chung Hwa Travel Service, Taiwan's unofficial consular entity, which list the flights destined for Taoyuan and the names of Chinese spouses on those flights who are first-time arrivals. The clerks print out relevant information available on these spouses from the NIA computer system, including transcripts of the citizen-spouse's in-country interview. They flag issues of concern (for instance, multiple domestic interviews, a substantial age difference, or a suspicious place of origin) and may track down additional information they feel would be helpful to the interviewer.[7] Once the Chinese spouse arrives at the counter, clerks collect and copy her travel documents and collate them with these other materials. Chinese spouses entering for the first time are called behind the counter to be fingerprinted, each finger carefully pressed into a digital sensor pad that creates a computer file tagged to the other documents. On subsequent entries, as Deng Lifang discovered, an imprint of her thumbprints alone will be used to confirm her identity. Once this process is completed, the clerks place the documents in an envelope and stack it in the interview queue.[8] Then the Chinese spouse (and her Taiwanese partner, if he has accompanied her on the flight) takes a seat in the rows of plastic chairs off to the side of the counter and waits, sometimes for as long as one to two hours, to be called for an interview.

The interview itself is not a clearly contained event but spills out beyond the boundaries of formal questioning. The interviewer calls out the name of the Chinese spouse and accompanies her across the arrival hall to a door marked "interview rooms." In this short span of a few minutes, the interviewer may ask the spouse informal questions about the marriage in order to begin classifying it in her mind (young couple with a child, marriage to a Taiwanese businessman resident in China, marriage to an elderly veteran, second marriage, pregnant woman, etc.). This informal questioning continues as the interviewer selects one of six starkly furnished interview rooms and begins entering basic information into the computer.[9] Often several minutes pass before the interviewer signals that the formal interview has begun by reading aloud a list of statements about the interview procedures and the consequences of giving false information, pausing after each item to ask the spouse to acknowledge verbally that she understands the content and consents to the interview.

During the typically hour-long interview, the interviewer asks detailed questions about the mainland spouse's life in China, how the couple met and courted, how often the Taiwanese spouse visited China and details of those visits, material exchanges between the spouses and their families (bridewealth payments of money and jewelry, gifts to parents or other family members, support payments after the marriage), details of the marriage registration process in China, how and with whom they celebrated the wedding, and what the Chinese spouse knows about the Taiwan spouse's job, family, and life in Taiwan. In particular, interviewers expect couples to know specific details about bridewealth (how much, how it was presented, when and where), wedding banquets (the time and location, the number of tables, who attended, whether alcohol was served), and the sending of support funds (the amount, frequency, and method of transfer). These expectations derive from interviewers' belief that Chinese spouses pay careful attention to financial arrangements and thus should be able to recall the specifics of monetary exchanges.

After this first round of detailed questioning, the same interviewer conducts a shorter interview with the Taiwanese spouse, asking him a subset of those questions to compare responses. Interviewers intentionally switch quickly between topics to prevent recitation of a memorized narrative and follow up on small details that they can use when comparing the two accounts. When an interviewer perceives the case to be straightforward (for instance, a young couple returning briefly to register the birth of their child or to hold a wedding banquet), the interview may be brief and the questions general. However, when personal or marital histories appear complicated, the questioning becomes more specific and intense, resembling an interrogation more than an interview.

EVALUATING MARITAL AUTHENTICITY

Subjective intentions are slippery indeed and especially difficult to evaluate through a formal bureaucratic encounter. Border interviews ultimately rest on the marriage's plausibility: in a context of unknowability, they aim to establish a plausible case for admitting or denying entry to an immigrant spouse based on the perceived authenticity of the marriage. In practice, however, interviews rarely determine the "truth" of a couple's marital intentions. The process of questioning couples and comparing accounts instead requires interviewers and interviewees to reevaluate their own understanding of what constitutes a legitimate marriage. Rather than coldly impersonal bureaucratic interactions, border interviews draw immigration officers into the messy, unpredictable features of cross-Strait couples' lives, even as interviewers seek to manage the disruptive effects of that variation through invoking cultural norms and expectations.

The interview creates an administrative conception of marriage and intimacy, a consequence of its reliance on a mode of questioning that demands certain kinds of responses from the interviewee, what elsewhere I have called "truth statements" (Friedman 2010a). Interviewers' expectations about what constitutes a real marriage emphasize *norms of conduct* over emotional bonds: they structure interview questions around a set of assumptions about a similar cultural heritage and ritual practices shared by Chinese and Taiwanese. It is not that interviewers are deaf to expressions of marital intimacy, but they do not rely on emotions to determine marital authenticity.[10] The interview itself becomes what Shuman and Bohmer term a "cultural performance"

(2004, 410), and yet it is not always clear that both parties share the same cultural expectations about marital norms.[11]

Marriage in both China and Taiwan is a relationship whose significance, goals, and practices vary across generations, urban and rural areas, and sectors of the population. Although love and romance signify "modern" marriage on both sides of the Strait, they often represent only one dimension of marital decisions oriented around practical considerations of economic livelihood and housing, family compatibility, and a potential husband's family composition and intergenerational commitments in contexts where patrilineal values and expectations of patrilocal residence remain salient features of many couples' lives (Davis and Friedman 2014). Although both love and instrumental motives feature prominently in many contemporary marriages, domestic couples are freer to integrate them in ways that often make the latter less explicit. Transnational marriages bring tensions between emotional attachments and material desires to the surface precisely because such marriages are presumed to facilitate social and economic mobility across borders.

Interview questioning generates a particular understanding of an authentic marriage and its component parts that creates an essentialized Chinese marriage defined by material exchanges and social and bureaucratic rituals. This construction reflects what Taiwanese interviewers think they know about Chinese spouses' marital motives and the conditions of their lives in China, despite the fact that most interviewers have never been to China and only interact with Chinese citizens in their professional roles. Although some interviewers explain divergent accounts as the result of customary differences and are willing to overlook what they view as minor discrepancies, they consistently ask a regular set of questions that shore up basic assumptions about a shared cultural heritage. Those assumptions and the stances from which interviewers initiate questioning (suspicion versus trust) also shape bureaucratic definitions of sham and real marriages. As a result, the burden of proving marital authenticity rests on cross-Strait couples themselves who must show that their behaviors conform to this model of real Chinese marriage.[12]

Border officers' emphasis on shared cultural conventions may, however, cause difficulties for interviewers because conformity to customary practice makes it hard for them to deny admission even when they suspect marital fraud. Many border officers argued that the presence of the husband's parents and other family members at the mainland wedding ceremony or at his in-country interview offered strong support to the authenticity of the marriage, especially given traditional views of Taiwanese families as oriented around a male descent line. For example, one interviewer described a case in which he had admitted a Chinese wife because the Taiwanese husband's parents and paternal grandparents had attended the wedding in China, identifying this kind of patrilineal support as a typical sign of an authentic marriage. And yet the woman was later arrested in Taiwan for engaging in prostitution.

Bureaucrats' concerns that cross-Strait marriages might be a pretext for engaging in sex work, often facilitated by a human smuggling or "snakehead" gang, permeated the interview system. The ubiquitous expression "sham marriage, actually prostitution" (*jia jiehun zhen maiyin*) made the association of sham marriage with sex work virtually unquestionable during the early years of the twenty-first century when the interview system was being established. But even when I observed interviews later in the decade, the specter of sex work emerged on a regular basis. And when it did, whether in interviews or during casual conversations among interviewers, it enabled interviewers to rearticulate their own assumptions about marital conventions and proper gendered behavior for "truly" married women.

During a meeting at central NIA headquarters in Taipei with former police officials turned NIA civil servants, I encountered Mr. Zhang, a midcareer bureaucrat who had been a key player in the initial planning for the interview system and who himself had conducted many interviews and trained new interviewers. His explanation for the purpose of the interview focused at first on the goal of discovering whether an immigrant spouse was likely to engage in illegal activity after entering the country. Mr. Zhang drew a fine line between the legality of a marriage and the intentions of the immigrant spouse, much like the definition in the second epigraph that distinguished a marriage's objective legal basis from the couple's subjective intentions. As Mr. Zhang explained, "Our most important [tasks] are twofold: marital authenticity is only one factor we consider in [deciding] whether to issue . . . a permit [for entry]. The other is whether the person will engage in illegal activity after coming to Taiwan" (interview Feb. 4, 2008). The perceived threat here was sex work, although Mr. Zhang was reluctant to name it as such: "She [a Chinese spouse] is clearly coming here to engage in, she might just. . . ." But instead of taking the sentence to its logical conclusion (she is clearly coming here to engage in sex work), he substituted the less controversial job of health aide (*kan hu*), a common form of employment for older Chinese women. Because this hypothetical Chinese spouse is not qualified to apply for entry as a migrant worker, Mr. Zhang continued, "She uses marriage to enter the country (*suoyi ta yong zhege jiehun jin lai*). So of course we're not going to issue her [an entry permit]!" By pairing concerns about undocumented labor and immigration loopholes with the goal of determining a Chinese spouse's "true" intentions, Mr. Zhang generated a model of marital authenticity that could then be evaluated through the interview system.

Up to this point in our conversation, I had found Mr. Zhang's distinction between truth and intention persuasive. His authoritative bearing, honed through years of police work and immigration control, coupled with his clear, compelling manner of speech, combined to create an image of a competent bureaucrat committed to transmitting his knowledge and experience to his subordinates. At the end of his explanation, however, he suddenly uttered a remark that undermined the careful definitional work he had performed up to that moment. Turning to his superior as if for confirmation, Mr. Zhang concluded, "Because as soon as you see it, you know that it is a sham (*yinwei neige na chu lai yi kan, kan le jiushi jia de ma*)."

This concluding sentiment permeated the remainder of our conversation, and I began to notice it in my discussions with other immigration officials. We might sum up its core sentiment as "I know a sham marriage when I see one." The signs are obvious, or ostensibly so: the attire and bearing of an immigrant spouse who is really a sex worker, limited or conflicting information about how the couple met or courted, significant age and status differences, or evidence of a sudden decision to marry. Mr. Zhang and his superior literally performed the physical signs of a sham marriage for me as they proceeded to mime the appearance of an immigrant wife-sex worker, drawing their hands up their legs in an exaggerated fashion to demonstrate the height of the slit in her skirt and sweeping their hands across their chests to suggest a revealing neckline. Mr. Zhang and his superior's performance reflected their taken-for-granted understanding of gender conventions by emphasizing how such norms were enacted on the surface of the female body. For them, a Chinese wife who failed to conform to the conventional standards of dress and comportment expected of married women indicated a sham marriage that was, they assumed, a pretext for sex work. By identifying sham marriages, bureaucrats such as Mr. Zhang not only aimed to block the instrumental use of marriage to enter Taiwan, but they simultaneously shored up societal standards for authentic marriages and socially condoned marital roles that cut across the citizen-immigrant divide.

Despite Mr. Zhang's assertion that sham marriages were easy to identify, however, the interviews I observed often revealed complicated marriage situations that required interviewers to adjust and refine their understanding of what characterized an authentic marriage. By the time I observed airport interviews in 2008 and 2009, interviewers claimed they could not discriminate against couples who had met through marriage brokers or matchmakers (especially given how accepted these practices were in Taiwan's recent past), but they simultaneously viewed such arrangements with suspicion and typically questioned the spouses more intently.[13] Similarly, caretaking unions involving elderly men and middle-aged or even young women might be subjected to greater scrutiny, but as long as the Chinese spouse appeared committed to her caretaking responsibilities (either exclusively or in addition to employment other than sex work), interviewers generally looked the other way. These negotiations show how the categories of sham and authentic marriage are not immutable but come into being in particular moments of discourse shaped by the bureaucratic encounter. The specific characteristics of any given encounter, including the identities of the participants, create a space for bureaucratic discretion in the very definition of sham and real marriage.[14]

DEFERRING JUDGMENT

As interviewers quickly discover, societal norms and standards of marital authenticity fluctuate over time and circumstances, and spouses' intentions prove notoriously difficult to establish through a brief, liminal encounter in the airport control zone. In the absence of definitive evidence of a sham marriage—such as a frank admission of collusion (which occasionally does happen), the use of fraudulent documents, or a falsified identity—interviewers who are suspicious about marital intentions typically admit the Chinese spouse but extend her visa for only thirty days and require a second interview by the NIA special operations brigade within that time period. By deferring judgment, they acknowledge the limitations of what can be achieved by the border interview, in effect calling into question the sovereignty work promised by this powerful bureaucratic practice.

One evening in late March 2008, I quietly slipped out of the matter-of-fact interview I had been observing after hearing Ms. Wu raise her voice as she closely questioned a Taiwanese husband in the room next door. Having observed Ms. Wu's interviews on several occasions, it was clear to me from the tone of her voice that the couple had aroused her suspicions. Ms. Wu's petite build and attractive appearance hid a fierce questioning style and a strong aversion to being taken for a fool. On paper, the forty-something Taiwanese man she was interviewing claimed to be an expatriate Taiwanese manager in the mainland, but his darkly tanned skin and awkward, almost boyish appearance and mannerisms suggested a more working-class background. He shifted uneasily in his chair, refusing to look directly at Ms. Wu, his gaze wandering around the small room. Occasionally, he turned his head slightly to check whether I was still sitting behind him.[15]

When I entered the room, Ms. Wu had been asking the man detailed questions about the bridewealth payment he had given to his wife, including when and where he had handed it to her and how the money had been packaged. She then printed out the interview transcript for him and excused herself while he read through it. I accompanied Ms. Wu to an empty room at the end of the hall, where she phoned her team head. In her brief summary, she emphasized that although the husband claimed to have known his wife for four years, he couldn't remember her birth date or the details of the bridewealth, which he had presented only a few months earlier. Whereas the wife stated that he accompanied her to and from work every day, he said she went to work alone. In sum, Ms. Wu concluded, the interview was marred by multiple discrepancies.

The team head's first response was that the Chinese spouse should be deported, but he came down to the interview room to question the husband himself. Standing next to the desk in the cramped space, he asked rapid-fire questions about how the man had met his wife, where they had worked, and when they had begun to live together. He pursued this line of inquiry while Ms. Wu spoke again with the wife, who was seated outside the interview rooms. Ms. Wu soon returned, irate because she had discovered that the wife had not been forthcoming in her interview: "Your wife admitted she lied to me," Ms. Wu burst out. "She was married and divorced once before." The husband acknowledged that he knew she was divorced and added that he didn't know why his wife hadn't told the truth. He then continued, as if viewing the situation from the interviewers' perspective, "speaking truthfully, there are some who come over through sham marriage." Hearing this, Ms. Wu retorted, "I always start from the position of believing you. Therefore, I must check and verify [all the details]."

As if to affirm her statement, Ms. Wu and her supervisor then initiated another round of questioning directed at the various points on which the spouses' accounts had differed. Exasperated by the inconsistencies in their statements, the team head accused the man, too, of lying: "Why would your wife say this? A sham story to swindle us?" As Ms. Wu spoke on the telephone with the husband's father to verify the couple's report of a New Year holiday phone call, her supervisor admonished the husband, "The two of you [he and his wife] have problems with communication!"

Despite Ms. Wu's suspicions about the marriage and the team head's initial instruction to deport the wife, in the end they admitted the woman but required the couple to submit to a follow-up interview with the NIA office in the husband's hometown. Ms. Wu's interview report included five reasons for requiring a secondary interview, most of which underscored discrepancies in the couple's accounts. Ms. Wu admitted that she still suspected the woman was being brought over by a snakehead organization, but she had no way to prove this unless the couple confessed. As I followed the couple back to the mainland arrivals counter, I was struck again by how ill-matched they appeared: she dressed stylishly in jeans and a leather jacket and he in casual attire with the darkly tanned skin of a rural laborer. Yet the sense that something was not quite right with the couple and the interviewers' concerns about gaps in their stories were insufficient to conclude definitively that the marriage was a sham.

A few months later I encountered a case that was similarly inconclusive, although for different reasons. Even before Ms. Feng, an experienced interviewer in her forties, began the interview at 10:30 p.m. on a Friday night, the case had already been flagged by the desk staff. The Taiwanese husband had gone through five in-country interviews before receiving approval to sponsor his wife, a consequence of his staggering credit card debt. When his wife arrived at the airport, the desk staff noted how young and pretty she was and raised concerns that the husband, more than ten years her senior, might sell her into prostitution to resolve his debt or had been hired by a snakehead gang to serve as a "fake husband" (*rentou laogong*) while she entered the sex industry. Regardless of the small likelihood of either outcome, anxieties about both human trafficking and sex work justified the attention given to the case, placing Ms. Feng under great pressure to determine the authenticity of the marriage, despite the late hour.

Ms. Feng's tension was palpable as I accompanied her and the young woman from Guangxi across the empty arrival hall to the interview rooms. The woman looked tired, but she replied calmly to Ms. Feng's questions, delivered abruptly and somewhat testily, as if Ms. Feng was trying to disrupt a possibly memorized account. The woman told Ms. Feng that she had met her husband when he ate at the restaurant where she worked and had asked for her phone number. After that first meeting, they communicated via telephone and QQ, a Chinese social networking website. He visited her three more times before they decided to marry, and on one occasion they vacationed in the tourist city of Guilin for a few days. Ms. Feng confirmed that he had met her father and stepmother, that he had given her father a bridewealth payment of RMB10,000 (roughly US$1,450), that they had gone out to dinner with her relatives after registering the marriage, and that they had taken a series of formal wedding photos.

The young woman rubbed her temples wearily at this point, but Ms. Feng plunged ahead with more detailed questioning about their celebratory meal after registering the marriage and the husband's visits to the wife's home. She also interrogated the young woman about the husband's employment status, housing situation, and family members in Taiwan. Only toward the end of the interview did Ms. Feng ask her whether her husband had any debt, to which she replied yes, although she did not know how much.

Because of the late hour, I did not observe Ms. Feng's questioning of the Taiwanese husband outside of immigration, but when I telephoned her a few days later to ask about the result, she informed me that she had admitted the Chinese spouse but required the couple to submit to a follow-up interview. The spouses' accounts were largely in accord, she added, but the husband simply owed too much money to the bank. Because the man had gone through five in-country interviews, he understood that she couldn't allow the couple to pass without arousing attention from her superiors. Ms. Feng then added that the young woman was both surprised and frightened when she learned the exact amount of her husband's debt, and she asked Ms. Feng to teach her how to place a phone call to China so she could discuss the situation with her father.

In this case, the signs of sham marriage did not emerge from inconsistencies in the spouses' accounts but from their statuses and life situations. Although a first marriage for both of them, the wife's youth, primary school education, and apparent naiveté made Ms. Feng and the desk staff suspicious about the husband's intentions and raised concerns about the young woman's fate in Taiwan given her husband's heavy debts. In the end, Ms. Feng's decision to require a follow-up interview was less about the wife's marital intentions and more about the husband's precarious financial state and potentially nefarious plans. Here, the secondary investigation was intended to serve a protective purpose through a subsequent evaluation of the marriage.

When interviewers decide on the outcome of an interview, they must do so according to specific procedural guidelines that may limit their ability to distinguish real from sham marriages with any clarity. Interviewers at the border generally rely on two categories to assess their interactions with immigrants and citizen-spouses: whether there are significant discrepancies in the couple's accounts (*shuoci you zhong da xiaci*) or whether there is sufficient positive evidence to recognize the marriage as authentic (*wu jiji shizheng zu ren qi hunyin wei zhenshi*).[16] The successful evaluation of marital authenticity hinges on the relevance of these bureaucratic categories to the nuances and complexities of everyday life and cross-Strait relationships. Not all cases fit neatly into one category or the other, nor do the categories themselves necessarily provide the rationale that interviewers need to justify an immediate deportation. As the NIA came under pressure from NGOs and the public to regularize its interview procedures, these evaluation categories took on a life of their own by establishing fixed parameters for border decision making that did not always correspond to more fluid marital histories and life circumstances.

On my first visit to the airport in February 2008, I observed an interview that revealed how these procedural categories might prevent interviewers from deporting an immigrant spouse even when they harbored deep suspicions about the authenticity of the marriage. This marriage was a second one for both spouses, and the timing made the interviewer suspicious. Both had divorced within days of one another and then remarried shortly thereafter. The Taiwanese husband's first wife had the same surname as his new spouse, and the latter admitted that they hailed from the same village in rural Hunan province. Through the intervention of a more senior airport official, the interviewer discovered that the two wives were not merely neighbors but sisters, at which point both the interviewer and the official began to interrogate the woman aggressively to determine whether her sister had divorced strategically to bring her to Taiwan. The senior official paused his questioning at several points to reiterate that he did not approve of the couple's actions, adding that both the woman and her sister were married with children, and yet she had begun an affair with her sister's husband. When he asked again why the interviewee had lied to them about her sister, she replied, "It wasn't an honorable thing [to do]," admitting the moral questionability of her actions, while continuing to assert that her current marriage was "real" (*shishi*).

After a second bout of questioning the Chinese spouse, the interviewer called in the Taiwanese husband. He clearly had guessed what had transpired because he admitted immediately that the two wives were sisters. His attitude was contrite and accommodating, and the details of his account accorded closely with those of his wife, with a few discrepancies. Both admitted that what they had done was not "honorable," but they also explained that they had been unhappy in their first marriages and were simply following their hearts.

This interview showed how the confessionary impulses compelled by bureaucratic examinations encourage border crossers to expose intimate details about both their status and character (Salter 2007, 59–60). Although both spouses confessed readily to character faults (not being honorable or moral), they refused to admit to status defects by denying that their marriage was fraudulent. Their willingness to confess to faults of character but not to a fraudulent marriage created what Susan Coutin (2001, 84n19) terms a "plot gap" in the interview narrative itself. This gap made it difficult for interviewers to justify immediate deportation based on the procedural categories at their disposal.

In the end, the interviewer and senior official decided to allow the Chinese spouse to enter the country but required the couple to submit to a second in-country interview within thirty days. The female interviewer was torn about this decision: "This one should be sent back," she said to me, to which the senior official replied, "Forget it." He admitted that he had been swayed by the husband's frankness, but allowed that a stricter interviewer might have judged their accounts to have "significant discrepancies" and therefore deported the woman. According to the standards of the past when he himself had worked as an interviewer, she likely would have been sent back to China.

Despite many hours of repeated questioning, in the end immigration officers were unable to determine without a doubt that the marriage was a sham. They did find that it deviated significantly from their recognized standards of morality and convention, and they were deeply suspicious about the couple's motives, especially because the first wife was already a Taiwanese citizen and therefore would not lose her legal status as a result of the divorce. Yet the interview process itself failed to provide the specific kinds of proof they needed to support those suspicions. The discrepancies in the spouses' accounts were not significant enough to warrant deportation, nor were the interviewers' moral objections to the marriage sufficient to override repeated assertions by the couple that their marriage was real. By passing on responsibility for deciding marital authenticity to the next interviewer in the NIA, the interviewers privileged the procedural formalization imposed by the interview guidelines over their own discretionary power.

Whether interviewers choose to mold their decisions to procedural guidelines or whether they feel they have no choice but to do so, the end result is a bureaucratization of decision making through formal categories that do not always support the aim of the airport interview to distinguish sham from real marriages. And even when interviewers opt for deportation, they do not necessarily explain their decision using the language of real versus sham. During one visit to the airport, I asked the NIA team leader in charge about a deportation case that had happened earlier that evening. The case involved a young couple in their twenties who had flown to Taiwan together and were met by the Taiwanese husband's father. All three individuals offered dramatically different accounts of how the couple had met, courted, and married. In the end, the husband confessed to downloading information from the Internet because, so he claimed, he feared their "real" story would not be convincing enough. When I asked the NIA team leader whether he saw this as a case of "sham marriage," he responded, "One can't say whether it is real or sham. Their statements did not accord [with one another]; they falsified documents (*shuoci bu fu, weizao wenshu*)" (March 14, 2008). Despite the ostensible goal of the airport interview to weed out those in sham marriages, the official in charge that night refused to characterize the marriage as a sham, choosing instead to frame the couple's responses and actions through the formal procedural categories that justified the Chinese spouse's deportation.

THERAPEUTIC ENGAGEMENT

Interviews are productive interactions, but they do not always produce what they claim or intend to, such as definitively identifying sham marriages and true spousal intentions. Nor, as McKeown (2008, 268–69) suggests, do they simply generate the kinds of fraud they aim to prevent, although they may very well do that as well, as in the case of the young couple just described. Interviews also provide a setting for interactions between state actors and cross-border couples that affirm desirable marriage roles and behaviors. These interactions enhance the power of interviews to promote ideal models of cross-Strait family formation and to educate Chinese spouses about the responsibilities they will face in Taiwan.

Some interviewers openly defined their role as being akin to that of a therapist who listened to stories about people's personal lives. On many occasions I noticed that interviewers, especially women, encouraged couples to reveal more about themselves by responding to accounts of moving life experiences and offering advice or, on occasion, affirmation of key decisions. Sometimes this happened when interviewers discovered that a mainland spouse would have demanding care obligations in Taiwan, and they aimed to discover whether the woman knew what was expected of her.

One notable case involved a senior female interviewer and a Chinese woman in her early thirties who had married a Taiwanese man nearly thirty years her senior. This was the wife's second marriage to a Taiwanese and her third marriage overall. She had divorced her mainland husband with whom she had a son, now age fifteen, and her first Taiwanese husband had died before she acquired citizenship. She had originally assumed she could remain in Taiwan after her husband's death and continue to work legally, but eventually she was arrested and deported, with the stipulation that she was barred from entering Taiwan for one year. Before leaving, however, the woman had been introduced to her current husband through his sister, and the couple married in China and waited until she was eligible to enter the country again.

Through careful questioning, the interviewer determined that the wife would assume caretaking responsibilities for her husband's infirm mother. The interviewer responded to this information by adopting an advisory role, warning the wife that caring for a sick patient required professional nursing skills and questioning whether she felt up to the task. Upon learning that the husband's daughter from his first marriage opposed their relationship, the interviewer warned the woman that she might have adjustment problems because her husband had not resolved this issue with his children.

The interviewer's attitude throughout the encounter was tough but also supportive, as she sought to determine not only that the marriage was authentic but also that the wife would be able to handle the demanding responsibilities she would face as a caretaker and new member of her husband's family. When she moved on to question the husband, the interviewer's demeanor changed noticeably, her facial expressions and tone of voice conveying sympathy as opposed to sternness. Immediately after sitting down in the interview room, the husband launched into an emotional account of the sad plight of his family, and he quickly broke down in tears as he described how his daughter, a college graduate, was unemployed; how his younger sister suffered from depression; and how his mother, bedridden now for forty-three years, qualified for monthly visits from a doctor and nurse but saddled him with heavy medical fees. Caring for his mother was such demanding work, he declared, that it literally had killed his first wife, and he had frankly shared his family obligations with his new spouse. He confessed to feeling sorry for her because of the burden she would face, and he had purchased a house for her in China in case his children did not allow her to remain in the family home after his death. Throughout the husband's emotionally narrated tale, the interviewer rarely interrupted him or asked direct questions. She simply listened as he poured out his difficulties, nodding sympathetically. His interview ended after a mere fifteen minutes, in stark contrast to the hour-long interrogation of his wife.

Over the course of this interview, the female interviewer moved between diverse roles, from investigating the authenticity of the marriage to advising the Chinese wife about how to handle the care burdens and family dynamics she would face to sympathizing with the Taiwanese husband about his sad and overwhelming responsibilities. These roles generated different kinds of engagement with her interviewees, both authoritarian (in its investigative and advisory modes) and egalitarian (in its therapeutic mode) (Illouz 2007). These modes of engagement drew the interviewer into intimate details of the couple's life together and put her in the position of reflecting on and affirming certain aspects of their relationship beyond simply ascertaining its authenticity.

Through this more personalized engagement, interviewers also wrestled with societal norms and values that served as the basis for determining marital authenticity. Some cases forced interviewers to confront relationships that were difficult for them to comprehend because they challenged their own assumptions about why Taiwanese chose to marry mainland Chinese. On one occasion, a middle-aged female interviewer, after questioning a couple in their early thirties who were marrying for the first time, expressed surprise to the Taiwanese husband about his choice of a wife. "You have good qualifications [as a spouse]," she said frankly to him. "Why did you marry a mainland woman?" (March 28, 2008). The husband replied that none of his previous relationships had been successful, in part because his mother did not like his girlfriends. Yet his mother approved of this woman, despite her homely appearance and only primary school education, and he was satisfied with her ability to manage the household.

Back at the mainland arrivals desk after the successful conclusion of the interview, the interviewer again expressed her difficulty understanding the husband's marital decision. Turning to me, she confessed, "I feel that his situation is quite good. He owns two homes, but he married a woman who isn't very impressive." As two other female colleagues joined the conversation, the interviewer added that she thought the marriage was unfortunate and was surprised that the couple appeared not to have had sexual relations yet. Another officer turned from the desk where she had been completing paperwork to offer a more positive interpretation of the scenario: "He's a gentleman; he wants to wait for their wedding night!"[17] The interviewer ignored her colleague, however, and simply concluded her train of thought: "In any case, their stories were the same, so there isn't anything we can do." The notion that they, as interviewers, might be able to intervene in a citizen's marital decision had less to do in this case with the authenticity of the marriage and more, as shown clearly in the interviewer's discomfort, with the sense among some interviewers that financially secure and well-employed Taiwanese should not be marrying mainland Chinese.

In contrast to interviewers' attention to couples' financial arrangements or bureaucratic and ritual formalities, they rarely assessed emotional bonds as part of interview evaluations.[18] I did notice, however, that interviewers might express appreciation when they came across a couple who displayed what they recognized as emotional maturity and mutual care and support. Sui and Chen were in their early thirties when they returned briefly to Taiwan from Shenzhen in 2008 to visit Chen's mother and participate in the annual Tomb Sweeping Festival to honor deceased ancestors. This was Sui's second marriage, and her daughter from her first marriage lived part of the year with the father in Sichuan Province. Chen had been married twice before and also had a twelve-year-old daughter, who now lived with the couple, along with Sui's parents, who had moved from Sichuan to help with housework and child care. The couple had met in 2006 in the Hong Kong airport when both were traveling to Singapore, and they married the following year.

During the first part of the interview, the middle-aged female interviewer queried Sui about how she had met her husband and how the couple had maintained their long-distance courtship. A turning point in the interview took place when Sui confessed that she had not encountered any suitable men in China prior to meeting her Taiwanese husband, with whom she had felt immediately simpatico. She then began to tell their story in a more personal manner, describing how her husband had promised her father that he would give her a better life in the future. Upon hearing this account of how honest Sui's husband had been with her father, the interviewer offered the following endorsement: "It's good to interact sincerely." In response, Sui opened up even more, admitting that she had become pregnant last summer, but their daughters had expressed concern that the couple would abandon them if they gave birth to a child of their own. Because of the children's anxieties and their own financial burdens, she and her husband had decided she would have an abortion. Clearly impressed by the couple's commitment to their parents and existing children and their emotional sophistication in dealing with a difficult situation, the interviewer praised Sui by concluding, "You're really something," to which Sui smiled modestly.

The interviewer continued with a few follow-up questions and then ended the interview by endorsing their marriage: "It's not bad—one good person meets another." The interview interaction proceeded as a dialogue rather than an interrogation, and the interviewer's tone and body language differed markedly from other interviews where she had adopted a more authoritarian and disciplinary manner. In this case, she transformed her role as state representative from regulator to supportive benefactor, repeatedly expressing approval of the couple's decisions and their maturity in considering their children's needs and financial stability. At the end of her brief interview with the Taiwanese husband, the interviewer assumed the position of well-wisher, as if she were a guest at the couple's wedding: "Congratulations to you both," she proclaimed, as the couple rose to leave the interview room. "I wish you much happiness."

This was a rare occasion on which I observed an interviewer praising a couple, and it showed me a new face of the interview as a productive encounter that generated societal ideals by affirming desirable roles and behaviors. In this mode, border interviews espoused new visions of cross-Strait family and marriage; they were, as McKeown argues, "less an investigation into how things actually were than an assertion of how things *should* be" (2008, 269). In the preceding interview, that assertion was made through encouraging behaviors and relationships that transformed otherwise troubling cross-Strait marriages into the kinds of unions that interviewers deemed necessary to build a healthy Taiwanese nation.

Border interviews may be more effective in realizing state goals when they mobilize emotional connections between interviewers and cross-Strait couples. Whereas the tasks of identifying marital intentions and distinguishing sham from real marriages encourage interviewers to adopt the position that these marriages are by nature abnormal or unhealthy, when interviewers engage with the intimate aspects of couples' lives, they transform the interview into a productive encounter that affirms desirable features of cross-Strait family formation. The therapeutic interview encounter may in fact better advance Taiwan's sovereign aspirations by empowering border officers to educate Chinese spouses about their expected roles as citizens in waiting and to mold the population so as to realize an idealized image of the Taiwanese nation.

SHAM MARRIAGES IN CIRCULATION

Although most Chinese spouses pass through the interview system relatively uneventfully, the experience teaches them about the power wielded by the category of sham marriage and how it may affect their own opportunities and status in Taiwan. Chinese spouses often responded to stories and accusations of sham marriage by affirming the authenticity of their own relationships and by asserting that they deserved better treatment as a result. Some of their statements were directed at the government, but equally relevant interlocutors were other mainland spouses who sat in judgment on their compatriots.

The day after I observed the airport interview with the Hunanese woman who had married her former brother-in-law, I met with Qiu Yan and Tao Weihong, two women from Henan Province who had become acquainted through the Taipei City government-sponsored acculturation class I attended in 2007. Qiu, originally from a small provincial city, had lived in Taiwan for six years by that point, and her four-year-old daughter watched cartoons as we chatted in my living room that winter afternoon. Tao, a mere twenty-one years old and of rural origin, had arrived in Taiwan less than a year earlier and was already pregnant. I described for them the basic details that had emerged from the airport interview I observed the previous day, eager to learn how Qiu and Tao would interpret the couple's relationship. As soon as I mentioned that the husband's first wife had obtained Taiwanese citizenship by the time of their divorce, Tao immediately asserted that the arrangement must be a ploy to bring the younger sister to Taiwan. Qiu then added that many mainland wives in Taiwan had motives that were far from pure or simple, unlike she, who had met and fallen in love with her husband in China where they courted for several years. These "other women" wanted money or had aspirations that had little to do with the marriage itself, neglecting their husband's financial burdens and spending money without a care.

By passing judgment on both marital authenticity and wifely behavior, Qiu and Tao discursively monitored the boundaries of conventional marriages and appropriate gender roles. For Tao, who had met her husband online and married him despite their twenty-year age difference and his four children from a prior marriage, discussions such as these reaffirmed her own honest marital intentions, especially given a marital situation that on the surface looked more questionable than Qiu's. Although their audience at the time was quite circumscribed (a foreign researcher and each other), their efforts resembled those of bureaucrats at the border who used interview interactions to shore up the power of conventional, respectable marriage through contrast with ostensibly less reputable and even fraudulent marriages. Moreover, Qiu's and Tao's narratives had the added effect of affirming for me and themselves the authenticity of their own relationships.

Discourses of marital authenticity circulate widely among Chinese spouses, in part because migrant wives and husbands continue to face bureaucratic evaluations of their marriages long after they enter the country and even on the cusp of acquiring citizenship. Yuan Mei and Xiao Hong had met through volunteering with a Taipei-based NGO and had become good friends despite different personal backgrounds and marital situations. Xiao Hong had delayed becoming a Taiwanese citizen for many years, in part because the Taiwanese government's requirement that she give up her PRC citizenship made her anxious about her ability to care for her daughter, who was still a student in China, and to manage her insecure living situation in Taiwan due to her elderly husband's complex family relationships (see chapter 6). Yuan Mei, too, had held off applying because she and her husband had lived and worked in China for many years, and she hoped they might return once their son finished his schooling. In the end, however, both women acknowledged that their lives in Taiwan would be much simpler with citizenship status, and they began the application process at roughly the same time.

After handing in their paperwork, they had been notified that a representative from the NIA's special investigation brigade would visit them to evaluate their marriage. Yuan Mei had never received a visit, but Xiao Hong was not at all surprised when officers came to both her husband's original home in elite northern Taipei and their current apartment in a working-class suburb in Taipei County. Their forty-one-year age difference had raised suspicions in the past, and Xiao Hong knew they would be investigated when she applied for citizenship. But the officer was perplexed by her decision to delay her application. He had never encountered a case like this, he claimed, with such a striking age difference and a mainland spouse who evidently wasn't certain she wanted to become a citizen. He carefully inspected the apartment, looking in the closets and bathroom to determine whether she truly lived there, and closely perused the photographs of Xiao with her husband and his many children at upscale restaurants and leisure venues. Concluding that "you wouldn't be in a sham marriage with these living conditions," the officer grew even more confused. Even after ending the investigation on a positive note, he remained unable to fit their marriage into his preconceived standards for sham and authentic relationships.

Hearing Xiao recount her experience with the NIA investigator, Yuan Mei grew increasingly agitated, especially when Xiao mentioned that the officer had taken photographs of the apartment and her personal effects to document the case. "Did he ask you first before taking the photos?" Yuan inquired, pounding the table in the tea shop where we had retreated to escape the summer heat. Although Yuan claimed she would have experienced such an act as an invasion of her privacy, she acknowledged that most mainland spouses would not challenge this kind of investigation for fear that the officer would accuse them of being in a sham marriage. Xiao Hong added that the officer's attitude was very harsh and that she certainly was afraid of offending him, as would others who had only recently arrived in Taiwan.

Women such as Xiao Hong and Yuan Mei were of mixed minds when it came to the role of the government in identifying sham marriages. Some worried that government investigations infringed on their civil rights and privacy. Others, however, demanded that the government do a better job of distinguishing sham from real marriages so as not to punish those in authentic unions for crimes they did not commit. By claiming the mantle of "real marriage," cross-Strait couples had to reckon with the slippery contours of the category of sham marriage. At a 2009 policy-education forum held in southern Taiwan, a Taiwanese man in his forties stood up with a small child in his arms and addressed the NIA representative with an accusatory question about the border interview system. He described the system as a rude interference in personal privacy and an obstruction of marital freedom.

I don't know what our government is safeguarding us from. My wife went through two interviews before she passed. And we now have a child. I'm really suspicious about what kind of reason was used for deporting her; was it sham marriage? If it was sham marriage, then is this child sitting here today also a sham? I feel that the problems with the interview should have been eliminated long ago. We have basic freedom of marriage. Whatever country I want to marry someone from, that is my own personal affair. The government absolutely has no right to interfere.

Although the NIA representative apologized to the man for his wife's trying interview experiences, he failed to address the basic critique that motivated the man's outburst—namely, the questionable status of the category of sham marriage itself.

The difficulty of distinguishing real from sham was raised again toward the end of the session when an older woman stood up and requested the microphone. Dressed in a shapeless cotton dress with disheveled hair, the woman spoke in heavily accented Mandarin and continued her tirade for nearly ten minutes before one of the organizers regained control of the microphone. Many in the room had difficulty understanding her, although it was clear that she had been inspired by the first man's accusations and was exercised about the prominence of sham marriages. This woman was married to an elderly veteran in his eighties, and the couple lived near a young Chinese wife who the speaker accused of being in a sham marriage.[19] She had money coming out of her ears, the older woman claimed, and had many protectors high in the government who had facilitated her return to Taiwan even after being deported in the past. Unlike the first gentleman who wanted the government to get out of the business of regulating all marriages, this speaker demanded greater government intervention so as to protect those in authentic unions.

Audience members listened attentively to both speakers as if they identified in some form with the concerns each one raised. Virtually every Chinese immigrant I met claimed to know someone in a sham marriage, an assertion through which they simultaneously identified themselves with the category of authentic marriage. Regardless of their position on governmental involvement, few challenged the notion that one could distinguish real from sham. Only on rare occasions, such as in the two statements at the policy-education session, did individuals recognize the ontological ambiguities created by the concept of sham marriage, including the status of children who might result from such unions. Underscoring, intentionally or not, the fluidity of the boundaries between the categories, the older woman at the policy session wrapped up her tirade with the pronouncement, "Real becomes sham [and] sham becomes real."[20]

If the ostensible goal of the interview system is to determine spouses' marital motives in order to block sham marriages, then the many permutations of cross-Strait unions constantly require interviewers to adjust their working assumptions about what qualities constitute authentic marriages. Despite the creation of a robust bureaucratic apparatus at the border since 2003, the categories of real and sham marriage remain notoriously difficult to define and recognize. Interviewers and cross-Strait couples alike acknowledge their fluidity, even as they strive to shore up categorical boundaries and the individuals encompassed therein. Given the pervasiveness of the concept of marital fraud in international border policing, it is unlikely that Taiwanese authorities will eliminate the interview system, although in recent years they have regularized interview procedures and formalized interview outcomes. The underlying questions of how to define real and sham marriages and what is at stake in organizing border control around such fluid distinctions rarely come to the fore, however, meaning that the assumption that sham marriages actually exist continues to shape immigration policies and, consequently, the lives of Chinese spouses in Taiwan.

PART TWO

Immigration Regimes

THREE

Exceptional Legal Subjects

September 21, 2007

Deng Lifang and I perched on the edge of the couch in the Mainland Affairs Council office belonging to Mr. Cai, the official responsible for legal affairs concerning mainland Chinese. This was merely one of many occasions on which Deng had come to petition Mr. Cai about pending policy reforms that would alleviate her liminal immigration status, the result of her husband's suicide two years earlier. In the midst of our meeting, Deng abruptly asked Mr. Cai, "So do we [Chinese spouses] count as foreigners or not?" She then explained that she had tried to apply for an ID-style residence permit, precisely the kind of card she would admire wistfully seven months later when we passed through immigration at Taoyuan airport on our return together from China (see chapter 1). But the civil servant at her local household registration office had told her she wasn't eligible to apply. "Why not?" Deng had asked her. "Don't the regulations include foreign spouses?" The bureaucrat's retort, succinct in its refusal, affirmed that mainland Chinese were patently not foreigners: "You aren't [foreign spouses]."

Mr. Cai laughed awkwardly at Deng's tale, clearly recognizing the contradictions in the government's position that mainland Chinese were not foreigners. As on other occasions when this topic arose in my meetings with bureaucrats and officials, Mr. Cai struggled to find a language to describe Chinese spouses' ambiguous status in Taiwan. He finally answered Deng's question by utilizing the concept of "official residence" in place of nationality: "You are people with official residence outside [Taiwan]," he explained, as if that confusing statement somehow settled the matter. Then, with a rueful expression on his face, he shifted uncomfortably in his seat and turned to address me, the only easily defined foreigner in the room. He explained that Chinese spouses could not be included under the Immigration Law, which governed foreigners in Taiwan and had introduced the ID-style residence permit Deng had failed to acquire. If Chinese spouses were encompassed under the law, Mr. Cai continued in an unexpectedly candid fashion, officials such as himself would be attacked from two sides. They would face ire

81

from Chinese authorities who would view the equation of mainland Chinese with foreigners as a statement of Taiwanese independence and respond accordingly, possibly with military force. And they would come under attack from pro-reunification politicians in Taiwan who refused to countenance any legislation that could be interpreted as supporting Taiwanese independence.

THIS BRIEF EXCHANGE NEATLY ENCAPSULATES the multiple conundrums faced by bureaucrats and Chinese spouses as they maneuver within an anomalous system of legal classification that identifies mainland Chinese neither as foreigners nor natives. When Deng walked into her local household registration office eager to apply for a resident ID, she encountered a civil servant whose categorical resources made it impossible for her to grant Deng's request. According to the laws and policies under which bureaucrats operated, Chinese spouses, and mainland Chinese more generally, were simply not foreigners, and therefore they did not qualify for that particular residence ID. Mr. Cai, an experienced official closely attuned to the history of these legal categories and their present consequences, did his best to put a good face on Deng's predicament by situating her categorical conundrums in their larger political context. Taiwanese lawmakers, he suggested, had no choice but to create an anomalous legal structure for mainland Chinese precisely because the stakes of doing otherwise were so high: domestic political conflict on the one hand and a potential military invasion by China on the other.

This chapter examines how the legal system governing Chinese spouses developed over the post-1987 period, beginning with its legislative origins and continuing through its expansion into an unwieldy array of administrative policies and practices that determine many aspects of Chinese spouses' lives in Taiwan. Initial legislative debates focused on the question of how to classify mainland Chinese, with assessments of the relative similarities and differences between Chinese and Taiwanese taking center stage. Over time, efforts to police the boundary between "us" and "them" produced a proliferation of legal distinctions and gradations that generated new kinds of legal subjects (such as "people of the mainland area") and new differentiations within existing legal categories (by creating distinct and unequal classes of Taiwanese citizens). These outcomes affirm how immigration policies produce—rather than merely recognize—categories of people and distribute access to rights and recognition unevenly among them (Anderson 2013).

The Taiwanese government has responded to the challenges posed by mainland immigrants in ways that reveal what is at stake when immigration law and policy become a crucial means for asserting fragile claims to national sovereignty. National origin myths create hierarchies of race and ethnicity that attach unequal value to individuals and communities and that become in turn the basis for inequitable citizenship rights and even exclusion from the national body (Chock 1991; Povinelli 2002; Williams 1989). Immigration policies are an important tool for defining borders of inclusion and exclusion that run through nations as well as between them (Dauvergne 2009). But in most nation-states, assumptions about difference determine the shape of those borders: embodied characteristics harden into racial categories, cultural beliefs and practices condense into ethnic or religious affiliations, and national origins are presumed to block identification with the host society. The anomalous legal classification of mainland Chinese, however, emerged from the conundrum of similarity, not difference, from a group of people whose otherness was not obvious and whose very presence in Taiwan channeled the cross-Strait political conflict directly into Taiwan's strategies for asserting sovereignty.

The second part of this chapter considers some of the unpredictable consequences produced by this atypical classification of mainland Chinese. Turning to the strategies used by activist groups dedicated to advancing immigrant rights in Taiwan, it examines how activists mobilize discourses of human rights to claim a shared humanity and equal protections for all migrants and immigrants. In Taiwan, however, these strategies frequently fail to achieve their objectives precisely because they cannot resolve the anomalous legal status of mainland Chinese immigrants. When activist campaigns incorporate both Chinese and foreign spouses under a single agenda, their appeals to human rights and equality under the law fall short for two reasons: not only do Chinese immigrants inspire less sympathy from the Taiwanese people, but their claims to recognition as rights-bearing subjects are thwarted by the atypical legal classifications that define them.

By creating an anomalous legal armature that rests uneasily on distinctions among and within categories of citizens and foreigners, the Taiwanese government has risked undoing its own efforts to use law and immigration policy to assert Taiwan's sovereign standing among a community of like-minded nation-states committed to democracy and human rights. State actors, activists, and Chinese spouses all struggled to define the terms by which law, policy, and international rights discourses could be made to assert sovereignty claims, while simultaneously advancing their own interests. Public protests became important sites for symbolic acts that spoke to audiences large and small, near and far, as part of diverse projects to forge a Taiwanese nation-state through appeals to shared international principles of rights and equality.

PRODUCING EXCEPTIONAL LEGAL SUBJECTS

Between 1990 and 1992, members of Taiwan's Legislative Yuan debated the Employment Services Act (*jiuye fuwu fa*), a law that would open up the country's labor market to foreign migrant workers. During these debates, legislators considered whether mainland Chinese should also be included in the category of foreign migrant worker, especially because recent surveys of Taiwanese employers had found that they overwhelmingly preferred to hire mainland Chinese over workers from other countries due to ease of communication and similar life habits (Tseng 2004, 25). A single question rose to the forefront: Were mainland Chinese foreigners or natives? How individual politicians responded to this question reflected their personal and party stance on Taiwan's future. Did they advocate reunification with the mainland or Taiwan's independence? Who did they consider a national of the ROC? How did they respond to the Constitution's controversial framing of ROC sovereignty as extending over the entire territory of China, including Mongolia and Tibet (see also Tseng 2004)?

Although the purpose of these legislative debates was to craft a law, they also constituted a moment "before the law," a time prior to the fixing of hegemonic social categories and legal classifications. Joan Vincent coins this expression to describe nonlegal, often unofficial settings that offer insights into "legal categories in the making" (1994, 119), but I suggest that legislative debates also reveal the broad range of discourses and legal categories that are possible before law's hegemonic inscription. As ethnographers have underscored, legislators (unlike their judicial counterparts) may actively question the bases for group identities as part of asserting their role as representatives of specific constituencies, even making claims to embody cultural attributes themselves (Chock 1991; Gershon 2011; Lazarus-Black 2003). Instead of the "mute ground" on which hegemony is established (Vincent 1994, 123), therefore, legislative debates speak in profuse detail about the ontological and political consequences of legal categorization for individuals, groups, and the nation as a whole. In the Employment Services Act debates, legislators explicitly engaged the question of what made Taiwanese different from mainland Chinese; through these discussions, they simultaneously raised pressing concerns about who was Taiwanese and what constituted Taiwan as a nation.

Pro-independence legislator Pang Pai-Hsien (Peng Bai-xian) identified what was at stake in the classification of mainland Chinese during a heated debate on December 3, 1991: "At present, we are still in doubt as to whether, if mainland laborers come to Taiwan, we want to see them as natives or foreigners. If we view them as foreigners, others will say we are engaging in Taiwan independence; if we view them as natives, then it is as if Taiwan is already unified [with the mainland]. In the end, is Taiwan unified or independent?" (*Legislative Yuan Bulletin* 80 (98): 31). Pang's wording suggested that the decision about how to legally categorize mainland Chinese was not a reflection of inherent differences between Chinese and Taiwanese; instead, legislators exercised "a demographic imagination" (Gershon 2011, 162) by deciding what features to emphasize and how to characterize them. Categories of native and foreigner were a product of perspective and desired political outcome: how Taiwanese chose to "see" mainland Chinese would establish both the latter's legal status in Taiwan and Taiwan's own political future.

Throughout these debates, legislators fixated on the similarities mainland Chinese shared with Taiwanese, and their stance on Taiwan's relationship to the mainland determined whether they viewed that similarity in positive or negative terms. For pro-reunification politicians, shared physical, cultural, and linguistic features could be used to assert racial and ethnic homogeneity as a basis for substantiating contentious constitutional claims that ROC sovereignty extended over the mainland, encompassing the residents of those territories in a single national space. Ethnoracial similarities, so these legislators argued, neutralized political differences inculcated under China's socialist regime, thereby supporting the pro-reunification position that mainland laborers should be allowed into Taiwan (in a controlled fashion) but not as foreigners.

Conversely, pro-independence politicians portrayed the similarities that mainland Chinese shared with Taiwanese as a liability: common language and similar physical features would enable mainland Chinese to blend into the local population, unlike foreigners whose more obvious racial and linguistic differences made it easier to expel them once their contracts ended (see also Tseng 2004). In addition, these legislators argued, mainland workers would become a drag on Taiwan's economic development as a result of their formative years spent under an "iron rice bowl" socialist system that fostered unproductive dependency. The potential risk of assimilation coupled with fear of slowed economic growth led pro-independence legislators to oppose the entry of mainland Chinese workers.[1]

These early legislative debates initiated a conversation about what consequences might emerge as a result of mainland Chinese laborers' ability to "blend in" with existing populations in Taiwan.[2] On June 12, 1991, Lee Yeou-Chi (Li You-ji), one of the few Nationalist legislators adamantly opposed to importing mainland labor, described one kind of social threat that such similarities might produce: "[Mainland laborers] will easily adjust because of [shared] language and life habits, and will integrate with locals. If, when the time comes and they intermarry, this will produce a great social problem" (*Legislative Yuan Bulletin* 81 (13): 117). The threat of intermarriage and, implicitly, of childbearing loomed large in Lee's opposition to allowing mainland laborers to enter Taiwan, and he explicitly portrayed these undesirable outcomes as a consequence of easy integration facilitated by a common language and cultural traits. Lee went on to argue that intermarriage would also undermine social stability, although he never explained precisely how or why. His opposition to both intermarriage and the children that such unions might produce reflected widespread concerns in some political quarters that mainland immigrants would degrade the quality and productivity of Taiwan's national body.

These debates revealed powerful anxieties about mainland Chinese that pivoted on the threatening consequences of their perceived similarities with Taiwanese. In turn, these anxieties fed fears of shared blood as a potentially contaminating force, of socialization under state socialism as fostering unproductive subjects who would slow economic growth, and of the potential to "blend in" through intermarriage and childbearing as destabilizing Taiwanese society, perhaps even creating a politically invidious Fifth Column. These fears ultimately decided the fate of the Employment Services Act. When it was promulgated in May 1992, it explicitly excluded mainland laborers from the categories of foreigners eligible to enter Taiwan on short-term labor contracts.

The question of whether mainland Chinese were foreigners or natives so hotly debated during these legislative sessions was finally put to rest a mere two months later. In July 1992, Taiwan's Legislative Yuan passed the Act Governing Relations between the People of the Taiwan Area and the Mainland Area (hereafter, the Act), legislation that classified all post-1987 Chinese visitors and immigrants to Taiwan under a new legal category: people of the mainland area. The threat of similarity did not disappear with this categorical legerdemain, however, and the anxieties about intermarriage and child-bearing that made only a brief appearance in the Employment Services Act debates assumed greater relevance once cross-Strait marriages increased and growing numbers of Chinese spouses obtained the rights to reside in Taiwan and ultimately to become citizens. In other words, passage of these two pieces of legislation did not make struggles over definitions of difference "recede to the background," as Gershon (2011, 168) more optimistically suggests for Anglo-American multicultural democracies. Nor did law as implemented on the ground simply begin to diverge from law as ideally envisioned by legislators (Lazarus-Black 2003), although there were certainly instances of this as well. Instead, the foundational categorical ambivalence at the heart of the Act was reenacted over time as the anomalies of the legal category "person of the mainland area" became more pronounced, despite (or, perhaps, as a consequence of) the rapidly expanding set of regulations intended to contain Chinese spouses' feared impact on Taiwanese society.

The Act created a social and political reality in which Chinese spouses became intelligible as legal persons through their mainland origins, and it marshaled the power of law to forge new worlds that bridged juridical, social, and political spheres (Bruner 1986; Fitzpatrick 1992). By collapsing legal and spatial categories, however, the Act established a neat binary between people of the mainland area and the Taiwan area that became increasingly difficult to uphold. Categories multiplied over the years, producing ever-finer gradations and permutations, and the bilateral principle of spatio-legal personhood gradually dissolved in the face of state efforts to police access to different citizenship rights and to shore up the privileged category "person of the Taiwan area."

Over time, the Act has functioned as a "mother law" (*mufa*) spawning multiple offspring, its legal fecundity instantiating the sovereign power so desired by the Taiwanese government. As a generative piece of legislation, the Act set the principles guiding cross-Strait mobility and created basic guidelines that defined which categories of mainland Chinese were eligible for entry to Taiwan and under what statuses. Yet it left the detailed work of regulation and implementation to a vast array of subsidiary administrative policies.³ These policies expanded the scope of the Act's address by creating categories of eligibility and legality tied to societal expectations for the kinship statuses that legitimated Chinese spouses' migration pathways: as wives, husbands, mothers, and fathers. Through this vast legal apparatus, Chinese spouses became recognizable subjects whose legal personhood was defined by their place of origin, the characteristics associated with that place, and their conformity to presumed norms for gendered kinship roles in Taiwan.

The legal regime spawned by the Act developed in fits and starts as cross-Strait marital migration gradually took off and then grew rapidly in the late 1990s and early 2000s. Throughout this period, administrative policies played an especially powerful role in shaping the everyday lives of Chinese spouses. They determined who could work and who could not, who could sponsor a child or parent from China, who passed the border interview, who faced deportation, who continued to endure spousal abuse rather than risk separation from children, who divorced and stayed, or who divorced and was forced to leave the country. Influenced by the political orientation of the party in power, these regulations were crafted through the complex workings of diverse bureaucracies, subject to political in-fighting, backroom negotiations, and, at times, foot-dragging. Although the Mainland Affairs Council (MAC) was charged with crafting cross-Strait related law and policy, it had to work together with other relevant government units in the Ministry of the Interior, the executive and legislative bodies, the various security agencies, and the Council of Labor Affairs.

Sensitive to the potential national security concerns created by an influx of mainland Chinese, the legislators who drafted the Act included an article that exempted it from the regulations of Taiwan's Administrative Procedure Law (*xingzheng chengxu fa*). Therefore, both the Act and its subsidiary policies have been protected from certain kinds of public oversight applied to other legislation such as the Immigration Law. Over the years, both immigration and MAC bureaucrats have relied heavily on administrative policies to refine mainland-directed immigration regulations and categories, especially because legislative revisions to the Act were often politically contentious and could be drawn out over several years.⁴ These administrative policies conducted the sensitive work of immigration regulation largely free from public and, at times, legislative review. But this scenario began to change in the early years of the twenty-first century, when the MAC proposed major revisions to the Act and a draft plan for restructuring the entire immigration bureaucracy began to circulate beyond government circles. These two events sparked new forms of activism that propelled immigration regulation into the public spotlight.

ACTIVISM AND THE RIGHTS-BEARING SUBJECT

The 1987 end to martial law in Taiwan paved the way for a democratic political system and robust civil society to emerge by the end of the century. The slogan "a country established on the foundation of human rights" (*renquan liguo*) rose to prominence in the new millennium as the government, then led by the Democratic Progressive Party, applied on several occasions for Taiwan's admission to the United Nations as an independent nation-state. By foregrounding the country's commitment to human rights, the DPP government simultaneously positioned Taiwan as an integral member of a like-minded community of sovereign states dedicated to eradicating rights abuses—a position that also enabled Taiwan to distinguish itself from China's more authoritarian regime. Immigration rights activists, therefore, appealed to human rights to hold the Taiwan government accountable to its "human rights-as-sovereignty" claim, and they did so by demanding that the government uphold United Nations covenants that protected the rights of migrants and immigrants.[5] In short, the discourse of human rights served two purposes: on the one hand, the state's espoused commitment to human rights undergirded its sovereignty claims (exemplified by campaigns to join the UN), while on the other hand, NGOs appealed to an international discourse of human rights to support demands that the government formulate a more humane set of (im)migration policies.

NGO activism in support of immigrant and migrant rights initially took shape along constituent lines, with separate organizations advocating on behalf of migrant workers, foreign spouses, and Chinese spouses. The only organization explicitly devoted to demanding greater rights for Chinese spouses was the Cross-Strait Marriage Promotion Association (*Zhonghua Liang An Hunyin Xietiao Cujinhui*, hereafter the Association), an organization formed in the 1990s by aging veterans who had married Chinese women. Although a small group that operated on a shoestring budget, the Association attracted public attention in 2002 and 2003 when it mobilized large numbers of Chinese spouses to participate in street protests against proposed revisions to the Act that would have extended the citizenship wait for Chinese spouses from eight years to eleven (Chao 2006; Lu 2011).[6] Covered widely by the press, the

EXCEPTIONAL LEGAL SUBJECTS · 89

protests drew public attention to the unequal treatment of Chinese and foreign spouses in Taiwan, and the legislature ultimately decided not to approve the extension. By the mid-2000s, the head of the Association had become a figure well known in bureaucratic circles for his persistent, and by some accounts troublesome, petitions on behalf of individual Chinese spouses.

Despite the Association's public protests and active petitioning, it remained a marginal player in the larger community of activist NGOs dedicated to migrant and immigrant rights. Its largely veteran leadership, men who had fled to Taiwan with the Nationalist army in the late 1940s, represented a population historically isolated from both local Taiwanese society and more elite Mainlander communities. Their social marginalization made it difficult for Association leaders to forge connections with other NGOs, some of which were suspicious of veterans' political allegiances given their renewed connections with the mainland in the post-1987 era. When Taiwanese activists did become involved in the Association later in the first decade of the new millennium, they tended to hail from labor organizations that advocated closer ties with China on the basis of shared socialist commitments. Some younger Taiwanese men gradually joined the Association leadership because they, too, had married Chinese women.

The most prominent organization dedicated to promoting the human rights of all migrants and immigrants was the Alliance for Human Rights Legislation for Immigrants and Migrants (*Yimin yizhu renquan xiufa lianmeng*, hereafter the Alliance). The Alliance was established on December 12, 2003 as a coalition of diverse activist groups opposed to the overarching emphasis on policing and security in the government's recent proposal to create a National Immigration Agency (NIA).[7] These groups contended that a police-heavy NIA would merely exacerbate the existing tendency to criminalize immigrants and migrants instead of treating them as full human beings with legitimate needs and rights. As a result, they formed the Alliance to strengthen their collective voice as they demanded both greater government transparency and a role for citizens and NGOs in the NIA design process (Hsia 2008, 194–96).

None of the groups involved in the Alliance had participated in the Association's protests in 2002 and 2003 against extending Chinese spouses' wait time to citizenship. Nor did the Alliance invite the Association to join its ranks when it formed a few months after the last of those protests. Instead, the Alliance represented the interests of Chinese spouses through a Taiwanese academic and a Chinese wife who had already obtained Taiwanese citizenship. Only much later in the decade would the Association join the group, partly as a result of changes in the leadership of the Association itself, as well as in the composition of the Alliance.

In its initial years, the Alliance focused primarily on the needs of foreign spouses and foreign migrant workers in Taiwan. Chinese spouses would benefit from a less police-heavy NIA, but they were not the subjects of the Immigration Law, the reform of which occupied the Alliance's attention throughout the mid-2000s until the revised law was passed in 2007.[8] Some of the issues addressed by the Alliance, such as undocumented status, poor conditions in government detention centers, and abuse by citizen spouses, were relevant to Chinese spouses, but others, such as statelessness or migrant worker abuses, spoke more directly to the needs of foreigners in Taiwan. Only later in the decade did the Alliance gradually—and, in some cases, reluctantly—begin to address the specific burdens imposed on Chinese spouses as the result of their exceptional legal status, as well as the forms of discrimination they shared with other immigrant spouses.

Through introductions from constituent organizations and academic members, I began to participate in Alliance events and planning meetings in summer 2007. At that time the group was gradually broadening its agenda to address concerns directly relevant to Chinese spouses. But this was not an easy shift, as several members admitted to me. When the Alliance was first established, many NGOs in Taiwan were uneasy about supporting immigrant and migrant causes, and quite a few openly refused to join the Alliance if it intended to support Chinese spouses. Although Chinese spouses could be rendered sympathetic through class-based frameworks that identified them as poor and disempowered (Lu 2011), these frameworks clashed with equally prominent stereotypes of Chinese spouses as gold diggers in search of easy wealth, as sexual operators, or as dubious victims who used the welfare system and legal protections to their advantage (Chen 2010; Friedman 2012; Shih 1998). Their presumed associations with Maoist socialism and its legacy of political authoritarianism also made it difficult for activists to imagine how to incorporate Chinese spouses into a futurist vision of a democratic, progressive Taiwan without simultaneously invoking Taiwan's own militarist Cold War past.

As Alliance members grew more attuned to the needs of Chinese spouses, they strategically used the organization's overarching emphasis on human rights to unite Chinese and foreign spouses under a shared activist agenda.

More than a mere rhetorical tool, this reliance on human rights discourse also strengthened the Alliance's own affiliations with a global activist community and legitimated its efforts to pressure the Taiwanese government to treat migrants and immigrants as fully endowed human beings. By challenging stereotypes that portrayed both groups as disembodied labor, reproductive machines, or criminals, the Alliance advocated for rights that migrants and immigrants shared with citizens, such as the right to marry (even if you were poor) or to preserve existing family bonds.

As a coalition of NGOs dedicated to protecting human rights, the Alliance aspired to create a social, legal, and policy environment in Taiwan that treated both citizens and foreigners humanely, and it promoted the rights-endowed subject as the foundation for legal reforms. But mainland Chinese did not always align neatly with such progressive visions of the rights-bearing subject, in part because they did not fit easily into categories of citizen and foreigner. The Act, as noted above, created a separate law and policy regime that undermined the integrity of these categories and denied constitutional equality guarantees through affirming the taint of mainland origins regardless of an individual's legal immigration or citizenship status.[9] As a consequence, activist appeals to equal treatment under the law and human rights protections could always be rejected by invoking the specter of China's political threat and the resulting need to place national security concerns above all other interests. For groups such as the Alliance, human rights advocacy might fail as a pragmatic strategy for collective struggle because it could not resolve the anomalous legal standing of Chinese spouses in Taiwan or fully neutralize the vast array of anxieties their presence evoked among Taiwanese citizens.

In the remainder of this chapter, I discuss two major Alliance initiatives that illustrate the difficult compromises made by activist NGOs when using a rights-based framework to advocate for exceptional immigrants. These compromises reflect both the existing legal and political configurations that NGOs confront in their daily practice and the fissures that emerge when groups strive to reconcile the ideals espoused in human rights discourses with the concrete goals of activist campaigns. As Aihwa Ong suggests, "NGO missions must be translated and negotiated within particular alignments of institutional power, and the ethical outcomes are not solely predetermined by human rights. In order to be effective at all, NGOs must work with and thus become subjected to the conjunctural force of overlapping political, moral, and economic systems" (Ong 2009, 180). My discussion shows how the dilemmas faced by activist NGOs in Taiwan emerged in large part from an anomalous legal structure that distinguished Chinese from foreign immigrants. Moreover, these dilemmas echoed some of the challenges encountered by the Taiwanese state as it used the regulation of exceptional immigrants to assert its own sovereign status.

NO MONEY, NO CITIZENSHIP

In July 2007, a coalition formed under the auspices of the Alliance to protest policies that they argued discriminated against the poor by interfering in their right to marry and to acquire Taiwanese citizenship. Called the Coalition against the Financial Requirement for Immigrants (CAFRI, *mei qian mei shenfen lianmeng*), the group challenged a financial requirement recently imposed on foreign spouses that required marital immigrants to show proof of their economic worthiness when they applied for naturalization (the requirement had been in effect for Chinese spouses since 2004). The coalition argued that this requirement did not protect marital immigrants from economic insecurity, as the government claimed, but instead discriminated against the poor and working classes by imposing excessive burdens on those who married across national borders. As an example of how the very procedures for naturalization define the desired composition of a nation's citizenry, the financial requirement affirmed Taiwan's image of itself as a hardworking, productive nation that demanded the same (if not more) of its new members and their citizen spouses.[10]

Although Chinese spouses had complained about the burdens imposed by the financial requirement, most were able to mobilize resources when the time came to show the necessary proof of economic self-sufficiency.[11] Revisions to the Immigration Law passed in 2007 imposed the financial requirement on foreign spouses as well, many of whose households engaged in informal employment, agricultural work, or fishing, occupations that made it difficult for them to accumulate the savings required or provide the necessary proof of resources. As a result, some foreign spouses were forced to turn to loan sharks or further delay naturalization until they could amass the required resources, which by 2007 had increased to NT$400,000 (US$12,320). These challenges spurred the Alliance to action, and under the auspices of CAFRI, it planned for a major street demonstration in September 2007 to protest the financial requirement faced by all marital immigrants.

Making Common Cause

On a hot August morning in 2007, I made my way down a dimly lit staircase to the basement office of the Cross-Strait Marriage Promotion Association located on a narrow alley in the oldest section of Taipei city. The office was sparsely furnished with a few desks and chairs, the walls plastered with newspaper articles documenting the Association's history of public protests. Ceiling fans spun furiously overhead in an effort to ward off the heat in the humid, un-air-conditioned space. I was greeted by Mr. Li, the retired head of the Association, who still performed most of the day-to-day work and continued to petition the government on behalf of Chinese spouses. He had arranged several rows of cheap plastic stools in the open interior area of the office, facing a long table with four office chairs arrayed behind it. The setting was formal despite the rundown surroundings, made even more so by the schedule printed up by Mr. Li that listed the meeting's four speakers in order of appearance.

I had come to attend a planning session for the upcoming demonstration against the financial requirement, the first major protest in which the Association collaborated with the Alliance. Several older Chinese women gradually filtered into the room, milling about and chatting in groups, until Mr. Li called the meeting to order and all moved to take their seats. Speaking in heavily accented Mandarin that revealed his mainland origins, Mr. Li opened the meeting by urging the ten or so women present to unite and use their collective power to force the government to pay attention to them and their needs. He then turned over the proceedings to Mr. Pei, a forty-something Taiwanese man with a Chinese wife. Pei had recently replaced Li as the official head of the Association.

Mr. Pei stood up, speaking hesitantly at first, as he encouraged the attendees to join forces with foreign spouses in speaking out against the government. Although Pei advocated cooperation across the two groups, he also emphasized that Chinese spouses faced even more discrimination than their foreign counterparts, pointing specifically to the quotas that restricted their access to residency status and ultimately to citizenship. The women sitting around me nodded their heads in affirmation, and a few whispered among themselves about other Chinese wives they knew who had suffered from the quota system. After Mr. Pei sat down, the new secretary of the Association, a Taiwanese labor activist, continued with a similar line of argument, calling on the audience to collaborate with their Southeast Asian counterparts to overturn the financial requirement, while also elaborating on the additional forms of discrimination imposed on mainland spouses. As the secretary admitted in his closing words, "Foreign spouses oppose class discrimination. In addition to this, we also have the unfair quotas; we must also oppose [this kind of] discrimination."

The organizers of the meeting faced a basic conundrum as they sought to inspire the attendees to participate in the upcoming protest and to spread the word among other Chinese spouses. Because the protest was organized around the single issue of the financial requirement, the organizers struggled to wedge the diverse forms of oppression faced by Chinese spouses into a narrow framework of class oppression. And yet concerns unrelated to class erupted constantly in the organizers' narratives, especially the proliferation of quotas that delayed Chinese spouses' progress through the immigration process and the interview requirements that threatened to derail that process altogether. The whispered conversations among the older women who attended the meeting confirmed that the quota imposed at permanent residence provoked the greatest anxieties, particularly for those married to ailing elderly veterans who might not survive the quota waiting period, putting their wife's citizenship application at risk. To contain these tensions without losing focus on the "core issue" of the financial requirement, the organizers invoked an umbrella term flexible enough to render commensurate the various forms of discrimination faced by Chinese and foreign spouses: "basic human rights."

Given how difficult it was to contain the tensions among the different inequalities faced by the two immigrant groups, I did not expect Chinese spouses to turn out in large numbers for the protest against the financial requirement. A mere two weeks later on a Sunday afternoon, however, clusters of foreign and Chinese spouses massed in front of the offices of Taiwan's executive branch in roughly equal numbers. They lined up in rows accompanied by husbands and Taiwanese activist supporters, many with young children in tow. They carried banners identifying their organizations and signs written in Chinese, English, Vietnamese, and Thai proclaiming messages such as "Protect Basic Human Rights, Eradicate the Financial Requirement"; "The Financial Requirement, Class Oppression"; "Oppose Discrimination, Demand Human Rights"; "Poor Sisters Are Also Good Sisters"; and "Oppose the Restrictions of the Residency Quotas" (figure 4). Evoking a nexus of class and immigrant oppression, the slogans used the concept of human rights both to assert the right of the poor to marry across borders and to reconcile the demands of different immigrant groups under a unified protest.

FIGURE 4. Protester carrying a sign with the slogan "Protect Basic Human Rights, Eradicate the Financial Requirement." Photo by author.

But opposition to the residency quotas—faced only by Chinese spouses— was the most difficult message to contain within this rubric of shared immigrant struggle.

During the demonstration, representatives from CAFRI and the Alliance spoke out against the financial requirement and demanded more equitable treatment for marital immigrants, their voices blaring from loudspeakers mounted on a small truck parked by the entrance to the Executive Yuan.[12] Responding to President Chen Shui-bian's campaign to acquire a seat for Taiwan in the United Nations, the speakers argued that before Taiwan could enter the UN, the government first had to prove its commitment to human rights by protecting them at home—and immigrants were the place to start. By explicitly addressing the UN campaign, activists called upon multiple audiences to bear witness to their protest that day: some physically near and others distant spectators invoked through mediated images such as the banner advocating Taiwan's entry to the UN hanging from a building in the background (figure 5). In so doing, they simultaneously asserted and enacted their own legitimacy as voices of a transnational civil society committed to protecting human rights for all.

Activists' appeal to an international norm of human rights, although a cause around which all could rally, was less successful in containing the different interests of the two immigrant constituencies or equalizing their commitment to the cause. After the first stage of the protest concluded, the crowd of several hundred protesters moved on in a motorcade of buses, cars, and motorcycles to the street in front of NIA headquarters, where they sat on the ground in front of a stage set up at one end of the block. As I spoke with protesters throughout the afternoon, I was struck by the comments of Chinese spouses, most of whom did not see themselves as playing a central role in the demonstration. They had attended to support those who had trouble meeting the financial requirement, and they endorsed the main message of the protest: that the requirement was discriminatory rather than protectionist. But in my many conversations with Chinese women of different ages and backgrounds, not one was overly worried about her ability to fulfill the financial demand.[13] Instead, they invoked a more general sense of unfair treatment as marital immigrants by characterizing the policies that regulated their presence in Taiwan (the financial requirement included) as infringements on basic human rights.

How Long Must We Wait?

Although Chinese spouses spoke frankly in private about their sense of discriminatory treatment, the vast majority were not willing to do so on a public stage. Some were reluctant to call attention to themselves, while others knew that public speaking put them at risk of immigration infractions under an expansive article that banned "any activities not in accordance with the purpose of entry to Taiwan" (*yu xuke mudi bufu de huodong*).[14] So as to avoid endangering the security of any participating immigrants, the Taiwanese men who led the Marriage Promotion Association articulated the demands of Chinese spouses through a vivid protest skit.

Standing on one side of the stage, the secretary of the Association shouted into a microphone as he directed the protesters' attention to a man dressed in

FIGURE 5. "UN for Taiwan" banner promoting Taiwan's entry into the United Nations. Photo by author.

the garb of an imperial Chinese official who was dragging a "bride" wearing traditional red wedding attire to the front of the stage. Three characters inked on a white strip of paper hanging down across the official's face identified him as a representative of the Ministry of the Interior. The bride's upper body was immobilized by a cangue-like board, on which were plastered statements of the many inequities faced by Chinese spouses, from the refusal to recognize PRC university degrees to the denial of work rights. The narrator proceeded to read these aloud to show how the bride's entire being was "shackled" once she arrived in Taiwan. Each mention of this oppressive immigration regime was accompanied by blows from the official who lorded over the bride a sign on which was written "national ID," symbolizing the forever-deferred goal of citizenship (figure 6).

Pausing his recitation, the narrator reminded the audience that Chinese spouses do not suffer this disciplinary regime passively; they strive to acquire citizenship, only to be met by more obstacles thrown in their path by a determined Ministry of the Interior. The narrator then handed the official one square, black "burden" after another: beginning with the financial require-

FIGURE 6. "Bride" shackled by oppressive restrictions, aspiring to the goal of acquiring a national ID. Photo by author.

ment, he quickly added the interview system and the quotas imposed at the different residency stages. Climbing onto a ladder, the official held the national ID just out of reach as the narrator urged the bride to rise up and seize her citizenship rights, despite the heavy weight of her burdens. As she struggled to stand, the bride performed what the narrator described as Chinese spouses' lifelong inability to acquire citizenship. "How long must we wait?" the narrator called out, leading the audience in reciting the protest's core slogan again and again until his voice broke, hoarse from shouting.[15]

This powerful skit broadened the scope of the protest that day by making the financial requirement merely one among many burdens imposed on Chinese spouses by a government intent on delaying their access to Taiwanese citizenship. In so doing, it showed how difficult it was to contain the scope of discriminatory policies within a narrow framework of class oppression. The skit also affirmed powerful parallels between immigration control and patriarchal oppression by portraying the official-patriarch as physically dominating the immigrant bride and blocking her inclusion in the family-nation. A version performed three months later to commemorate the twentieth anniversary of renewed cross-Strait ties emphasized even more prominently the potential violence unleashed by harnessing patriarchy to immigration regulation.

Performed once again by male Taiwanese activists affiliated with the Association, this subsequent skit vividly enacted the oppressive policy restrictions faced by Chinese spouses through the figure of a bride garbed in traditional wedding attire who lay splayed out on the steps of NIA headquarters, her ankles and wrists shackled by chains held by four masked men representing the Ministry of the Interior, the National Security Bureau, the National Immigration Agency, and the Council of Labor Affairs. Each chain was marked with its corresponding burden: the financial requirement, suspicion of spies, the "black-hearted" interview, and restrictions on legal work rights. An official wearing traditional dress stood above the bride, grasping a chain wrapped tightly around her neck, her veiled head drooping limply to the side. Representing the Mainland Affairs Council, the official "strangled" the bride with the chain of citizenship.

The Association had not obtained a permit to hold the protest that day, and because it was during the workweek, a team of police had arrived in full riot gear to form a barricade separating the protesters from the NIA entrance. The effect was a vivid image of state violence, as the rows of riot police were absorbed into the skit itself, as if to shore up the sovereign power of the "official" who held the shackled bride-immigrant's life and citizenship status in his hands (figure 7). The protesters could not have planned such a felicitous convergence. The visual effect of bureaucratic power backed up by state-controlled means of violence enhanced the protesters' indictment of mainland-directed immigration restrictions by exposing the oppressive configuration of gender and nation that compromised the government's sovereignty aspirations. The protest's slogan, "I want happiness, return my human rights," underscored the consequences of this particular mode of sovereign assertion by affirming how it foreclosed immigrants' own aspirations for happiness in Taiwan.

Despite the well-attended CAFRI protests and subsequent demonstrations by the Association, the Ministry of the Interior ultimately rejected activists' demand to abolish the financial requirement. It also refused to shift the timing of the requirement to marital immigrants' first entry into the country, a stage when, activists argued based on international precedents, the financial requirement made more sense as protection against abuse or economic vulnerability. Government officials' intractability on this issue reflected their commitment to the particular form of sovereign assertion through immigra-

FIGURE 7. Shackled "bride" strangled by an imperial official with riot police in the background. Photo by author.

tion regulation.[16] By refusing to alter the timing, the Ministry affirmed the power of immigration policy and naturalization procedures to assert sovereignty effects through fostering productive citizens and regulating access to that privileged status. In its own public statements, the government also invoked international precedents to justify the merits of the financial requirement and to assert that such policies put Taiwan on equal standing with other sovereign states that made similar demands on permanent immigrants. Taiwan was by no means, as one newspaper statement argued, "an exception" (Taiwan Ministry of the Interior 2007).

CAFRI and the Alliance, by contrast, identified human rights protections as a core commitment shared by like-minded international actors. In so doing, they appealed to an expansive model of sovereignty premised on the equal and fair treatment of immigrants and citizens alike. Although an admirable goal in theory, this model failed to redress the multiple oppressions faced by Chinese spouses or the anomalous legal regime that consigned them to an immigration status that fit uneasily at best with rights-based activism. Seen from one perspective, both the Ministry's framing of the financial requirement as an international "standard" of immigration regulation and CAFRI's appeal to the international paradigm of human rights protection affirmed that immigration policy making (both actual and aspirational) was a sovereign act. The government and its protesters might disagree about the content and overall orientation of those policies, but both groups agreed that immigration policy and support for human rights situated Taiwan in a community of sovereign nation-states that crafted those policies in dialogue with one another. From another perspective, however, neither the government nor activist groups were able or willing to confront the ways that Chinese spouses' anomalous legal status undermined those very sovereign aspirations.

THE SHADOW OF CHAIN IMMIGRATION

A few months after the financial requirement protests, the Alliance did turn its attention to the exceptional legal status of Chinese spouses. Cognizant of mounting electoral tensions in Taiwan that might lead to victory for Nationalist presidential candidate Ma Ying-jeou, who had made a campaign promise to equalize the treatment of Chinese and foreign spouses, the Alliance focused its efforts on revising the Act itself. From January through June 2008, I was part of a small group of Alliance members who met every few weeks to pore over the Act, comparing specific articles with the revised Immigration Law, evaluating them for political and gender biases, and debating how each item affected Chinese spouses specifically. We then moved on to the more detailed regulations governing implementation of the Act, as well as related policies regulating residence and citizenship for mainland Chinese.[17] This careful work produced a set of proposed revisions to the Act that was submitted to the legislature at the end of 2008 by Nationalist legislator Shyu Jong-Shyoung (Xu Zhong-xiong) and thirty other supporters.[18]

The version of the Act that finally passed the legislature on June 9, 2009 (taking effect on August 12, 2009) contained several revisions proposed in the Alliance draft, although it failed to realize President Ma's campaign promise to equalize the treatment of all immigrant spouses.[19] One item on the Alliance's agenda grew in prominence over the course of the legislative debates in spring 2009. As younger, divorced Chinese women married Taiwanese men, they faced major obstacles reuniting with minor children from their previous relationships whom they had left behind in China. In its proposed revisions to the Act, the Alliance advocated abolishing the article that prevented Taiwanese from adopting children from the mainland if they already had birth or adopted children of their own (a change that would have enabled Taiwanese husbands to adopt their wife's existing children and sponsor them for citizenship).[20] Although legislators were not willing to reform the adoption article, they passed a supplementary resolution urging that procedures be established for granting visitation, residency, and citizenship rights to the minor children of Chinese spouses.

Exceptional Legal Objects

All parties involved recognized that it would not be an easy task to alleviate the difficulties faced by Chinese women who sought to sponsor their children for residency and citizenship in Taiwan. Officials and bureaucrats across Taiwan's immigration and policy-making bureaucracies were deeply ambivalent about loosening controls on chain immigration from China. Prior to the 2009 reforms, a Chinese spouse only became eligible to sponsor a birth child from a previous relationship after she herself obtained Taiwanese citizenship, at which point she still faced formidable quota and age restrictions.[21] In September 2007, the NIA issued a new quota table for residency and citizenship that effectively eliminated the right to sponsor a minor birth child, not by banning the practice altogether but by classifying naturalized mainland Chinese as a subcategory of Taiwanese citizens and by applying administrative restrictions to that subcategory alone.

On the face of it, the 2007 quota table was quite straightforward. It was divided into three main sections by type of residency and citizenship (defined as permanent residence). Each section was subdivided into categories of eligible mainland Chinese, with the yearly quota for each category listed in the third column. Category four under the permanent residence section referred to birth children of "persons of the Taiwan area" who were under twelve years of age and faced no quota restrictions. Depending on how a "person of the Taiwan area" was defined, this category constituted a potential source of chain immigration.

An explanation of the new table appended to a Mainland Affairs Council (MAC) policy paper described the different types of "persons of the Taiwan area":

> In order to avoid people of the mainland area who have received permanent residence applying for other mainland relatives to come to Taiwan, producing a growing population and effectively squeezing out social welfare [resources], therefore the quota table clearly states that if *a so-called person of the Taiwan area is a person of the mainland area who has changed her status to a person of the Taiwan area*, she must have established residence in Taiwan for a full five years [before becoming eligible to apply for residence for other mainland relatives]. (emphasis added)[22]

The policy paper refers to a footnote appended to category four in the table that created a special subcategory of naturalized Taiwan citizens—"a person of the mainland area who has changed her status to a person of the Taiwan area"—and imposed a five-year waiting period on those in this subcategory alone. The MAC's rationale reiterated the discriminatory view of mainland Chinese as unproductive immigrants who would drain Taiwan's welfare reserves, and it described the waiting period as a means to stem the feared flow of unproductive dependents such as children and the elderly. For Chinese spouses with birth children from a previous relationship, however, the new waiting period effectively foreclosed the very possibility of reunification. The additional five years meant that a child would be older than twelve by the time the mother waited the eight years required to become a citizen and, therefore, would be ineligible for family reunification. Put simply, the five-year delay closed off this channel of chain immigration without banning it explicitly.

I raised the status of the quota table and its new restrictions in a 2008 interview with bureaucrats in the residency division of the NIA. Their responses clearly distinguished between the state of affairs "before" and "after" the September 2007 quota table went into effect. As one experienced bureaucrat admitted:

> Before with regard to children under twelve, the mother only needed to establish permanent residence and then she could apply [for the child]. So there were many children from previous marriages dragged over to live with new husbands (*tuo youping*). But now with the restrictions, those who were born in the mainland, those kids born to a previous husband who want to come to Taiwan, they have even less of a chance! . . . [These] cases likely have no hope; we've effectively cut off this possibility.[23]

This woman's frank admission that they had eliminated this channel for virtually all cases made her colleague, Ms. Lin, pause, and she quickly intervened to reassure me that former mainland Chinese now had other avenues they could pursue to reunite with their children, such as "special permission for societal considerations" (*shehui kaoliang*). But Ms. Lin also added another rationale for the new restrictions:

> So the current policy position is, we don't want so many mainland children coming here. . . . Therefore, the regulations derived from this particular policy formulation will also take this direction. . . . Because after chain immigrants enter the country, once they have grown up, their jobs, education, we

all need to . . . ah, [I] can't put it this way, saying it this way does discriminate against them.[24]

Ms. Lin's comments are striking both for their frankness and for the way she catches herself and tries to rectify her remarks. She states explicitly that the current policy direction dictated to bureaucrats is to restrict chain immigration, especially the entry of "mainland children." Ms. Lin and her colleague assume that these children will become a drain on Taiwanese society: despite their linguistic competence and cultural similarities, they will require additional resources in order to compete successfully in Taiwan's educational and employment system. A large-scale influx of chain immigrants, these women suggest, will undermine Taiwan's population quality and national productivity.

The bureaucrats' statements also identify a specifically patrilineal vision of the Taiwanese family as the basis for denying Chinese wives' immigration claims. The first woman uses the derogatory expression "*tuo youping*" (literally, lugging a jug of oil) to describe a Chinese wife bringing a child from a previous marriage to live with her new husband. The expression connotes both the burden of raising another man's child and the assumption that the child belongs to its birth father in a patrilineal family organized around a male descent line. Her negative portrayal reaffirms that such children lack a culturally recognized kinship tie to a native citizen (either through blood or marriage) and she uses a patrilineal family model to undermine an immigrant wife's appeal to birth parentage as the basis for a reunification claim. These comments echoed an official stance that viewed mainland Chinese women's reproductive capacities as desirable only when they produced recognizably Taiwanese children.

The quota table itself fell under the category of an administrative order that derived its authority from a policy chain originating with the Act.[25] As the outcome of administrative policy, the table's content represented the decision-making capacity of bureaucrats, not elected officials, and it disguised its discretionary features in its status as an official object: it was published on the NIA website and was cited by bureaucrats to justify immigration decisions. The choice to use a footnote in the quota table was also intriguing here. Footnotes were not common in other policy documents regulating mainland Chinese, and therefore, as several Alliance members charged, their legal status was highly questionable (could a footnote be challenged in court or through administrative appeal?). Moreover, its very form resembled an afterthought, albeit one with powerful consequences. The footnote enacted the exceptional standing of mainland Chinese in Taiwan both by creating the rule—the five-year waiting period that on the face of it simply deferred the right to sponsor a child—and by holding that right forever in abeyance. The exceptionalism of Chinese spouses, enacted here through de facto denial of their rights-bearing status, was reaffirmed by the use of the footnote as the form of exclusion.

The Alliance openly challenged the legal standing of the footnote and the quota table's creation of distinctly unequal categories of Taiwanese citizens. In response, the MAC and NIA issued a new table on December 31, 2008.[26] The new table eliminated both the five-year waiting period and the distinction between types of Taiwan citizens. However, it also divided the original category four in the permanent residence section of the table—minor children of persons of the Taiwan area—into two separate categories. The first retained both the wording from the previous table and the lack of a quota applied to "birth children under age twelve of people of the Taiwan area." But this category was now followed by a new one: "birth children under age twelve of persons of the mainland area who received permanent residence after being permitted to enter the Taiwan area and who have established household residence" (*dalu diqu renmin jing xuke jinru Taiwan diqu dingju, bing she you huji*). The yearly quota for this new category was set at sixty persons.

The second category created a new legal status in Taiwan and applied a quota to the minor birth children of this group alone. Yet in fact this new status was none other than a Taiwan citizen. The individual entered the country legally, had received permanent residence, and had established official household residence, fulfilling all the requirements for citizenship. Rather than call this status "Taiwan citizen" or "person of the Taiwan area" and then distinguish among types of citizens, the revised table created a new category derived from the individual's mainland origins. Although the revisions redressed the critique of second-class citizenship leveled at the 2007 quota table, they further differentiated citizenship from within by introducing discrimination based on place of origin, making this subset of Taiwan citizens forever "people of the mainland area."

Publicizing the Human Faces of Immigration Restrictions

The December 2008 quota table reflected deeply rooted bureaucratic anxiety about chain immigration flows from China. Recognizing that it would have little luck overturning the quota system altogether, the Alliance shifted its strategy to publicizing the human costs of blocked family reunifications. Individual Chinese spouses had already embarked on this path by petitioning the government directly. Their pleas redefined the Taiwanese family so that it encompassed members on both sides of the Strait, and they repositioned Chinese women as active initiators of migration flows rather than as passive recipients of their Taiwanese partner's beneficence.

Chen Ying-long had met and married his Fujianese wife in 2005, knowing that she already had a one-year-old daughter. Before Chen could begin adoption proceedings, his wife became pregnant and later gave birth to their son in Taiwan. Because Chen now had a child of his own, he could not legally adopt his wife's daughter or apply for citizenship on her behalf. Only when his wife became a Taiwan citizen could she sponsor her daughter as a birth child under twelve years of age.

The quota table and five-year waiting period implemented in September 2007 dashed their dreams. Angry and distraught, the couple petitioned legislators and bureaucrats, and they posted their tale on immigrant websites and their own blog. Their petitions and blog entries were written in the wife's voice, and every sentence was permeated with her pain at the enforced separation from her daughter and her anger at the heartless policies that had destroyed the future of an innocent child. At its root, her appeal used both emotional bonds and assertions of financial independence to claim her daughter as an integral member of a Taiwanese family: "We have the ability to raise and provide for our children (including [our] daughter born in the mainland); both are [our] own children carried for ten months in my womb, not a child adopted from someone else."[27] The typical absence of pronouns in the Chinese makes it difficult to determine definitively whether she meant "our" or "my" here, but the overall assertion was clear: both are her birth children, and therefore both are part of her and her husband's family (and as parents they have the resources to care for both equally). Her rhetoric skillfully elided contradictions in the presence and absence of biological ties (she stressed that their children were not adopted from someone else, but did not reiterate that her husband had no biological tie to her daughter). Moreover, she solidified her argument by including herself, at least obliquely, as part of the Taiwanese people, chastising the government for its refusal "to permit its own people to reunite their entire family (*bu zhun ziji de renmin quanjia tuanyuan*)."

Newspapers picked up the story, and the couple's heartbreaking tale of a now four-year-old girl left behind in China unleashed a flood of similar accounts from other Chinese women with young children on the mainland, most of whom had assumed when they married that they would be able to bring their children to Taiwan. These women sought to redefine the national family so that it encompassed their children born before they married a Taiwanese, a model that challenged traditional family structures organized around patrilineal descent from a male Taiwanese citizen. Immigration policies shored up this patrilineal family by legitimizing only certain roles for an immigrant Chinese wife: she was assumed to marry into her husband's family where she might bear children with him or care for his children from a previous marriage but where there was no place for children she conceived with another (ostensibly Chinese) man. As the NIA bureaucrat asserted, these children were "born to a previous husband" and were subsequently "dragged over to live with new husbands." The patrilineal bias of this family model effectively excluded mainland children from any claim to belonging in their mother's new family and denied Chinese women an active role in initiating future-oriented migration chains. The very presence of such children, by contrast, was portrayed by bureaucrats as drawing a mother back to her mainland origins. In response, women with children in China invoked their ability to produce and nurture families that they portrayed as stretching across the Taiwan-mainland divide, thereby refusing state efforts to deny them "the intimacies [others] take for granted as integral to family life" (Pratt 2012, xxiv).

The adoption ban and quota tables reaffirmed traditional gender biases within cross-Strait marriages by inscribing them in law and administrative policy. Thirty-year-old Yu Hua bitterly criticized these inequities over lunch one June day in 2009 as she described for me how her husband's family assumed he had been duped by a mainland woman simply looking for someone to support her and her child. Yu Hua had given up a successful bank job in China to marry her Taiwanese husband following a divorce. At the time, she had assumed she would be able to bring her young daughter with her to Taiwan, and she had made arrangements for the child to live with her sister in the meantime. Five years later, she acknowledged that her daughter might never be eligible to come to Taiwan, and the pain of their forced separation was compounded by the poor treatment she received from her husband's family members and friends:

> I've suffered a lot of unfair treatment marrying into this family. My husband
> is more than ten years older than me. My family—my older sister, for

instance—they say, "Your husband is so lucky to marry you!" But his people don't think this way. They think that if you marry someone from the mainland, that person is coming in search of fortune. And then the money you [the husband] earn, she sends home to support her mainland family, to support her mainland child. My husband's friends will say, "Ah, you married this wife, but you still have to support someone else's child?"[28]

After several years of failed attempts to resolve her daughter's plight, Yu Hua began to participate in activist circles through the Association and the Alliance. She quickly realized that she was not the only mother separated from her child, and she eagerly reached out to other Chinese women she met through these groups and through contacts she made online. In the hope of publicizing the painful experiences of immigrants such as herself, Yu Hua agreed to participate in a press conference organized by the Alliance on May 8, 2009, Mother's Day, timing that also coincided with the Legislative Yuan debates about revising the Act. The Alliance press statement clearly explained the two articles of the Act that needed to be revised in order to allow mothers to reunite with their children, and it pointed out at every step that foreign spouses did not face similar restrictions. Calling on legislators and the MAC to approve the revisions proposed by the Alliance, the press conference statement urged the government to reverse the tragedies it had caused.[29]

Media coverage of the press conference described in poignant detail the pitiful plight of the four mothers featured by the Alliance, Yu Hua included. What ultimately drew attention from the press was not these women's willingness to speak out against the regulations that separated them from their children, however, but their tearful suffering as mothers. Framing their desire to reunite with their children as a basic human right was ultimately a less effective strategy than underscoring their maternal commitments and painful separation from their children. Officials and the public responded favorably to Chinese women's emotional appeals as mothers, recognizing motherhood more generally as the means through which Chinese wives could transform their ties to a mainland past into claims for belonging and equitable rights in a future Taiwanese nation.

During the feverish legislative sessions and closed-door bargaining meetings that took place throughout the month of June, MAC bureaucrats, legislators, and Alliance activists debated how to grant residency and citizenship to these children and what age standard to use for defining minor status. The result was a decision to revise administrative policies so as to permit Chinese spouses with residency status to sponsor birth children under age fourteen first for a visitor visa and later for residency and citizenship.[30] By the time I left Taiwan in August of that year, Yu Hua and several other women had brought their children to Taiwan, a successful conclusion to their struggles that was celebrated with much public fanfare by MAC chairwoman Lai Shin-yuan herself.

LEGAL ANOMALIES

The expansion of Taiwan's law and policy regime regulating Chinese spouses has produced an array of contradictions and unforeseen consequences over the past two decades. Despite what appeared at first to be a straightforward spatio-legal distinction between categories of legal subjects based on place of origin, the designations "people of the mainland area" and "people of the Taiwan area" have proven difficult to hold in place. Categories have multiplied over time or become differentiated from within, and legal regulations have fostered conflicting interpretations of Chinese spouses as unproductive drains on the nation's economy and vital contributors to its reproductive future. Resorting to atypical legal forms such as the footnote or supplementary resolution, bureaucrats and lawmakers simultaneously expanded the terrain of legal subject-making, while undermining both its coherence and potential legitimacy as an assertion of national sovereignty.

As Chinese spouses move through a prescribed sequence as visitors, residents, and ultimately citizens, they experience firsthand the challenges created by this anomalous system of legal classification, especially when they seek to claim rights they perceive as fundamental to human happiness and fair treatment. When activists incorporate mainland Chinese into rights-based agendas, they struggle to render commensurate the diverse forms of discrimination faced by foreign and Chinese spouses. Not only are Chinese spouses less easily assimilated into the popular imagination as sympathetic victims who suffer from racism and class oppression, but the anomalous laws and policies that regulate their immigration trajectories are also more difficult to overturn through claims to human rights protections and equal treatment under the law. As a consequence, reform initiatives have often utilized a combination of public protest and behind-the-scenes negotiations in order to identify—often uneasily—Chinese spouses with the rights-bearing subject and to make claims on the basis of that uneasy association.

Both Taiwanese state actors and activist organizations such as the Alliance envision a political future in which specific forms of immigration policy making and human rights advocacy consolidate Taiwan's status as an independent nation-state. By appealing to international precedents—whether with respect to widely adopted immigration and naturalization requirements or a shared commitment to protecting human rights—both groups in their own way advance the cause of Taiwan's sovereign recognition. Yet because they do so without overturning the anomalous legal structure that defines mainland Chinese as neither foreigners nor natives, they find themselves with few options for imagining new political possibilities that do not simply reenact configurations of space and time rooted in the Cold War past.

FOUR

Risky Encounters

ON A GLOOMY JANUARY AFTERNOON IN 2008, I entered a small conference room in the Taipei office of CARES, an NGO that offered support services to Chinese spouses. I found it neatly arranged for the group of immigrants soon to arrive, with each place at the long conference table set with a microphone and a steaming cup of tea. CARES was hosting a symposium on behalf of the Mainland Affairs Council (MAC), which had commissioned an advertising company to produce a sitcom-style DVD to educate mainland Chinese about the policies regulating Chinese spouses in Taiwan and to introduce typical Taiwanese lifestyles and societal norms. The DVD was intended to resolve the lack of accurate information in the mainland about these topics, an information gap produced in part by the absence of official Taiwan government offices in China.[1] This was the second such symposium sponsored by CARES to help the producers solicit suggestions from Chinese women already in Taiwan about what they thought their counterparts in China most needed to know when considering a cross-Strait marriage.

Six women in their thirties and forties participated in the discussion that day and they represented a heterogeneous group who hailed from urban and rural areas across China. One or two of them were college graduates who had held white-collar jobs prior to migrating, but the rest had ended their educations after junior middle school or high school. The circumstances of their marriages and life trajectories in Taiwan also varied significantly, with some married to elderly veterans and others coupled with younger men with whom they had borne children. One woman had divorced in Taiwan and was able to remain in the country because she had obtained child custody. Others were previously divorced in China, and one woman had been separated from her young child for several years. These diverse life experiences produced the wide-ranging perspectives and concerns that the women brought to the symposium that day.

The producers had structured the informational DVD around a dramatized portrayal of one cross-Strait couple's shared life. The stylishly dressed Taiwanese producer opened the session that afternoon by describing the content she had planned for the drama: the legal regulations faced by Chinese spouses in Taiwan, including the initial ban on work rights; basic lifestyle disparities that new immigrants might encounter; and cultural differences that could produce tensions in interactions with husbands, in-laws, and even children. As she asked the six women present what they would want to tell their compatriots contemplating a cross-Strait union, she made it clear that she hoped their comments would fit into these broad content categories. Their initial suggestions did just that. Several women emphasized the difficulties they experienced adjusting to new cultural expectations, such as sharing a home with in-laws or worshipping traditional gods and spirits. Others urged the producer to underscore the social services and educational opportunities available to recent arrivals during the period when they were unable to work legally.

As the session proceeded, however, the participants quickly launched into accounts of marital conflict, divorce, child custody battles, and family separation, issues that certainly had broader relevance for all marital immigrants but could also be dismissed as too specific to individual circumstances and twists of fate. The calm exchange of ideas aspired to by the organizers rapidly devolved into emotional and sometimes heartrending narratives as participants relayed their own tales of hardship or added poignant commentary to others' accounts, frequently speaking over one another in an effort to be heard. At several points, the CARES representatives intervened to guide the discussion back on track by chastising speakers for focusing on "individual cases" irrelevant to the larger task at hand. Yet the women in the room failed to see a clear distinction between individual cases and general policy or adjustment issues. Regardless of personal experience, they sympathized deeply with tales of employment discrimination, societal alienation, divorce and child custody battles, and separation from children left behind in China.

As I listened to these heated exchanges and observed the fruitless efforts of the producer and CARES employees to contain the scope of the discussion, I began to wonder who the participants saw as the audience for their comments. Their own distressing accounts of how government policies supported abusive husbands or forever sundered ties between mothers and their children certainly were not going to inspire confidence in Chinese women contemplating marriage across the Strait. Nor would watching a DVD help those women make good choices when selecting a spouse, for, as several participants pointed out, even Taiwanese men who seemed to be good husband material during visits to China might later turn out to be uncaring or even abusive partners. Reiterating how government policies made it more difficult for couples to become better acquainted before they decided to marry, participants took the opportunity provided by the planning session to promote a short-term fiancée visa that would allow potential Chinese spouses to see their husband's living situation in Taiwan firsthand before embarking on a legal marriage. By the end of the two-hour meeting, I became more convinced that the women had used the session's stated goal of soliciting their opinions to convey to the MAC representative sitting quietly in the room their criticisms of where the government was falling short in its espoused commitment to protect and assist Chinese spouses.

The unfolding of events at the DVD planning session showed how encounters between Chinese spouses and Taiwanese bureaucrats often swerved from their intended track and led to unpredictable outcomes. The session participants refused to contain their narratives within the parameters outlined by the organizers: they insisted that individual cases were not narrowly personal but instead had wider application, and they described in moving detail how policies mattered to them in ways both large and small. In essence, Chinese spouses used individual cases to make broader claims about policy inequities and the structural disempowerment they faced as marital immigrants, but this approach also enabled organizers and bureaucrats to dismiss their concerns for being too specific to individual circumstances. In addition, the planning session foregrounded how some NGO representatives supported state actors by invoking law and policy precedents and by affirming the value of neutral application of the law in the face of immigrants' requests for personalized adjustments. The final response from the MAC representative who observed the session revealed one possible outcome of such encounters. When asked to comment on the participants' statements as the discussion drew to a close, she ignored their more searching criticisms of policy inequalities and returned to the safer terrain of cultural and linguistic differences between mainland Chinese and Taiwanese.

The planning session and the final DVD enacted a particular kind of exchange between Taiwanese bureaucrats and Chinese marital immigrants that I saw replayed time and again during my research. This mode of interaction reflects more than what bureaucrats believe needs to be shared with potential immigrants still in the mainland. It constitutes an effort to instruct immigrants how to engage with the Taiwanese state, how they should think about the policies that govern their lives, and, in some cases, how they might maneuver around or strategize in the face of policy restrictions. This chapter examines how these encounters between bureaucrats and immigrants unfolded at large policy-education forums and in the more intimate settings of law and policy sessions included as part of government-sponsored acculturation classes. I analyze face-to-face interactions as powerful moments when bureaucrats' law and policy directives confronted immigrants' diverse life circumstances and when both parties endeavored to create a structure of recognition expansive enough to account for their disparate needs and desires.

Formalized exchanges between bureaucrats and immigrants required participants to anticipate the audiences for their statements, in effect calling forth a particular kind of audience empowered to enact a specific relationship to the speaker and his or her claims. These interactions provided marital immigrants with an opportunity to tell their stories, mobilizing emotion and sympathy in the hope of inducing policy reform or procedural exceptions. Bureaucrats, however, typically responded by invoking the precedents established by a robust immigration law and policy regime, calling upon Chinese spouses to acknowledge this regulatory authority and, by extension, Taiwan's sovereign statehood. But this goal was inherently risky, for immigrants might reject the state's authority and refuse to act as the necessary mirror to bureaucrats' sovereign assertions, instead demanding that bureaucrats adapt policies to address their own special circumstances.

Although these interactions often led to unpredictable outcomes, they generated a range of productive effects. In their responses to Chinese spouses' queries and pleas, bureaucrats instructed Chinese spouses on how to work around policy constraints and taught them strategies for forging a more secure status in Taiwan, in effect guiding immigrants through the intricacies of Taiwan's state apparatus in ways that naturalized the state's right to govern those within its territory. And Chinese spouses, even when demanding better treatment on the basis of shared ethnoracial ties with Taiwanese, nonetheless advocated using foreign spouses as a model, in effect asking to be treated *as foreigners* and thereby recognizing the government's power to regulate them as outsiders to the polity. When considered cumulatively, therefore, these encounters show how state actors called upon Chinese spouses to play a critical role in the drama of asserting a fragile Taiwanese sovereignty and how spouses, in turn, used the twists and turns of this sovereignty plot to demand state recognition of their own needs and aspirations.

MEDIATED ENCOUNTERS

The DVD ultimately produced by the MAC, titled *Hold Hands with Taiwan, Make a Date with Happiness*, presents an idyllic portrayal of Yuqing and Qixue, a young, urban, and middle-class cross-Strait couple whose love marriage, harmonious family relations, and financial security make them an aspirational ideal for those considering a cross-Strait marriage.[2] The plot follows the attractive Qixue as she marries and moves to Taiwan, quickly adjusts to life with her in-laws, learns new skills through taking advantage of training classes, and struggles to find employment, her job search ultimately put aside when she bears a son and assumes her celebrated role as mother of a Taiwanese child.

The narrative intersperses the couple's life of comparative ease with brief scenes that introduce potential threats to marital harmony and immigrant integration, such as domestic violence, employment discrimination, and separation from children left behind in the mainland. Throughout the video, the dialogue reiterates the policy regime regulating cross-Strait couples, beginning with the multiple steps couples must go through to marry and apply for the Chinese spouse to enter Taiwan and continuing with detailed descriptions of the visa and residency stages and the various rights and protections afforded by each. This heavy-handed dialogue is interrupted regularly by fly-ins that reiterate key information in bullet form and list the names and contact information for relevant Taiwanese government offices and NGOs. The combined effect of these elements is to portray an effective yet benevolent government and civil society committed to guiding Chinese spouses through a complex immigration system and offering training and support services in the process. Glossing over sticking points that might obstruct that smooth progress—the border interview, conflict between mother- and daughter-in-law, job discrimination, domestic violence—the video depicts the constraints imposed on Chinese spouses as a form of governmental care, not discipline.

The citizens and immigrants portrayed on screen openly affirm the value of this governing regime and the performance of Taiwanese sovereignty it enacts. The audience conjured by the video—Chinese contemplating marriage to a Taiwanese and Chinese government officials who might distribute the DVD—are thereby called upon to witness (and, in an ideal scenario, acknowledge) the sovereign claims made within. Audiences, however, are tricky interlocutors; rarely unified in their response, they often interact in unpredictable and perhaps unexpected ways. Danilyn Rutherford (2012) astutely points out the essential role of audiences in sovereign claims, but she also highlights the play of dependency and risk that makes the outcome of sovereign encounters so uncertain. As "moments when sovereignty makes an appearance, and in making an appearance, puts itself at risk" (Rutherford 2012, xi), the scenarios portrayed on screen mirrored the face-to-face interactions that I observed during policy forums and acculturation classes.

Hold Hands with Taiwan enacts this risky dance of sovereign assertion and audience acknowledgment most forcefully in its concluding section, composed of three testimonials from Chinese women who are all long-term residents of Taiwan.[3] The women are filmed outside in a natural setting, looking off at an angle to the camera as they speak sequentially about different features of life in Taiwan and describe how they have overcome personal obstacles to achieve a greater sense of societal integration.[4] One speaker, appearing at both the beginning and end of the testimonial section, speaks more frankly than the other two about her feelings of loneliness, her painful separation from family and friends in China, and the daily challenges she has faced in Taiwan despite her previous experience as a professional woman in urban China. She uses her closing remarks to remind those contemplating a cross-Strait marriage that they will have to adjust to their new environment, for it won't adjust to them. "Once you have the right mindset," she says encouragingly to the imagined viewer, "you will live as happily and fortunately as I have in Taiwan."

No smile softens her face as she utters these final lines, however, and the words sound forced, as if she is struggling to end her testimonial on a positive note. Instead of a message of hopeful encouragement, the viewer is left with a powerful feeling of dislocation and even alienation that is exacerbated by repeated mention of the hard work needed to adjust as an immigrant and build a new life. An undercurrent of tension runs through the testimonials—evidenced by tightness in the speakers' faces, their unease at speaking on camera, and the forced quality of their speech—and it creates an embodied subtext that undoes the reassuring work of the women's narratives and the idyllic sitcom plot that preceded them.

These closing testimonials leave the DVD viewer feeling unsettled, unsure of what message to believe and how to interpret the statements from women who have actually married a Taiwanese and relocated to Taiwan. In the first part of her narrative, the speaker whose comments bookend the other testimonials describes the experience of waking up one day and realizing that she is in a completely strange place. It felt, she explains, "as if I had gone to a foreign country." With this simple expression, "as if," the speaker unravels the sovereign assertions woven throughout the video. Her utterance calls into question the DVD's enactment of a robust yet caring immigration regime as the bedrock of Taiwan's sovereign rule, but it also introduces the possibility that Taiwan could potentially be seen as sovereign by virtue of its status as a "foreign country." The speaker's testimonial does not resolve these conflicting interpretations. Instead, the audience is left with a lingering sense of powerful difference for which there is no ready label at hand.

MASTERING IMMIGRATION POLICY

When Chinese spouses first arrive in Taiwan, they typically know very little about the laws and policies that will govern their new lives. The PRC government blocks access to Taiwan's government websites and official media sites, and only the most savvy computer users navigated successfully around these Internet obstacles. Some Taiwanese partners will research policies in advance, but in many cases even they are not familiar with the full panoply of restrictions faced by mainland Chinese in Taiwan or the complex immigration sequence that awaits their spouse upon arrival. Many immigrants were unaware that they would not be permitted to work legally in Taiwan for several years (in effect through August 2009) or that their postsecondary degrees from PRC universities would not be recognized. Others were unfamiliar with the requirements for progressing through the various visa and residency stages. And as I described in chapter 3, those with dependent children still on the mainland did not realize that it would be very difficult, if not impossible, to sponsor those children for residency and citizenship in Taiwan before the 2009 reforms took effect. During the long decade (1992–2004) when residency status for Chinese spouses was allocated through a quota system, some Taiwanese husbands found the system so confusing that they failed to put their wives on the quota list when they first became eligible, thereby delaying their progress toward citizenship. Others did so inten-

tionally to keep their wife at a more insecure immigration status or to prevent her from acquiring the independence that came with becoming a
citizen. These trends were common among couples otherwise distinguished
by age, educational level, and class status.

The insecurities produced by policy unfamiliarity were exacerbated by constant revisions to the policies in question. The status quo when a Chinese
spouse first entered Taiwan might be obsolete by the time she became eligible for residency or work rights; in fact, her very criteria for eligibility might
have changed dramatically, altering her time clock to citizenship without her
knowledge. In response to this ever-changing landscape of immigration regulation, the DPP government and its Nationalist successor implemented a na-
tionwide program to educate cross-Strait couples about relevant laws and
policies. They incorporated policy introductions into acculturation and training classes run by local governments and NGOs, all with funding from a
national government fund created in 2005 to provide guidance and support
services for Chinese and foreign spouses. Under the auspices of the MAC and
CARES, the government sponsored policy-education forums for cross-Strait
couples who lived across the island, the largest of which attracted several hundred participants. Between 2007 and 2009, I attended five of these public
forums held in northern, central, and southern Taiwan, as well as six policy
information sessions that were part of acculturation or training classes or that
were organized by CARES and conducted at their Taipei office.[5]

Regardless of location, policy forums adopted a similar structure. They began with a brief introduction from relevant local and national government
units that outlined the services each office provided for Chinese spouses and
explained recent policy reforms (figure 8).[6] Speakers then moved to individual stations set up around the building and fielded questions from immigrants
and their family members. This component of the forum continued for upward of two hours, providing enough time for attendees to interact directly
with bureaucrats as they sought answers to questions or resolutions for
difficult situations. In each of the forums I attended, the NIA station
attracted the largest audiences and frequently led to emotional and at times
confrontational exchanges between bureaucrats and immigrants or their
citizen partners.

During these face-to-face interactions, NGO organizers used question-
and-answer formats and microphones (which could be taken away from
verbose or confrontational speakers) to limit the scope and length of exchanges. They quickly discovered, however, that statements often exceeded

FIGURE 8. Main auditorium of Chiayi policy-education forum. Photo by author.

desired narrative forms and conceptual boundaries. Questioners presented lengthy narratives that took winding paths before arriving at the "main point"; some immigrants or elderly husbands were unable to speak clearly in Mandarin, requiring interventions from neighbors or volunteers who might add their own details to a query; and others were so distraught that they broke down in tears and were unable to articulate their request succinctly. As at the DVD planning session sponsored by CARES, organizers sought to police the distinction between individual cases and general policy inequalities and to prevent speakers from expanding their specific points to general critiques of immigrant disempowerment. Attendees, however, regularly challenged any illusion that these boundaries could be fixed for all. As a result, participants were often drawn into conflictual and emotional interactions, as bureaucrats affirmed principles of legal impartiality as part of shoring up state authority, while immigrants challenged, through accusations of heartlessness, the moral foundations of the very immigration policies that formed the bedrock for sovereign claims.

The questions posed to NIA representatives at policy-education forums consistently showed that cross-Strait couples wanted immigration policies to be more flexible so as to account for their own difficult or unusual circumstances. They articulated their desire for an exception through moving accounts that emphasized, for instance, immigrants' commitments to their children near and far, the consequences of marital discord, the challenges of poverty, and the risks posed by life-threatening illnesses to an immigrant's security in Taiwan. In response to demands for policy flexibility, bureaucrats at policy forums and acculturation classes instead reaffirmed the importance of precedent and impartiality in Taiwan's legal system and immigration regime, instructing Chinese spouses how to engage more effectively with the state and its many moving parts. In the process, however, many bureaucrats also suggested strategies for maneuvering around inflexible policies and exploiting contradictions in the gaps that arose between different government bodies.

Underscoring the inflexibility of existing immigration policy was not merely a tactic of bureaucratic avoidance or "indifference" (Herzfeld 1992); these responses both oriented immigrants toward a governmental system based on the rule of law and invoked the sovereign foundations of that system. Precisely because immigration policies shored up Taiwan's fragile claims to sovereign status, changes to those policies—especially those forced through as a result of pressure from immigrants and their activist supporters—might also undermine their sovereignty effects. Making policy flexible enough to account for the exceptions demanded by Chinese spouses required that Taiwanese officials and bureaucrats adjust their assertions of sovereign rule in response to the care challenges posed by changing configurations of power on the ground (Dunn and Cons 2013). Yet as I argued in chapter 3, officials and bureaucrats showed little willingness to make such adjustments, whether in response to activist protests or individual cases. On the rare occasions when state actors did yield some ground, they contained revisions within narrow parameters that did not threaten the important role of immigration policy as a sign of sovereign decision making. The encounters at policy-education forums displayed a similar commitment to a rigid armature of policy rationales and procedural requirements, regardless of the tragic consequences that might result.

The three short vignettes that follow illuminate the dynamics of encounters premised on requests for exceptional treatment. Buttressed by tears and poignant tales of personal tragedy, these requests moved many participants at the forums—immigrants and citizens, bureaucrats and laypeople—because they underscored the acute human consequences of policy inflexibility. Although very few bureaucrats in these public settings would acknowledge the possibility of making policy more flexible, on occasion they did offer potential strategies for resolving painful outcomes or hint at possible reforms on the horizon.

I Will Die before She Is Eligible to Stay

The 2008 Yunlin forum held in a sleepy county seat in central Taiwan happened to fall on a rainy Sunday afternoon in late May, and the organizers worried that turnout would be low because participants needed to travel, often by moped or motorcycle, from outlying villages and towns. The event took place in the large assembly hall of the local high school, and CARES organizers and volunteers spent the morning arranging rows of metal chairs facing a wooden stage, its surface scuffed by generations of high school students. The forum began with introductions from the government representatives, and then participants dispersed to locations around the hall where staff from each office addressed individual queries. The local officer from the county NIA station, a stocky, middle-aged man dressed formally in his white uniform, set up shop at one end of a long table near the edge of the stage, and the organizers herded the large group forming just below into a line that snaked down the aisle of the main hall.

Early in the session, a young couple slowly approached the table, the Taiwanese husband, gaunt and very pale, leaning heavily on his wife. He explained that he suffered from late-stage liver cancer and feared he would not live long enough for his wife to obtain extended residency, at which point she would be eligible to remain in Taiwan even after his death. The couple adopted a traditional petitioning stance—with their heads bowed and hands held in front, one clasped around the other—as they pleaded with the NIA officer to backdate the wife's eligibility to redress their earlier delay in applying for her kin-based residency status. They were not asking for special treatment, they asserted, but merely an adjustment of her timeline so that it corresponded to her date of eligibility and not the later date when they had submitted her paperwork. As the young man swayed with the effort of standing for so long, he added one more point of support for their case: the fact that his wife would continue to care for his parents after his death.

After the man finished his plea, the group seated at the table looked at one another and sighed, distraught by what they had just witnessed. I quickly realized that the couple's appeal could only rest on a procedural exemption because the wife did not meet the existing qualification for granting citizenship in the case of the citizen-spouse's death: having a citizen-child. Lacking evidence of their commitment to the future provided by childbearing, the couple instead emphasized the idiosyncratic nature of bureaucratic procedural time to justify their request. The NIA officer's reply, however, affirmed the intractability of procedural temporality. He quickly pointed out that current policy did not permit the agency to readjust the timing of an immigrant spouse's eligibility for each immigration stage: eligibility was determined by the date when the paperwork was processed.

Nonetheless, the bureaucrats around the table were moved by witnessing a young man so obviously ravaged by disease and his distraught wife, and they offered an alternative to compensate for the rigidity of procedural practice. The MAC representative gestured to the NIA officer, and after the two conferred in hushed tones, the latter suggested that the couple submit a "special case" (*zhuan an*) petition explaining the circumstances and details of the wife's request. The MAC would evaluate the petition in accordance with existing policy guidelines and issue a decision on the case. The emphasis on existing policy guidelines was intentional, I surmised, because it would enable bureaucrats in Taipei to put aside the emotional impact of the case in favor of policy precedent. Given that the couple did not have children, only their relatively young age and the claim that the wife would care for her in-laws might lead to a favorable outcome.[7]

No Government Wants My Child!

The NIA session at the Taoyuan forum held in May 2008 took place in a large auditorium in the county government complex, and the space was filled to capacity for much of the afternoon. Late arrivals had no choice but to sit on the floor or stand in the aisles, and the noise of children running about added to the sense of mayhem. Not long after the session began, a woman of indeterminate age rose from her seat to ask a question. Holding the microphone tightly in both hands, she explained in a halting voice that this was her second marriage; her first husband had died, leaving behind a child who could not come to Taiwan. "My question is this: can we adopt a mainland child?" She then added that she had given birth to a second child with her current Taiwanese husband, and the government had told her husband that he could not adopt her mainland child if the couple already had a child of their own. At this point, the speaker's voice cracked and tears began to run down her face. Only a few muffled words escaped audibly through her sobs: "I'm so heartbroken. Because my previous husband died, . . . my child couldn't go to Macau. . . . I only married a Taiwanese after my previous husband died, but we can't adopt my child. My child is suffering so much."

The audience members murmured among themselves and shifted uncomfortably in their seats as the full scope of the woman's pain became apparent. The CARES employee running the session intervened and urged the woman to calm down so the NIA officer could hear her question. The officer interrupted to say that he had understood, despite her emotional breakdown. The woman stemmed her tears long enough to ask the question again: "Why can't I apply for my mainland child to come over?" The officer's response was brief, and he stuck closely to the letter of the law, while also encouraging the woman to pursue other avenues. Acknowledging that the Act did not permit a Taiwanese to adopt a child from the mainland if he or she already had another child, the officer suggested that the woman go to the local court to apply for the adoption. He knew of another case, so he claimed, where the court had ruled in favor of the adoption because of special circumstances. Speaking in a pedantic tone of voice, the officer used this opportunity to remind the audience that the power to decide on adoption lay with the courts and not with the NIA or the Ministry of the Interior. Assuming, perhaps, that mainland Chinese would not appreciate these jurisdictional distinctions, the NIA officer instructed them on the different institutional actors responsible for implementing specific features of immigration regulation and the rule of law more generally.

By this time, the speaker had regained her composure, and she tried again to explain her situation in greater detail. Her previous husband had hailed from Macau, but the mainland government did not permit the child to go to Macau. After her husband died, she married a Taiwanese, but the Taiwan government also refused to grant entry to the child. By now she was growing upset again, and her voice quivered as the tears began to flow. "I say, my child is so pitiful. How is it that three governments don't want my child? The Macau government doesn't want my child, nor does the Zhuhai government [on the mainland]. And now the Taiwan government doesn't want my child either!" As the CARES representative sought to end the exchange, the woman interjected a final call of despair: "Why is my child in this situation? No government wants her!"

Whispered expressions of support circulated among the audience members sitting around me as the organizer took the microphone away from the woman and urged her to take her seat. The organizer sought to manage the woman's outburst by reiterating that the NIA officer had already instructed her to apply for a special exemption from the courts. Interestingly, the NIA officer had failed to ask the woman important questions such as how old the child was and what immigration stage the woman herself had reached. By directing her to the court, he, in essence, sidestepped the NIA's role in crafting and implementing regulations that made it virtually impossible at the time for Chinese spouses to sponsor children from a previous relationship. By reaffirming the intractability of the Act, the bureaucrat allowed that only a major exception granted by the court would enable the couple to adopt her child, an outcome that most Chinese spouses felt was unlikely.[8] The CARES employee confirmed the inflexible power of the law and existing policy regulations by reminding the audience that these policies were already in effect before they came to Taiwan. Because the law preceded and took precedence over exceptional circumstances, it could not adapt to individual demands, regardless of the tragic consequences that might result.

I Stay for My Son

The 2007 Taipei County forum was the first policy-education forum I attended, and I had cajoled Liao Lijing, Tao Weihong, and several other members of the Taipei City acculturation class into joining me that Sunday afternoon. Upon entering the massive hall in the county government complex, we were approached by CARES employees and volunteers in white vests who directed us to the registration tables and handed out packets of information. We settled into plush red seats in the main auditorium and listened to the introductory presentations by representatives of various government agencies. Lulled into a state of passivity by the dry speeches, the audience only slowly roused itself after the large space was then allocated to the NIA station for the question-and-answer session.

The first few questions for the NIA officer did little to enliven the crowd, focused as they were on routine issues of processing paperwork and applying for visitor visas for family members in China. But then a volunteer handed the microphone to a thin woman roughly thirty years of age, with deep lines of worry etched in her face and her hair escaping in tendrils from her ponytail. She stood and grasped the microphone with trembling hands, while her young son pulled anxiously at her skirt. Speaking in a soft voice, the woman described how her husband beat her regularly, but she was unwilling to divorce him because she knew she would be forced to leave the country. "I stay for my son," she added, explaining that her husband was familiar with existing policies and had refused to grant her child custody (which she needed in order to remain legally in Taiwan after a divorce). She grew increasingly agitated as she spoke, and the mood in the room became tense as the audience waited for the NIA bureaucrat to respond.

A wan smile was fixed on the female officer's face, and she gently urged the woman to calm down. But the woman continued to plead with her, asking what she could do to protect herself. Calling the police was no help, she argued, and she did not know how long she could continue in this situation, despite her commitment to her son. Shaking her head, the NIA officer replied that there was nothing she could do given the current regulations (which did not yet offer an exemption in cases of divorce due to domestic violence). This was a matter between her and her husband, the bureaucrat continued, and the CARES organizer chimed in to suggest that the woman speak with the local representative from the domestic violence prevention office.

By the end of the exchange, the woman's son was in tears, and he was clawing frantically at her clothing. The two of them left, presumably to speak with a social worker, and as I turned to look at Liao Lijing sitting next to me, I noticed that her eyes had filled with tears and she was dabbing at the mascara that threatened to run down her cheeks. The woman's plight was so sad, she complained, and there seemed to be nothing she could do to end the abuse, unless she was willing to abandon her son. It was true that even with a court-issued protection order, a Chinese spouse still required child custody to remain in Taiwan after a divorce, and this was not the first time I had heard of Taiwanese partners using this regulation to their advantage. Only in 2009 would the regulations be revised to permit Chinese spouses with minor children who had divorced because of domestic violence to maintain legal residence in Taiwan, regardless of whether they had obtained child custody.[9]

A similar vein of questions followed this distressing exchange. Many audience members talked about cases where the Taiwanese spouse wanted a divorce but the Chinese partner was unwilling to acquiesce for fear of being deported.[10] The NIA officer remained calm throughout, responding in turn that these were personal conflicts between the couple and not something that the NIA could resolve. By keeping her responses safely within the parameters established by existing policy, however, she failed to acknowledge how the state, through both crafting and enforcing such policies, assumed the role of disciplinary patriarch who shored up the power of citizen-spouses (in essence, condoning their abuse).[11] Instead, she attributed the NIA's inability to act in such cases to the current status of the policies in question.

At some point in this line of questioning, the NIA officer, with a growing note of frustration in her voice, tersely mentioned the possibility of future policy reform as a solution to immigrants' dilemmas. By redirecting audience members' hope toward an unspecified time in the future when regulations might be revised (*chufei na yi tian xiufa*), she also introduced them to legitimate means of obtaining redress in a state governed by the rule of law. Her wording was intentionally noncommittal, however, merely alluding to the possibility of future reforms without providing any specific information.[12] As an observer at these events, it was unclear to me whether NIA officers actually knew of policy revisions under discussion or whether they simply assumed that immigration policies were subject to constant change (and therefore might be revised to resolve the emotionally wrenching scenarios they faced at policy-education forums). Regardless, the suggestion of future reform (actual or aspirational) encouraged immigrants to see policy reform as a solution to their pleas, while simultaneously freeing NIA officers from any professional responsibility for the tragic situations they confronted in their encounters with Chinese spouses. These encounters created a powerful sense of contradiction among audience members and presenters alike: bureaucrats and officials relied on the support of policy precedents and the generic form of law when faced with immigrants' specific demands, but they also regularly suggested strategies for working around inflexible policies to make the system more responsive to individual cases and immigrants' perhaps not-so-exceptional circumstances.

REGULATIONS ARE HEARTLESS

These encounters at policy-education forums left attendees with an enduring sense of the rigid impartiality of immigration policies—their ostensibly equal application to all—and the immigration bureaucracy's general imperviousness to requests for exceptional treatment. Many bureaucrats admitted to me in private that they were moved by immigrants' appeals but felt powerless to act, especially in public forums where their charge was simply to convey information. I did learn of some instances when the MAC offered special dispensations to Chinese spouses in desperate circumstances, and NGO activists were able to extract concessions in other cases. But individual bureaucrats could do little in these public settings where they represented the immigration system as a whole, especially because that system was indispensable to Taiwan's claims to a fragile sovereignty. In the tense encounters that often ensued, Chinese spouses interpreted bureaucrats' commitment to the *form* of sovereign assertion as heartless inflexibility. The robust law and policy infrastructure of Taiwan's immigration regime, the bedrock of efforts to assert sovereignty despite the general absence of international recognition, responded indifferently to outside challenges or distressed pleas, even though individual bureaucrats might offer strategic suggestions when faced with the painful consequences of policy impartiality.

Some Chinese spouses and their family members came to view immigration policies as heartless because they were unable to resolve their individual problems and offered few provisions for flexible treatment. The female officer at the Taipei County forum, however, had replied to individual cases of domestic abuse and divorce by directing the audience's attention to the possibility of future policy reform, thereby recognizing, albeit implicitly, that these ostensibly individual experiences of oppression and inequality might in fact affect Chinese spouses collectively. Although policy reform represented an alternative to the exceptional individual case approach, it did not promise immediate redress. As the NIA officer herself acknowledged, policy reform existed as a future potentiality, its endless deferral signifying for many the government's dominant stance of heartlessness and lack of care.

For immigrants whose lives were stalled by their unusual circumstances, shifting from an individual case strategy to advocating for policy reform was a difficult process. After her husband committed suicide in 2005, Deng Li-fang described herself as stuck in an endless present, forever banned from seeking Taiwanese citizenship. I first met Deng a few short months after her husband took his own life. She used her public performance at a Taiwanese dialect language contest I attended to pour out her tale of woe following her husband's premature death, hoping to elicit sympathy for her case from the bureaucrats and officials presiding over the competition. Only in her late twenties at the time, Deng had learned to present her story to great effect. Nothing in her background had prepared her for the challenge of petitioning the Taiwanese government, but despite her upbringing in a northern Fujian village and only junior middle school education, she spoke clear Mandarin and had rapidly mastered Taiwanese dialect, skillfully incorporating evocative words and phrases into her speech. With experience gained through months of petitioning officials across the state bureaucracy, she had honed her narrative skills so that her self-presentation elicited maximum sympathy from her audience and provided compelling arguments for why the government should restore her citizenship eligibility.[13]

Yet despite Deng's powerful presentation, the response she had received from all government bodies was the same: her husband's death had dissolved their marriage and, with it, her eligibility for citizenship. She could only remain in Taiwan as a legal resident. This decision hewed closely to existing policies, which granted a widowed spouse citizenship only when she had a dependent citizen-child, and Deng's childlessness meant that her repeated efforts to obtain redress ultimately led nowhere. From Deng's perspective, however, the government's response punished her for an act that was beyond her control.

During our first meetings that spring and in subsequent e-mail correspondence before we met again in 2007, Deng lamented that she was being blamed for her husband's death. "During this period I can't stop thinking, what did I do wrong? These past years, I've lived in this land, loved it and the people. Moreover, I've abided by the regulations, progressing from feeling strange to becoming familiar, leaving time and again, living such a hard life" (e-mail correspondence, July 10, 2005). Deng had conscientiously observed the onerous requirements necessary to maintain her legal status in Taiwan, and she portrayed that obedience as a sign of her "love" for the country and her devotion to becoming a citizen.[14] When she received extended residency status in 2004, she believed that her struggles would soon come to an end and she would finally feel at home in Taiwan. But that hope was stolen from her on the April morning when her husband leapt from a window of their highrise apartment building.

Deng Lifang described the regulations that denied her citizenship as "heartless" (*wu qing de*), their inflexibility reinforced by bureaucrats and officials who claimed their hands were tied by existing policies that offered no recourse for more humanitarian treatment. "I am sure that I'm not the only person in this kind of situation," Deng argued, "[but] I hope that for those of us who identify with this place, law can provide fairness and justice, an opportunity" (e-mail correspondence, July 10, 2005). Deng clearly recognized the power of law in a democratic society, and on numerous occasions she lambasted the Taiwan government for policies toward Chinese spouses that she argued contravened democratic ideals. Despite her appeal to justice through the law, however, she failed to see how the very qualities of a system based on the rule of law, such as impartiality and precedent, might work to her disadvantage. For Deng's initial strategy was not to advocate for the reform of policies that held her citizenship eligibility in abeyance (potentially uniting with others "in this kind of situation") but instead to seek an individual exemption through portraying herself as an ideal "citizen in waiting" and inspiring compassion and care from the state.

To convey the depth of her commitments, Deng emphasized her invest-ment in her Taiwanese family and through it, in Taiwan's own future, re-peating in her public presentations how she had become pregnant with her husband but had miscarried and failed to conceive again. Expressing love for her new homeland despite the tragic outcome of her marriage, Deng sought to spark a sympathetic response from her audiences and spur them to make an exception in her case. During our correspondence over the fall of 2005, however, Deng slowly began to recognize that policy reform might be her only option, but she was deeply dissatisfied with the proposed substance of the revised policy:

> This [proposed revision] is a little better than before, at minimum I can have the opportunity [to become a citizen]. But I must wait five years; five years is really too long! . . . If I must complete five years [of extended residence] be-fore I can apply [for citizenship], this comes to eleven years. And during these five years I'm not permitted to marry. . . . Then I will be at least 35 before I can have a baby. (e-mail correspondence, October 25, 2005)

Deng was incensed by two restrictions in the proposed revisions: the re-quirement that she spend five years at the extended residence stage (instead of the usual two) and the ban on remarrying during this period, both of which further delayed her desire to have a child and realize the promise of integra-tion such a child might bring. The marriage ban was particularly invidious, Deng argued, because it resembled traditional Chinese proscriptions against widow remarriage, a remnant of a feudal past that seemed to have no place in a modern Taiwan that identified itself with ideals of equality and democ-racy (e-mail correspondence, August 18, 2006). Deng's astute critique of the contradictory logic underlying this restriction exposed in poignant detail how patriarchal values and gender inequalities infuse immigration policies in liberal democracies in ways otherwise deemed unacceptable in the sphere of domestic civil law (van Walsum and Spijkerboer 2007).[15] Although Deng gradually accepted the message that policy reform was the only viable solu-tion to her liminal status, she nonetheless rejected reforms that enforced pa-triarchal inequalities for immigrants alone.

Deng deeply resented the restrictions imposed by the revised policy, but she grew more despondent as even this reform appeared endlessly deferred, entangled in institutional transitions and bureaucratic wrangling over min-ute details. This delay motivated her visit to Mr. Cai that I described in chap-ter 3, as Deng began to fear that citizenship eligibility was slipping from her grasp. During the three years she waited for the regulations to be revised, Deng struggled to go on with her life, training for a new career and setting up her own business under the name of a Taiwan citizen. But despite her perseverance and remarkable business success in Taipei's competitive service sector, other aspects of her life stalled in the meantime, especially her desire to marry again and have children.

The long years of waiting attenuated Deng's ties to Taiwanese society and diminished her confidence in her own identity. "Where am I from? Where do I belong?" she asked me in a pained voice, as we huddled in a side room in her company's office to escape the prying ears of her employees, from whom she had hidden her mainland roots. "I don't know when that regu-lation will be approved," she continued, affirming how powerfully the im-migration policies that determined her fate had affected her very sense of self. "Wherever I go, I am asked: 'Where are you from?'" Deng despaired of finding an answer to this pressing question, and her silence weighed heavily in the room, her identity and sense of belonging intimately tied to what seemed, not unreasonably, like the endless deferral of immigration policy reform.

Revisions to the relevant policy were not announced until March 7, 2008, and they granted citizenship eligibility to Chinese spouses in Deng's situa-tion provided that they met the restrictive conditions Deng herself found so distressing.[16] Deng's changing stance over the years showed how she came to accept policy reform as the best strategy for resolving her plight, but she remained dissatisfied with the substance of the reform and the ad-ditional burdens it imposed. Throughout, Deng refused to relinquish her belief that immigration regulations should not be heartless and that the Tai-wanese state should express its care for Chinese spouses by being flexible enough to accommodate exceptional cases. Her stance did not deny the gov-ernment's power to regulate immigrants such as herself, but she refused to accept a logic of policy impartiality that failed to redress her unusual circum-stances. By expressing her love for Taiwan, Deng was, in a sense, demanding that the government live up to its standing as a sovereign power by creating egalitarian, caring immigration policies and acknowledging the commit-ments of its deserving citizens-to-be.

The additional three-year waiting period imposed on widowed Chinese spouses without children was a political compromise intended to assuage the concerns of politicians opposed to an influx of mainland immigrants. Without marital or parental ties to substantiate their bond with the nation, widowed spouses such as Deng could only rely on time spent waiting to prove their commitment to their new home. Time mediated an immigration system based on privileged kin relationships by ameliorating certain obstacles that might arise as an immigrant spouse progressed through the system, but it could not replace marital or parental ties altogether. Therefore, when bureaucrats and officials at policy-education forums faced pleas for more humane flexibility in policy application, they evaluated what kinds of relationships best affirmed an immigrant's commitment to Taiwan and what bonds were excluded from that privileged status. Some cross-Strait couples appealed to shared ethnoracial roots as a rationale for demanding better treatment for Chinese spouses, but the logic of common roots also prompted responses from bureaucrats that narrowed the scope of immigrant inclusion even further, in effect hardening the borders of the nation and projecting an image of a contracted national body far into the future.

In the vast auditorium that housed the Taoyuan forum on a warm May day in 2008, a young woman took the microphone and, speaking softly but forcefully, asked the NIA officer why Chinese spouses had to wait eight years to become citizens, but wives from Southeast Asia only required four years. The audience members sitting around her began to cheer and clap in support, urging her to go on. "We are all one people (*yici tongren*)," she added, her voice growing stronger. "So why do those from Thailand only wait four years, but we wait eight years?" The woman then continued, "We're not two countries (*bu shi liang guo*); we are mothers of Taiwanese children." By collapsing the subjects of her statement so that political entities (countries) merged with Chinese spouses (mothers of Taiwanese children), she appealed to shared roots and familial bonds to affirm the ambiguous features of the Taiwan-China relationship and to use that ambiguity to challenge Chinese spouses' unequal treatment by the government.[17]

This woman employed the powerful expression "we are all one people" to assert Chinese spouses' shared ethnic and racial ties with Taiwanese, appealing to their status as brethren to contest their harsh treatment as immigrants. At other policy forums, both Chinese and citizen spouses invoked their shared status as "Chinese" (*women dou shi Zhongguo ren*) to dispute policies they argued were unfair and discriminatory. Regardless of the specific framing of shared heritage, however, several inconsistencies undermined this strategy. Asserting common roots raised the specter of similarity that made Chinese spouses' ostensibly shared features—language, cultural norms, physical appearance, even "blood"—more threatening than reassuring, especially because they might be viewed as disguising other salient differences such as political commitments and values cultivated under a socialist regime. The very claim that Chinese and Taiwanese were the same people was itself subject to contestation, moreover, with the assertion of shared origins challenged in diverse quarters across Taiwanese society.[18] Finally, Chinese spouses (and their citizen partners) undercut their own declarations of shared heritage when they demanded that Chinese spouses be treated the same as foreigners. In effect, these assertions contested Chinese spouses' anomalous standing in Taiwan's immigration regime not by rejecting the government's power to regulate them as immigrants but by insisting that they be recognized as equal to foreigners.

At the Taoyuan forum, the woman's claim to shared roots prompted enthusiastic expressions of support from audience members, and their bursts of applause drowned out her voice at several points. The NIA representative initially struggled to grasp the substance of her complaint, but he then began to address in a surprisingly frank manner her point about the ambiguous relationship between Taiwan and China and the status of their people:

> Actually, one could say that the relationship between Taiwan and the mainland is a special relationship, a very unusual relationship. One could say that they are two countries, but they also are not two countries. We have said, "one country, two systems."[19] I think phrasing it this way is more comfortable. Just like laws which gradually move forward, it was like this from the very beginning. The laws have become more flexible. Actually I know that they have created many inequalities for everyone.... Foreign spouses can work as soon as they receive a residence permit, so why must you apply [for a work permit] when you receive kin-based residency? The law has gradually become more flexible, gradually. You must have patience.

By acknowledging the not quite state-to-state relationship between Taiwan and the mainland, the NIA officer affirmed that he had heard the woman's assertion that they were not two separate countries, but he also held back from fully endorsing this denial of Taiwanese sovereignty (*they are* two countries, but *they also are not*). Moreover, he admitted that in the past, this awkward political relationship might have made life more difficult for Chinese spouses in Taiwan. Stepping back from the basic political conundrum, he urged the audience to adopt a long-term perspective by recognizing that policy restrictions had loosened over time, meanwhile admitting that bureaucrats such as himself agreed that such regulations were often inconvenient and even inhumane. Despite invoking these shared sympathies, he reminded his listeners that progress could only be gradual. "The law cannot change in one fell swoop to conform to everyone's needs," he added, and encouraged all in the audience to give the laws time so that they could slowly be revised.

The NIA officer's response, both supportive and deflective at the same time, neutralized the speaker's confrontational tone but left untouched her implicit demand that Chinese spouses be treated equally to foreign spouses. Instead of addressing the larger question of whether mainland Chinese were (or should be regulated as) foreigners, he emphasized the government's caring attitude and its investment in policy reform as a means of addressing immigrant spouses' needs. Reiterating how much policies had improved over time, he closed with the claim that they would only grow less restrictive as cross-Strait tensions eased: "I think that progress will speed up with the relaxing of cross-Strait relations, it won't stagnate, march in place. I think it will now move forward in ever bigger steps. Because no matter what, as long as you have given birth to a child, one type is . . . the mother of a Taiwanese child, right? So it will slowly, this law will slowly conform to everyone's needs, okay?"

With this closing comment, the NIA officer affirmed the power of a future-oriented perspective attuned to the inevitable march of progress. Encouraging the audience to step outside the conditions of their own lives, he asked them to adopt a different kind of relationship to the problem described by the speaker by recognizing the progress that had already taken place and the better future that such progress portended. Instead of viewing immigration policies as rigid and heartless, the NIA officer portrayed them as changeable, their flexibility a reflection of the kind of immigration bureaucracy he conjured in his reply, one attentive to the needs of immigrants such as those in the audience.

Improving policy flexibility required other conditions, however, the most important of which were more harmonious relations across the Strait. Despite the NIA officer's initial framing of cross-Strait ties as something other than a state-to-state relationship, his subsequent emphasis on the inevitable relaxation of political tensions suggested that future policy reforms depended on Taiwan's increased confidence in its own political authority. Although he skillfully sidestepped any overt mention of Taiwan's sovereign challenges, his call for patience intimated that a better future for Chinese spouses was tied to a more secure future for the Taiwanese polity as a whole.

The integration of Chinese spouses into this national polity was possible in its fullest form only through realizing another form of immigrant futurity: reproducing the next generation of Taiwanese children. The first speaker evoked this promise by demanding equality between Chinese and foreign spouses on the basis of Chinese wives' status as "mothers of Taiwanese children." The NIA officer acknowledged that childbearing added value to Chinese immigrants' demands for better treatment, but he also resisted collapsing all Chinese spouses into the category of mother of a Taiwanese child. As merely "one type" of Chinese immigrant, mothers were clearly privileged in his vision of a more flexible policy future, but he knew all too well that not all Chinese spouses fit this ideal type. Just looking around the room at the sea of women and men in the audience—young, middle-aged, and elderly— was enough to confirm this point.

Shared blood, in short, evoked different responses, depending on what kind of blood ties were at stake and what claims were being made in their name. Assertions of ethnoracial unity prompted uncomfortable memories of a not-so-distant past marred by forced migrations and the high stakes of Cold War conflict. Such assertions also motivated bureaucrats to acknowledge how the unusual political relationship across the Strait required the government to impose harsher policies on Chinese spouses, despite their shared features with Taiwanese. In response, Chinese spouses asked to be treated as well as foreigners, a stance that implicitly affirmed Taiwan's independent standing and its sovereign authority to regulate them as immigrants. Ultimately, however, Chinese spouses could most legitimately make claims for equitable and flexible treatment through their status as parents of citizens, for childbearing substantiated their commitment to Taiwan through reproducing Taiwanese citizen-children.[20]

INVESTING IN THE FUTURE

Chinese women and men who attended the boisterous policy-education forums or more staid acculturation classes quickly learned that they best demonstrated their investment in Taiwan's future and justified their equality demands when they bore or fathered Taiwanese children.[21] This message left a deep impression on many Chinese spouses I knew, especially those anxious about the stability of their marriage or the health of their citizen-spouse. Bureaucrats openly promoted the protections gained through having a child and, in so doing, shaped the very composition of cross-border families and the strategies of immigrant spouses searching for greater security and inclusion.

Tao Weihong, the young Henanese woman who attended the Taipei County forum with several other women from the acculturation class, frequently discussed with me her concerns about her marriage during class breaks and when we socialized outside of class. Over time, she came to realize how much she felt like an outsider when she was with her husband and his four sons from a previous marriage. Not only did they exclude her by speaking in Taiwanese dialect, which she did not understand, but she recognized that her husband's primary commitment would always be to his children, not to her. She even suspected that he had married her largely to help care for the household. The practical benefits of having a child—as emphasized by the NIA officer at the Taipei County forum—were compounded in her case by her growing sense that a child would also enhance her standing and claims to belonging in her new family.

When a female bureaucrat from the Taipei City NIA Service Station made a presentation to the acculturation class a few weeks after the forum, class members repeatedly interrupted her to ask how to remain in Taiwan in the event that their marriage ended. The bureaucrat initially responded by emphasizing how important it was to have a child and obtain child custody. When similar questions followed, she grew impatient and sought to stem the flow of interruptions by forcefully asserting the benefits of childbearing: "Children can resolve quite a lot of problems. Therefore, many people have a child as soon as they get married." The class burst out laughing in response to this statement, but those who were still childless had obviously absorbed the officer's lesson. Tao and Liao Lijing, both of whom wanted children but were not yet pregnant, turned to urge each other on, mischievous smiles spreading across their faces: "You have a baby, you have a baby (*ni sheng, ni sheng*)!"

Over the next few years, Liao Lijing would struggle with infertility and would eventually give up on having a child, but Tao discovered she was pregnant a mere month after the NIA officer's presentation. Despite growing awareness of the security provided by childbearing, Tao initially debated whether or not to continue the pregnancy. Her husband responded in a lukewarm fashion to the news, and he argued that it was ultimately her decision to make, a position that on the face of it was not unreasonable given that he was already in his forties and had four children to support. What he perhaps failed to recognize, however, was how his response fueled Tao's fears that he viewed their relationship merely in pragmatic terms, whereas she claimed to have an emotional commitment to the marriage. His inability to sympathize with her dilemmas or communicate his feelings to her ultimately encouraged her to adopt a more instrumental attitude toward the pregnancy. When she and her husband were about to depart for her hometown in Henan to visit her parents prior to the Chinese New Year, she admitted to me that she planned to determine the sex of the fetus in China and would keep the baby only if it was a girl, on the assumption that her husband would want a daughter given that his existing children were all boys. If, however, her husband's attitude toward her and the child did not improve over time, she would wait until she became a citizen and then leave the marriage to raise her child herself. Having learned from immigration officers that a child provided her a chance at future security and recognition from the state, Tao decided that this strategy was her best option.[22]

Through their presentations at acculturation classes and responses to queries at policy forums, NIA and MAC bureaucrats influenced Chinese spouses who were making critical life decisions about whether and when to have a child. Their explicit messages also fueled growing anxieties about an immigrant's future in Taiwan in cases where a spouse was unable or unwilling to bear children. Nonprocreative spouses were well aware that childbearing shored up claims of marital authenticity and smoothed the path to citizenship. As a consequence, they worried deeply about how they might express a commitment to a future in Taiwan in the absence of children. By underscoring the benefits of childbearing as part of the ostensibly neutral charge of providing information about immigration policies, bureaucrats and officials used these exchanges to define what kind of family tie substantiated a claim to belonging in Taiwan and what bonds failed to perform the necessary work of demonstrating commitment to a shared future. They taught spouses that state recognition was more secure from a position as mothers or fathers, as opposed to "merely" wives or husbands.

As I discussed in chapter 3, however, not all mother-child relationships were equally valued. When Chinese women tried to reunite with children left behind in the mainland, their efforts evoked for bureaucrats the opposite of future promise; instead, they affirmed a Chinese spouse's ties to the mainland and sparked official anxieties about immigration chains that might degrade the quality of Taiwan's population. Exchanges at policy forums about how to reunite with children left behind in China provided an opportunity for bureaucrats to drive home the message that these parental bonds were not only undesirable from the perspective of the Taiwanese state but failed to establish (and even undermined) an immigrant spouse's commitment to a future in Taiwan.

Injunctions to bear specifically Taiwanese children enabled bureaucrats to rearticulate the policy logics that recognized certain kinds of families as the building blocks of the Taiwanese nation. By the same token, their reluctance to support Chinese spouses seeking to reunite with children left behind in the mainland excluded cross-Strait parent-child bonds from the promise of future integration.[23] As they explained the intricate details and consequences of these policies to audiences composed of immigrants and their family members, bureaucrats asserted the sovereign power of the state as they literally performed a robust immigration regime that aspired to regulate the minute decisions of family lives, both those that predated immigration paths and those that followed from them.

UNPREDICTABLE AUDIENCES

Bureaucrats and immigrants used their exchanges at policy-education forums and acculturation classes to advocate different relationships to the state. Bureaucrats called upon immigrants to recognize the distribution of jurisdictional authority and regulatory power, both to deflect responsibility for policies seen as particularly restrictive and heartless and to teach immigrants how to maneuver through a governmental system based on legal precedent and impartiality. Immigrants, however, insisted that the state respond flexibly to their needs and unpredictable situations, marshaling the emotional power of individual cases to demand exceptional treatment. Chinese spouses listened silently but attentively as bureaucrats droned on about policy details, alert to possible loopholes that might resolve their policy-induced dilemmas. Only in some cases did individual immigrants come to see policy reform as a solution to their woes, and even then they chafed at reforms that opened certain doors while closing others.

In addition to cultivating particular relationships to the state, these exchanges also showed how bureaucrats and immigrants anticipated each other as their relevant audience for claims and petitions. Bureaucrats depended on Chinese spouses to affirm, implicitly or explicitly, their assertions of sovereign rule through the government's right to regulate them as newcomers to the polity. And some spouses did just that but in unexpected ways, such as when they demanded that they be treated the same as foreign spouses. Some participants at forums and classes responded deferentially to bureaucrats' injunctions, occasionally taking the lessons bureaucrats imparted to them to heart by incorporating policy logics into their own family plans. But others used the opportunities for direct engagement provided by these settings to openly contest policies that were too restrictive, unable to account for the fluidity of cross-Strait lives and the diverse needs of marital immigrants.

When audience members bravely challenged NIA representatives about policy inequities, immigrant- and citizen-spouses alike clapped and cheered in agreement. But they also endorsed frank admissions from bureaucrats about the unusual status of the relationship between Taiwan and China and the illogical features of some policies developed in response. These exchanges provided bureaucrats with the opportunity to assert a fragile Taiwanese sovereignty through affirming the government's robust immigration regime, but they did not guarantee that immigrants would recognize this ideal image. In sum, Chinese spouses and their citizen partners were not uniformly obedient audiences: like the testimonial speaker on the MAC informational DVD who described Taiwan "as if" it was a foreign country, their responses showed how they might act less as a direct mirror for the state's sovereign claims and more as an unpredictable, strangely altered reflection.

PART THREE

———

Belonging

FIVE

Gender Talk

IN JUNE 2009, the Mainland Affairs Council (MAC) produced a ninety-second promotional film titled *New Age Taiwanese* (*Xin shidai Taiwan ren*) that aired in public service slots on television and in movie theaters. The film endorsed new policy revisions that were to take effect for Chinese spouses later that summer, and it focused on the legal work rights that Chinese spouses would receive shortly after their first arrival in Taiwan.[1] The film begins with a rapid succession of shots that introduce three Chinese wives through their Taiwanese children, husbands, and in-laws, portraying the women as embedded in a web of local kinship ties defined by patrilineal principles. Throughout the short vignettes, the film's voiceover—spoken in alternating sequence by a female narrator and MAC chairwoman Lai Shin-yuan—emphasizes Chinese women's reproductive capacities and celebrates their feminized, domestic roles in Taiwan as mothers, wives, and daughters-in-law.[2] When the women speak, they stress their emotional bonds with their husbands as part of affirming their authentic marital motives, and they describe the difficulties they initially experienced in Taiwan because they were banned from seeking employment. "Being able to work," one woman asserts, "is very important for our families because then we can share the burden with our husband, and he won't have to suffer so much."

The narrator switches from Taiwanese dialect to Mandarin toward the end of the short film as she justifies the recent decision to relax restrictions on Chinese spouses' work rights. Underscoring the government's ongoing commitment to obstructing sham marriages and praising the economic contributions made by Chinese spouses in authentic unions, the voiceover proclaims, "In the future, as long as [Chinese spouses] are in a legal, authentic marriage (*hefa zhenshi de hunyin*), they can work to support their families and together improve Taiwan's economy (*wei Taiwan pin jingji*)." The film celebrates these "new age Taiwanese" by subsuming their productive capacities in an idealized vision of feminine domestic responsibility. It foregrounds Chinese spouses' reproductive roles as childbearers and caretakers, and it reframes their desire to engage in paid work as a legitimate interest that supports the Taiwanese family, reduces the burdens placed on Taiwanese men, and enhances the overall economic productivity of the nation. This message affirms that Chinese spouses do not qualify for legal work rights as individual rights-bearing immigrants but as contributors to familial and national welfare (see also Lu 2011, 129–30).

By identifying Chinese spouses through their roles as mothers and wives, the film reinforces a dependency model of immigration that provides no legitimate basis for making nonfamilial claims to legal status or belonging in Taiwan. I use the term *dependency* to highlight two interlocking features of this immigration system: one, the system restricts the permanent immigration routes available to mainland Chinese primarily to a recognized kinship tie with a citizen, making Chinese spouses dependent on that kinship relationship to maintain legal immigration status; and two, it defines the authenticity of those privileged kinship relations according to gendered principles of feminized domesticity and care work, thereby enforcing Chinese spouses' economic dependence on their citizen partner.[3] As a core value promoted by Taiwan's immigration system, dependency limits the acceptable roles, behaviors, and imaginaries available to both spouses in cross-Strait marriages, foreclosing alternative possibilities by "narrow[ing] the range of framings that are thinkable" (Greenhalgh 2012, 144). In other words, dependency produces gendered consequences for men and women, immigrants and citizens, through the disciplinary effects of immigration policies framed in otherwise genderneutral terms.

The MAC's promotional film enacts an idealized vision of traditional gender roles by identifying the new Taiwanese family as exclusively patrilineal in orientation: a Chinese wife "marries into" (*jia gei*) her husband's family, bears children for his family line, and often resides with and cares for his parents. The vignettes ignore more complex marital histories by erasing family members who expose the potentially contentious underside of this patrilineal ideal, such as children from a previous marriage or an immigrant wife's natal kin who might also reside in Taiwan.[4] By celebrating this narrow vision of family, the film denies legitimacy to other family forms, including those that appear to mirror this reproductive ideal but include a Chinese husband.

In this chapter, I examine how gender norms and expectations shape the broad principles undergirding Taiwan's immigration system and, in turn, how these principles influence the internal dynamics of cross-border marriages and the struggles of Chinese spouses to build new lives for themselves in Taiwan. Taiwan's immigration policies guide marital dynamics by heightening attention to expected gender performances, influencing the tenor of spousal interactions, and narrowing the scope of potential marital roles for immigrants and citizens alike. As I showed in chapter 2, the bureaucratic performance of sovereignty through immigration regulation tightly links cross-border couples' management of their personal lives to state demands for specifically gendered performances of marital authenticity (see also Cole 2014; Neveu Kringelbach 2013). These state demands promote an ideal model of the national family built around a masculinized citizen-breadwinner and feminized immigrant-homemaker.

My discussion focuses on how different groups talk about these gender expectations both in the context of individual marriages and when assessing the behavior of Chinese spouses in Taiwan. I trace how official discourse—such as that conveyed in the MAC's promotional film—permeates everyday conversations and how, at times, those conversations offer alternative visions of desirable gender roles and behaviors. When Chinese spouses engage in this kind of "gender talk," they often express a profound sense of disillusionment about the possibility of happy marriages, exposing the compromises and hard work necessary to resolve both everyday and bureaucratic forms of intimate contestation. Certainly there are many couples who build fulfilling family lives despite their differences, and not all cross-Strait marriages are marred by tension and conflict. I choose to focus on points of contention in order to expose key gendered assumptions that cut across official state immigration models and Taiwanese norms of social interaction; in the process, I also show how Chinese women and men negotiate gender conflicts in their daily lives as marital immigrants in Taiwan. These negotiations establish a framework for working within the restrictions created by immigration policies, popular opinion, and cross-Strait political contestation. At the same time, however, these pervasive gender conflicts underscore the vast differences in the recent histories of marriage, family, and gender formation across the Taiwan Strait.

My goal is not to document empirical differences in cross-Strait gender roles and ideologies (as these vary over time and context) but instead to show how immigrants, citizens, bureaucrats, and officials in Taiwan mobilize the concept of gender discursively and through their everyday practices. A powerful discourse of different gender ideologies across the Strait sharpens anxieties about the "proper" femininity and masculinity of Chinese spouses and creates expectations that are, more often than not, prefigured to fail. Yet talk about gender expectations and differences also potentially mitigates concerns about Chinese spouses' political alterity by channeling those tensions into domestic relations and familial needs. In so doing, this gender talk provides an important register through which cross-Strait political differences (and the diverse forms of socialization they engender) may be discussed, managed, and, in some cases, neutralized to make them less threatening to the intimate domains of marriage, family, and the nation.

GENDERED DISAPPOINTMENTS

A growing body of scholarship on Western Europe has documented how gender and sexual relations are frequently invoked in debates about immigrants' perceived lack of integration, especially with regard to Muslim immigrant communities. Comparing public discourses in France and Germany, Rita Chin succinctly concludes, "Ultimately, both French and German debates about the gender relations of Muslim residents became a way to raise fundamental doubts about the compatibility of Muslim migrants with European culture and society" (2010, 572). Mayanthi Fernando (2013) argues that heightened attention to Muslim immigrants' gender and sexual "deviance" enables French national elites to disavow their responsibility for enacting neoliberal reforms that created crushing social and economic dislocation in immigrant communities, instead positing "cultural" differences as the explanation for male violence and criminal behavior.

These authors and others astutely illustrate how perceptions of gendered and sexual alterity constitute immigrants as a threat to European values and social cohesion (see also Beck-Gernsheim 2007; Neveu Kringelbach 2013).[5] In Europe, immigrant women become an object of concern because they are seen as victims of oppressive, traditional gender and sexual relations. Their presence threatens the gender equality and sexual liberation fought for by white European and secular immigrant feminists. This particular European response to Muslim immigration usefully highlights the distinctive features of cross-Strait marriage migration. In Taiwan, the gender problem posed by Chinese wives represents a very different kind of alterity: they are seen as already "too liberated" because they grew up under a socialist system that

ostensibly promoted gender equality. As a consequence, their behavior conflicts with models of traditional femininity associated with Taiwanese
women (although not necessarily subscribed to by all in practice). Chinese
women's outspokenness, reluctance to assume sole responsibility for domestic
tasks, and commitment to paid labor are read as signs of radical political
difference—as evidence of their commitment to ideals of gender equality
cultivated under state socialism.

Different gender role models in mainland China and Taiwan originate
from many sources, the most prominent being the principles of gender egalitarianism introduced by Chinese communists under the slogan "Women
hold up half the sky." After the Communist Party took control of the country
in 1949, it initiated widespread campaigns to liberate women by fostering
more egalitarian family relationships and encouraging women's nondomestic
workforce participation. The effects of gender and family reforms were felt
unevenly across China, however, with urban areas experiencing more rapid
and perhaps longer-lasting changes than rural communities, where women
continued to perform most household tasks and child care despite also engaging in agricultural and other nondomestic labor. Market reforms initiated
in 1979 eroded some of the gains of the Maoist decades by pushing women out
of comparatively secure state and collective sector employment, relegating
many to now-devalued agricultural work or the low-paying export and service sectors, and encouraging them to model new ideals of the glorified
housewife and sexualized femininity (Evans 1997; Farrer 2002; Gao 1994;
Honig and Hershatter 1988; Hung and Chiu 2003; Jacka 2006; Rofel 1994;
Wang 2000). Reform-era population control policies that limited couples
to one or two children also encouraged discrimination against girls in the
face of continued preference for sons, leading to increasingly skewed sex ra-
tios at birth in many parts of the country (Greenhalgh 1993; Greenhalgh and
Li 1995; Greenhalgh and Winckler 2005).

Despite these recent setbacks to gender egalitarianism and the persistence
of male privileges derived from patrilineal family norms, Chinese spouses of
all ages identified China with greater gender equality, especially in comparison to the immigration policies they encountered in Taiwan that encouraged
feminized domesticity by directing immigrant spouses' primary obligations
toward their citizen-partner and conjugal kin. The principle of dependency
that shaped those policies assumed its most powerful form in the restrictions
in place prior to August 2009 that limited Chinese spouses' right to work
legally outside the home. Bans on workforce participation have in turn

influenced both governmental and societal assumptions about how an immigrant spouse should express her commitment to her marriage and family, fostering a model of authentic marriage that could be used by bureaucrats and family members to discipline immigrants' behavior and aspirations. At the same time, these limits on immigrant spouses' access to legal employment also channeled citizen-partners into the role of sole family provider, exacerbating the financial pressures faced by many, especially those in working-class jobs.

Many Chinese women I met chafed at expectations from husbands and in-laws that they assume responsibility for cooking, cleaning, child care, and elder care, tasks that typically fall to wives and daughters-in-law in Taiwan or are outsourced to foreign domestic workers (Adrian 2003; Lan 2006). When coupled with policies that restricted access to legal work rights, these familial pressures created a pervasive sense of disparate gender ideologies on the two sides of the Strait. As a result, Chinese women came to experience their difficulties integrating into Taiwanese society in part as a result of conflicting gender role expectations, a process that was doubly painful for those who initially imagined that marrying a Taiwanese would liberate them from some of the economic and gender constraints they encountered in China. Faced with demands that they fulfill similar and at times even more domesticated roles in Taiwan, Chinese women narrated challenging experiences as immigrant wives through a language of competing gender ideologies (see also Parreñas 2008, 8–9).

In this context of heightened tensions between reproductive and productive labor, even mundane activities such as housework or a wife's physical deportment became sources of contention in cross-Strait marriages. I first met Liang Xiuyun and Wei Liping in 2007 at a CARES training course for volunteers who would provide support services for other Chinese spouses in Taiwan. Both were in their thirties and hailed from Guangxi Province in southern China. They had lived in Taipei for roughly a year at that point and had met their husbands in 2005 when the men traveled to Guangxi on matchmaking tours, although both women described these as fortuitous meetings and claimed they had never planned to marry a Taiwanese. At the time, Xiuyun, a Han woman who had the equivalent of a college-level vocational degree, held a steady administrative job in a work unit based in the small city where she had grown up, whereas Liping, a junior middle school graduate and member of the Zhuang minority, was a contract worker at a hospital in the provincial capital where she had migrated from her rural hometown. Xiuyun's husband—a never-married, second-generation Main-lander eight years older than she—had impressed her with his graduate degree. Liping, on the other hand, had married a native Taiwanese man twenty-nine years her senior who was divorced with two adult children. Both women had agreed to the marriage with the hope of changing their lives and finding opportunities they felt were unavailable to them in China. Both, moreover, acknowledged that they were rapidly finding themselves unmarriageable as they moved out of their twenties.

During a break from the formal lectures that made up most of the volunteer training, Liang Xiuyun admitted that although she knew coming to Taiwan would not be easy, she had not been fully prepared for her husband's expectations of her as a Taiwanese wife and daughter-in-law: that she speak more softly and gently, that she take sole responsibility for housework, and that she treat his parents respectfully, despite their initial opposition to the marriage and refusal to meet her.[6] "This is what it means to be a housewife," Xiuyun added. "Before I had relatives, friends, [my own] income. Now, however, I feel as if I am a useless person."

Both Xiuyun and Liping attributed their husbands' assumptions that they would perform household chores and other care work to Taiwanese men's patriarchal tendencies. A conversation at Liping's house a few months later quickly turned to frustrations with their husbands' refusal to assist with household tasks, and Xiuyun, now pregnant with her first child, exclaimed in exasperation, "Ah, they [Taiwanese men] are all like that. Frankly speaking, men from here are extremely patriarchal (*feichang da nanren zhuyi*)." By contrast, Liping added, Chinese men were more likely to be considerate of their wives and share household responsibilities.

Clearly disappointed with their current life circumstances, both women then launched into accounts of male relatives or friends in China who, despite holding down demanding and prestigious jobs, still picked up their wives and children after work, shopped for dinner, and even cooked and cleaned. Xiuyun observed, "Taiwanese men would never do this! Maybe men under forty, under thirty-five, they might help out a little bit. But those over forty, absolutely not." When one of her female cousins expressed interest in marrying a Taiwanese, Xiuyun recounted how she was quick to deter her for these very reasons:

"You want to marry here [Taiwan]?" I told her, "Men from here don't ever do housework!" She was shocked. "Really? Don't do housework?" I said, "In any case, he'll be lounging about (*qiao er lang tui*) while you rush busily in and out." She asked, "How could this be?" So I replied, "You need to think about it." . . . I said, "What's so good about [Taiwan]? In any case, when it comes to housework, he'll never lift a finger. Most [men] are this way."

Xiuyun urged her cousin to consider more seriously the benefits of a domestic marriage in China, reminding her that even older Chinese men helped out at home and took care of children, including her own father who had been a manager in a work unit. Wrapping up her account, she concluded dogmatically, "Our tradition there is the most gender egalitarian (*zui nan nü pingdeng*)!"

Gendered disappointments featured prominently in Xiuyun's and Liping's comparisons of married life in Taiwan and China, and their portrayals were punctuated by a language of gender inequality that Xiuyun in particular deployed to great effect, as seen in her use of expressions such as "patriarchal" and "gender egalitarian." This language spoke to their marital frustrations of the moment and heightened the sharp contrast in cross-Strait gender roles they sought to convey to me. As we chatted leisurely in Liping's immaculate living room that afternoon, I was struck by the powerful sense of regret that permeated the stories Xiuyun and Liping shared with me and each other. Accounts of kin, classmates, and colleagues in China who were "treasured" by caring husbands dominated their tales, together with numerous examples of Chinese men who unquestioningly performed household chores. Beneath the surface of their narratives lay several gender disappointments: the assumption common among Chinese women of their generation that both spouses would be employed and, consequently, their own anxieties about having given up jobs in the mainland, secure or otherwise, without the guarantee of employment in Taiwan; envy toward female classmates and colleagues married to Chinese men who shared household responsibilities or partnered with Western men (who presumably were well off financially); and, ultimately, disappointment that their lives in Taiwan had not, to date, provided the kinds of professional and personal opportunities that had inspired their cross-Strait journeys.

Taiwanese women who married Chinese men and relocated to China also underscored the different gender role expectations found across the Strait, but for many, these differences eased their transition to life in the mainland and made married life more enjoyable. As the exception to the typical pairing of a Taiwanese man with a Chinese woman, Taiwanese wives were eager to provide an alternative perspective on cross-Strait marriages, and they responded enthusiastically to queries I posted on websites or to introductions from mutual Taiwanese and Chinese friends.[7] Many of these women expressed pleasure in their husband's willingness to share household tasks and identified this trait as a striking difference from Taiwanese men. Female friends back home, they added, were envious of their Chinese husband's more egalitarian outlook, especially as those friends married and grew exhausted by the demands of residing with in-laws and performing domestic chores. Adjusting to life in crowded, competitive Shanghai was not easy, a group of Taiwanese wives complained to me when we met in a bustling Shanghai mall on a stifling hot July day in 2009, but their husband's domestic support and encouragement in the face of a tough job market had helped them feel more at ease in the city.

Over the years, I heard different versions of these accounts of comparative patriarchies and greater gender egalitarianism in China from immigrants and citizens on both sides of the Strait. This variation makes me cautious about concluding too hastily that Chinese society is necessarily less patriarchal than Taiwan's or that all Chinese men are caring and considerate husbands. The same Taiwanese wives who praised their mainland husbands for sharing domestic responsibilities also admitted that they had agreed to move to China only on the condition that they reside separately from their in-laws, fearful of the demands they might face as in-marrying daughters-in-law from the older generation. Moreover, not all experienced their Chinese husband's expectation that they work outside the home as empowering, their desire to stay at home producing, from their perspective, surprising tension in the marriage.

Similarly, some Chinese wives in Taiwan offered more nuanced and even radically different portrayals of mainland gender relations and role expectations from those conveyed by Liang Xiuyun and Wei Liping. Some explained what appeared to be a sudden decision to marry a Taiwanese man as the result of being moved by their husband's gentle, cultured tone of voice and caring behavior, in contrast to the coarse language and emotional distance of a mainland boyfriend or ex-husband. These affective strengths might not translate into a willingness to perform domestic labor after marriage or to side with a wife in intergenerational disputes, but they did explain why Taiwanese men might be seen as more desirable husbands than their mainland counterparts because of their communication skills and ability to provide emotional support (see also Chao 2004b; Constable 2003a).[8]

Taiwanese husbands, on the other hand, responded in different ways to the provider role required of them by state policies and to the various gender expectations encoded in a dependency model of marital immigration. Some took pride in their ability to "care for" (*yang*) their wife and children and expected in return that their spouse remain at home to perform domestic tasks and child care instead of "running around" outside. Older men, especially veterans marrying for the first time later in life, often feared that their younger wife would meet a more desirable husband if given the freedom to circulate widely. Other men had married a Chinese woman with the expectation that she would care for his aging parents or dependent family members, responsibilities that kept her tied to the home. But some Taiwanese husbands I met resented the restrictions that their immigrant partner faced and were angry about delays imposed on their spouse's ability to pursue a career or develop new skills. Many were willing to fudge their own earnings so their wife could qualify for a work permit at the first residency stage; others, however, saw testifying to low-income status and filing the necessary paperwork as humiliating evidence of their failure to fulfill the desired provider role that affirmed their own successful masculinity. In the context of Taiwan's recent economic downturn, even domestic couples found it difficult to survive on one salary, but cross-Strait couples often had no choice but to conform to the model of male provider–female homemaker given the restrictions on Chinese spouses' work rights in place prior to August 2009.

These diverse visions of Taiwanese and Chinese men's ability and inclination to perform affective and domestic labor show how gender discourses may be mobilized to speak to a wide array of issues, from conjugal incompatibility and intergenerational tensions to heterosexual desires, intimacy expectations, maternal responsibilities, and the delicate negotiations around material support that cross-Strait couples engage in on a daily basis. The malleability of these gender discourses affirms that an empirical comparison of relative patriarchies is less relevant here than an assessment of how talk about gender is used to articulate challenging dimensions of cross-Strait marriages and the difficulties Chinese spouses encounter as they seek to realize their own migration desires while managing the constraints imposed by Taiwan's immigration policies.

Conflicts over gender roles and expectations may become so severe that they lead cross-Strait couples down the path to divorce. By the time I met Hu Ying in 2007, she was a thirty-something single mother struggling to support her young son on her own in Taipei. Hu Ying was one of very few Chinese spouses I knew who had secured child custody after a divorce and thus was able to remain legally in Taiwan once her marriage ended. But Hu Ying's success was not without cost.

After arriving in Taiwan in 2000, Hu Ying bore two sons with her Taiwanese husband. The elder child was taken away by her mother-in-law, who cared for him along with two children from her husband's first marriage. After Hu Ying gave birth, her husband and his parents pressured her to continue running the profitable food stall the family had established for her in their hometown, a small city southwest of the capital. When Hu Ying became pregnant for the second time, however, her husband began to beat her, and she quickly realized that she could no longer remain in such an abusive marriage. But Hu Ying also feared that if she divorced, she would be forced to return to China and would forever lose contact with her children. Once her second son was born, Hu Ying learned that the government planned to change the policy regarding divorce to permit Chinese spouses who obtained child custody to remain in the country legally. After several difficult months of negotiating with her husband, she finally persuaded him to agree to a consensual divorce and grant her custody of their younger son.

On a blustery December day, Hu Ying and I met at a McDonald's near the apartment she shared with an elderly veteran from her hometown in China. Her plump face framed by wavy hair, Hu Ying joked playfully with her four-year-old son as he eagerly dug into his meal, but her expression grew wistful whenever she described the direction her life had taken.

Hu Ying attributed many of the conflicts in her marriage to the different gender role expectations she experienced on both sides of the Strait. Her father had died when she was quite young, and she and her younger sister had been raised by their mother, a low-level manager in a foodstuffs company, who encouraged them to pursue their own paths in life. Hu Ying grew up in a midsize city in China's interior, and she graduated from a communications university with a degree in Chinese literature, which she later supplemented with a two-year program in business administration. She became a party member and worked as a civil servant in the city's environmental protection bureau, where she was recognized for her writing skills.

Despite her good family background, education, and successful career, Hu Ying found herself unmarried in her late twenties, a state she attributed to her own tendency to find failings in all the men she had met. Realizing that she was quickly approaching an unmarriageable age in China, she agreed when a relative offered to introduce her to a Taiwanese man. Hu Ying was impressed by her husband's education and white-collar employment, and after knowing him for a year, she decided to marry him. But once she arrived in Taiwan, she discovered that her husband was not the man she had thought he was, and her new in-laws viewed her simply as a source of housework and extra income:

> When I had my first son, no one in the family helped me do the postpartum month (*zuo yuezi*). They looked down on people from the mainland. You [referring to herself] clearly feel that you're pretty hot stuff, but they use that kind of attitude. [They] say, "Go do housework." We have to endure [because] we don't have citizenship.

Especially painful for Hu Ying was her husband's attitude toward her labor and financial contributions to the family. No matter how hard she worked to conform to the traditional image of the "dutiful wife and loving mother" (*xian qi liang mu*), she claimed, he regularly derided the work she performed. "Coming to Taiwan has been eating bitterness," Hu Ying complained. "[If] I am going to suffer, then we should suffer together." But according to Hu Ying, her husband refused to share her burden; instead, "he wanted everything from me." Returning home from work, he would sit in front of the television and read the newspaper, refusing to help with household tasks. Moreover, he continued to demand money from her, sarcastically belittling her income-generating skills: "Who told you to be so capable? [I] married a money tree (*qu le yige yao qian shu*)." Although her husband praised her in front of others, to her face he called her a "pig" and an "idiot."

Hu Ying used a gendered framework of unequal role expectations to explain her husband's abuse and her failed marriage. Although in her eyes she had worked hard to become a devoted, industrious wife, mother, and daughter-in-law, nothing, she asserted, satisfied her husband or mother-in-law. Despite now struggling to survive on the low salary she earned as a waitress in one of Taipei's large hotels, Hu Ying was proud of her independence, and she looked forward to the day—not long in the future—when she would be liberated from her ex-husband by becoming a Taiwanese citizen. She planned to change her younger son's surname to her own and to sue her ex-husband for visitation rights to see her other child. In the midst of this bravado, however, Hu Ying's eyes filled with tears whenever she returned to the topic of her elder son, and she admitted that a wound still festered inside her. "I do my best not to think about it," she added, dabbing at her tears. "If I think about my child, I become so sad."

Hu Ying's experiences reflect many of the contradictions generated by a dependency-based immigration regime that constrains the rights available to Chinese spouses through policy restrictions defined by unequal gender expectations and patriarchal norms. In Hu Ying's case, her husband and in-laws clearly expected her to bear children for the family and to perform the care work necessary to sustain them. Not only did Hu Ying's husband denigrate her homemaking skills, however, but he also prevented her from forming strong ties with her children because he and his parents expected her to support the family through working in their family business. When her husband's abuse became unbearable, Hu Ying found that she had few options to leave her oppressive marriage without simultaneously being separated from her children. Government policies in effect at the time made her claims to legal presence in Taiwan contingent on a continuing marriage to a Taiwanese citizen; only when such policies were revised to offer an exemption through child custody was she able to pursue a divorce. Hu Ying herself experienced these conflicting demands as part of different cultural expectations for enacting proper gender roles as a wife, mother, and daughter-in-law, and she suffered deeply for these conflicts by being forcibly separated from her older child.

Ironically, the very bureaucrats who crafted and implemented Taiwan's immigration policies also appealed to this possible scenario of gendered oppression to justify the dependency principles that undergirded the country's immigration regime. Before the 2009 policy revisions that granted work rights to Chinese spouses at the first residency stage, government officials and bureaucrats often pointed to the potential abuse of Chinese women's labor to rationalize continued restrictions on legal work rights. At the 2007 CARES training session where I met Xiuyun and Liping, an NIA bureaucrat made this very argument as she explained why Chinese spouses were barred from working legally at the initial reunion stage. Beyond the government's desire to block "sham" marriages contracted for access to economic opportunity, the bureaucrat noted, it also aimed to protect recently arrived immigrant wives from unsavory husbands who, she cautioned, might force them to go out to work to provide financial support or even sell them into prostitution. The initial ban on work rights was intended to protect women from this abuse by making all paid work illegal, although it was debatable who was actually protected by this ban and who was harmed. For instance, bureaucrats were much less concerned about how this protectionist orientation might be used by citizen-spouses and conjugal kin to limit a Chinese wife's freedom to circulate outside the home, and they had few resources to intervene in abusive situations such as that faced by Hu Ying, beyond arresting a Chinese spouse for working without a permit.

There certainly are Chinese (and foreign) spouses who face excessive labor demands from family members or whose innocence makes them vulnerable to unscrupulous dealings. These experiences profoundly limit the opportunities available to these immigrants and greatly diminish their quality of life, as my discussion of Hu Ying's case makes clear (see also Chao 2004b). Yet protectionist justifications for bans on legal employment or freedom of movement rarely accomplish their stated goals, again as evidenced by Hu Ying's experience. Instead they strengthen the dependency principles that undergird a gendered immigration regime and its patrilineal and patriarchal foundations. This regime defines Chinese spouses' participation in remunerative labor as exceptional and suspect, irrespective of whether couples might depend on that income for survival. Meanwhile, by rewarding care work that reproduces Taiwanese families, immigration regulations confine Chinese spouses' legitimate activities to the domestic sphere and potentially exacerbate the burden of support faced by Taiwanese breadwinners. As Hu Ying's account of her marriage attests, both reproductive labor and paid employment thereby become sites of heated contestation in cross-Strait marriages, and Chinese spouses often struggle to reconcile their own needs and commitments with the differential value ascribed to their labors by immigration policies and Taiwanese society at large.

SHARP TALKERS, FORCEFUL PERSONALITIES

Middle-aged and older women, most of whom were previously married in China and many of whom form unions with elderly veterans in Taiwan, experience this conflict between reproductive and remunerated labor differently, in part because of how their gender identities are imagined by Taiwanese who emphasize such women's formative socialization experiences under Maoist state socialism. Born roughly between the 1930s and early 1960s, this group stands out in Taiwan because their accents and patterns of speech, dress styles, and modes of social interaction differ in often striking ways from local women of a similar age cohort.[9] A consistent stereotype of older Chinese wives that I observed in the Taiwanese media and in everyday conversations portrays these women as "sharp" talkers whose verbal skills and adeptness at achieving their own interests were honed through a decade of conflict during China's tumultuous Cultural Revolution (1966–76). Taiwanese women, by contrast, tend to describe themselves as more reserved and indirect, traits that reflect different models of femininity and gender socialization on the two sides of the Strait.

On several occasions I observed Ms. Chen, a young Taiwanese employee from the Employment Service Center run by the Taipei City Department of Labor, as she made presentations to Chinese spouses on Taiwan's labor market or conducted employment consultations with small groups of immigrant wives. Ms. Chen was responsible for assisting eligible Chinese spouses as they searched for suitable employment in Taiwan. Prior to August 2009, Chinese married to Taiwanese citizens who were over age sixty-five automatically received work rights after two years of marriage. As a result, middle-aged and older Chinese women (who typically married elderly veterans) represented a prominent constituency for Ms. Chen.[10]

While watching her interactions with these women, I had attributed Ms. Chen's tentative attitude to her relative youth and inexperience. But when she met with me in early 2008, having recently resigned from her position to prepare for application to graduate school, she admitted that older Chinese women made her especially nervous because they spoke so directly and their style of interaction differed so dramatically from Taiwanese, who tended to broach difficult topics indirectly and avoided criticizing people to their face. "Because they went through the Cultural Revolution, before, when I encountered them, I was very afraid," Ms. Chen admitted. "If you have something to offer her that is in her interest, she will treat you well. If you don't, she will criticize you." Although Ms. Chen sympathized with these women because many had married impoverished veterans who lived in dismal housing conditions, she also complained that their inability to change their patterns of speech and behavior made it very difficult for them to find desirable employment or integrate into Taiwanese society.

Over the course of our conversation, Ms. Chen returned repeatedly to the case of Huiling, a feisty Hunanese woman in her fifties, whom she had helped to find a job with the Veterans Affairs Council. In Ms. Chen's recounting, Huiling had difficulty understanding one of the information systems she was expected to use in her job, and instead of asking for help, she had decided to process the documents her own way. When she was reprimanded by her boss, she accused him of being a poor leader and criticized him to others. Her boss attributed her refusal to follow instructions to an abiding concern with maintaining face, and Ms. Chen, brought in to mediate, concluded that Huiling had resorted to stirring up interpersonal relations (*gao guanxi*). Dealing with this case troubled Ms. Chen because she felt she could never fully satisfy women such as Huiling.

Without Huiling's own perspective, we cannot know for certain how she experienced these interactions, but Ms. Chen described her negative reaction as a response to Huiling's forceful interpersonal style and strong sense of self-interest. There were, however, two sides to Ms. Chen's portrayal of this cohort of Chinese women. On the one hand, she clearly felt intimidated by their direct speech and what she perceived as their manipulation of personal relationships to satisfy their own interests. On the other hand, a cautious admiration also ran through Ms. Chen's comments. Near the end of our conversation that January afternoon, she attributed these traits to the strong sense of women's rights in the mainland that empowered these women to venture overseas. Her use of the adjective "tough and capable" (*lihai*) to describe Huiling and other middle-aged Chinese wives reflected her implicit admiration for their bravery in moving to a foreign society and suggested a note of wistfulness about her own lack of similar traits.

Just a few months prior, I had witnessed Huiling's public persona during a ceremony recognizing foreign and Chinese spouses who had participated in an employment seminar run by the Department of Labor. The tone of the event was largely celebratory, and participants painted a positive picture of immigrant spouses' work opportunities and successful employment searches. After the formal program of speeches, performances, and testimonials had ended, the master of ceremonies asked for comments from the audience. For a few minutes, no one moved to speak, but then Huiling stood up from her seat. Dressed simply in a blouse and slacks with her graying hair cut short, she prefaced her remarks by stating that she was speaking not for herself but for all Chinese spouses: "In the mainland, we are people with status and position. But this is not the case in Taiwan. I, personally, have great hopes of making Taiwan my home. I have already lived here for seven years, and I have only returned [to the mainland] three times. What we want is fairness and justice. We want to work for Taiwan (*wei Taiwan fu chu*)" (November 30, 2007).

Huiling's voice grew louder as she spoke, and by the time she reached her final demands for equitable treatment, she was shouting. The room was silent after she finished, and the organizers and participants shifted uncomfortably in their seats, uncertain how to respond. Huiling's remarks spoke to the difficulties of finding gainful employment in Taiwan and the discrimination that many Chinese spouses experienced seeking jobs and, afterward, in the workplace. At the same time, she also made a broader claim for rights and justice based both on mainland spouses' previous status in China and their desire to make contributions to their new home. The performative genre Huiling used to express those claims, however, confirmed Taiwanese stereotypes of Chinese women as forceful speakers educated in the crucible of Cultural Revolution–style struggle sessions. Regardless of Huiling's intentions at the time, her assertive style made it difficult for the Taiwanese present at the event (Ms. Chen included) to take her statement seriously.[11]

In other settings, however, middle-aged Chinese women were quick to emphasize values and behaviors that conformed more closely to the ideal of the caretaking wife enshrined in immigration policies and praised in official propaganda. I first met Huiling in 2003 when I participated in a group meal organized by several women who had attended a government-sponsored acculturation class held at their district household registration office. Huiling stood out at the gathering for many of the same reasons that she had appeared so forceful at the Department of Labor event: she clearly portrayed the pros and cons of life in Taiwan and analyzed the roots of the government's restrictions on Chinese spouses. She also took great care to describe her own privileged position in China as a college graduate who had been in charge of women's affairs at a state-owned oil company. After reaching the mandatory retirement age, she had been invited to join another company, where she assumed a managerial position and, according to her, greatly improved the company.

Huiling's husband was a former military doctor also originally from Hunan who had retired from the military soon after fleeing to Taiwan with the Nationalist forces and had established a private medical practice. Beyond their interpersonal rapport, Huiling described being attracted by her husband's never-married status, which meant she would not have to worry about complicated relations with children from a previous marriage (she had two grown daughters in China from her first marriage, which ended in divorce). Moreover, she emphasized that her husband was educated and boasted two college degrees. His letters to her were well written, and she described feeling "warm all over" when she talked to him. Despite the roughly twenty years in age that separated them, her expectations for the marriage had been realized, and she proclaimed herself quite happy with him.

Both during the group meal and later when I visited the couple at their home in a run-down public housing complex, Huiling also admitted that she felt torn between the need to earn money and her desire to care for her husband who was in frail health. Despite her husband's years of private medical practice, he subsisted exclusively on the minimal monthly pension he received as a veteran (NT$13,550 or roughly US$390), having lost his savings through poor investments in the stock market. Their finances forced them to live frugally, and she worried about covering her younger daughter's expenses as a college student in China. Nonetheless, as the three of us sat around a low table in their crowded one-room apartment, eating the meal Huiling had prepared, Huiling repeatedly emphasized that her primary obligation was to care for her husband. She expressed pride in the weight he had gained since their marriage, occasionally interrupting her narrative to select choice pieces of meat and place them carefully in his bowl. Huiling was quick to distinguish herself from other Chinese wives who earned money by caring for others but left their husbands to fend for themselves. "If I earn more, but his health is bad, then I will be uncomfortable," she explained, adding that her goal was to make her husband happy in his later years, even if it meant turning down lucrative jobs because they demanded long working hours.

Huiling's portrayal of herself as a caring wife invested in her husband's health and happiness affirmed the authenticity of her caretaking marriage by underscoring her conjugal commitments and downplaying her material aspirations. The diverse ways she managed her self-presentation in different contexts, both public and private, exposed the complex power of reproductive dependency principles, especially for older women who have existing family commitments in China and may be attracted to a cross-Strait marriage because of the income-generating opportunities Taiwan offered them. Like Huiling, many older women intentionally chose spouses who did not have children from previous marriages or, at minimum, who lived independently, because they were unwilling to assume additional caretaking responsibilities and feared being drawn into extended family conflicts that might result in their being treated simply as the family's maid or as their husband's nurse, instead of being recognized as a legitimate spouse.

For middle-aged and older women, therefore, an immigration system premised on reproductive dependency generates powerful contradictions. Those married to elderly veterans recognize that only by prioritizing care over paid work can they possibly legitimize their marriage and subsequent citizenship claims in the eyes of bureaucrats, officials, and Taiwanese society more generally.[12] In their self-presentations, some disputed portrayals of older Chinese women as instrumental and self-interested by claiming that their husbands had chosen them precisely because they were "simple and honest" (*pushi*) and satisfied elderly men's need for someone who would provide care and companionship.[13] Others, such as Huiling, took every opportunity to show how they put their husband's needs above their own, eschewing higher-paying jobs with long hours in order to fulfill their domestic responsibilities. Even immigrant wives who established a mutually agreed-upon, instrumental relationship with an elderly husband—providing money in exchange for completing immigration documents and appearing at NIA offices when needed—recognized that they might be judged by the standards of the caretaking model when interacting with state actors. In short, regardless of whether older women actively or implicitly conformed to immigration principles which emphasized dependency and care work, most had to reckon with their consequences at some point during their precitizenship period in Taiwan.

MASCULINE DEPENDENCE

Assumptions about spousal dependence and the value of reproductive care work guide the immigration policies that regulate cross-Strait marriages and shape the life opportunities, marital relationships, and self-presentation of diverse groups of Chinese wives in Taiwan. Similarly, this gendered immigration regime also establishes specific roles for Taiwanese husbands as male providers and recipients of Chinese women's care labors. Although some husbands enforce the gender hierarchy encoded in immigration policies as part of asserting their own desired masculinity, others struggle to fulfill demands that they act as household breadwinners or negotiate new divisions of labor with wives who refuse to remain confined to the domestic sphere. When conflicts over gender roles do arise, however, government policies give citizen-spouses the upper hand, for as their Chinese partner's legal guarantor, they have the power to derail her progress through the series of immigration stages or, as a last resort, to initiate a divorce, which frequently leads to deportation and sometimes forced separation from children.

How do Chinese husbands experience the gendered expectations of Taiwan's immigration policies? Increasing numbers of cross-Strait couples with a Chinese husband reside in China, but some settle in Taiwan (either temporarily or permanently), where the husband encounters the same bureaucratic restrictions and similar forms of social discrimination as those faced by his female counterparts. In addition, he risks the potential erasure of a previous sense of male patrilineal privilege by being subsumed in his wife's family and under her citizenship standing, adding the disempowerment of immigrant status to the societal disenfranchisement of an in-marrying son-in-law in what uncomfortably resembles a traditional uxorilocal marriage.[14] As a consequence, men who migrate through marriage often find that the migration experience forces them to adjust their own masculine ideals and previous expectations for male adulthood (Charsley 2005).

In 2003, I attended a job seminar for Chinese spouses at one of Taipei's district-level employment service centers, a small building wedged under an overpass for a major thoroughfare, where the sound of cars and trucks rumbling above punctuated the half-day program. The second part of the seminar included presentations by companies deemed suitable to provide employment to Chinese spouses, and one of these was a chain of beauty salons run by Xiao Lin Beauty Company. The representative of the company was Mr. Liu, himself from Beijing, who had moved to Taiwan three years prior. A lively, boisterous businessman, Liu peppered his presentation with appeals to shared homeland ties, repeatedly engaging the primarily female audience in a dialogue about where they hailed from in China. At the end of the session, as he was writing his phone number on the chalkboard, Liu paused and commented, "You have all married out to Taiwan (*nimen shi jia dao Taiwan lai*), [whereas] I have married in a Taiwanese 'little sister' (*wo shi qu le yige Taiwan mei*)."

Mr. Liu's gendered verb choice reflected the patrilineal orientation of Chinese and Taiwanese families, conveyed through the use of different verbs to describe the marriage of a man, who brings a wife into his birth family to continue the family line (*qu*), as compared to that of a woman, who marries out of her birth family to join her husband's family and reproduce his family line (*jia*). Mr. Liu distinguished himself from the Chinese women in the audience, despite their shared mainland origins, by emphasizing his masculine power to "marry in" a Taiwanese wife. The female audience members refused to accept Liu's distinction without comment, however, openly recognizing how cross-border marriages leveled patrilineal gender hierarchies among male and female marriage migrants. A middle-aged woman sitting next to me muttered (not so quietly) under her breath, "You also have married out to Taiwan." Another woman in the room confronted Liu openly: "You're the same [as us]. You also have married out to this place." Faced with the rejection of his male patrilineal privilege, Liu in the end appealed to a gender-neutral basis for their common bond by emphasizing their shared immigrant status and place-of-origin: "We are all compatriots," he added, laughing uneasily, and then quickly changed the subject by repeating his phone number for the group.

Liu's effort to deny the disempowering effects of marital migration to Taiwan (and his obvious failure in this context) affirms the strongly feminized character of the dependency principles that guide marital immigration and citizenship procedures. Despite the gender-neutral language of "spouse" in official government discourse, Chinese husbands in Taiwan must regularly negotiate the assumptions of feminized domesticity and dependence embedded in policies that make marital status the basis for their access to legal residency and naturalized citizenship.

As discussed in previous chapters, a cross-Strait marriage that produced children enhanced a Chinese spouse's ability to successfully navigate this marital path to residency and citizenship. Chinese husbands were not immune to the message that having children granted them greater security in Taiwan, although they responded with some ambivalence to the related assumption that having a child required caring for that child. Ma Jun, a Chinese man in his early thirties, was about to receive Taiwanese citizenship in 2005 after being married for only six years. His wife had borne a child during their first year of marriage in 1999, and Ma was able to take advantage of a policy change that allowed Chinese spouses who had children with their Taiwanese partner to skip the initial reunion visa stage and reduce their overall time to citizenship. In keeping with the gender-neutral language of the policy, the regulation also applied to Chinese men whose Taiwanese wives had given birth. As Ma Jun explained to me:

> The policy is formulated with respect to mainland people only, that is to say, regardless of male or female. Whether you have married out [to Taiwan] or married in [a Taiwanese], the only requirement is that you have a child who has established household residence in Taiwan.... Although I was applying

as a man, they didn't think that only women could apply, only mainland brides could apply. Therefore, at the time, I enjoyed what can be seen as a coincidence.[15]

Ma Jun's explanation neatly sidestepped the feminizing effect of benefiting from a reproductive exception by describing his successful application simply as a "coincidence." Yet as he continued with an account of how his daughter's birth had affected his own immigration trajectory and employment choices, Ma acknowledged the unusual path his life had taken as a result. After he married his wife, who was fourteen years his senior, he had intended to return to Guangzhou and resume his work as an editor and writer. When their daughter was born, however, his wife insisted that she be raised and educated in Taiwan, and he gradually came to accept this position: "So I gave up my plan to return to Guangzhou to work. Someone has to care for a child. So my job became "nurse-father" (*nai ba*). From the time our child was born until she went to kindergarten, I cared for her at home. My wife returned to work when our child was about six months old. . . . I basically cared for our kid full time by myself."

Ma Jun explicitly recognized the unconventional gender division of tasks that characterized his marriage. His use of the neologism "nurse-father," a play on the traditional expression "nursemaid," underscored how significantly his child care responsibilities deviated both from Taiwan's conventional male provider role and from the image of liberated Chinese men willing to "help out" with household tasks. At the same time, however, he downplayed any sense of discomfort with his gender nonconformity by adopting a joking tone and expressing pride in how well he had cared for his daughter and how active he had become in their residential community when she was little. Moreover, he was quick to point out that once his daughter started school, he resumed his work as a freelance writer and editor. Our interview concluded with his eagerly offering to send me some of the articles he had written and published recently. This emphasis on his productive, remunerated professional labor drew attention away from his reproductive care-work and diminished the centrality of gendered dependency to his immigration experience, reaffirming its merely "coincidental" impact on his life path.

Most of the Chinese men I met in Taiwan were quite anxious about the restrictions they faced with regard to legal employment and feared they would be unable to find work commensurate with their educational level and professional training. Those who lived in central and southern Taiwan encountered additional challenges because their inability to speak the local Taiwanese dialect made it harder for them to adopt appropriate patterns of masculine behavior and forge valuable social networks. Unable to fulfill their own expectations of themselves as family providers and independent economic actors, some of these men described the costs of immigrating through marriage as a loss of masculinity so profound that they became feminized dependents who had forgotten their male ideals and responsibilities (Friedman 2013).

Not surprisingly, Chinese men with advanced degrees and high professional ambitions often expected their Taiwanese wives to move to China. I interviewed several such men in the summer of 2009 in Shanghai and Beijing. Xu Lixin had met his wife while studying in a graduate program in Europe, and after they married, both relocated to Shanghai, where they had found employment. Although Xu had visited his wife's family in Taiwan on several occasions, when I asked whether he would consider moving there permanently, he replied brusquely, "I can't think of any reason to go to Taiwan."[16] His wife had a more secure position in Taiwan as a civil servant, he admitted, but his job opportunities would be greatly limited and their family's standard of living would decline precipitously as a result. When pressed about the sacrifice that his wife had made, Xu concluded sharply that she had no choice. He had no desire to live abroad and feel perpetually like a foreigner, but he saw no contradiction in expecting his wife to compromise in this manner. Xu, therefore, justified their decision to live in China by emphasizing his provider role in the family, but his response to my question about whether he would consider moving to Taiwan also conveyed his reluctance to assume dependent citizenship status in a place that—as his tone clearly implied—was secondary to China.

PRODUCING DESIRABLE FAMILIES

The examples I have discussed throughout this chapter illustrate the intense work required to produce the ideal families promoted by immigration policies, those organized around a citizen provider and immigrant homemaker and caregiver. The MAC's promotional film released in 2009 reaffirmed this ideal scenario by portraying Chinese spouses' legal access to paid work outside the home as conditional on their successful performance of reproductive domestic labor. Both the voiceover and the vignettes of family life confirmed that only by subsuming their productive capacities in a framework of contributions to the family and nation could Chinese spouses legitimately express a desire to engage in nondomestic paid work as they simultaneously progressed toward Taiwanese citizenship. Because their claims to citizenship are based on their kin-dependent status, they must simultaneously maintain at least the appearance of being dedicated to fulfilling the domestic responsibilities that substantiate gendered kinship commitments.

Conspicuously absent from the film's vignettes are Chinese wives whose caretaking marriages with elderly veterans dominate negative media portrayals of Chinese spouses and attract intense attention from immigration bureaucrats ever alert to "sham" marriages (Chao 2008). The one caretaking marriage portrayed in the film is interesting precisely because, on the surface at least, it seems to conform to the idealized model of a reproductive marriage. Sun Jie, the Chinese wife, appears to have borne a child with her elderly husband. In actuality, however, her family composition looked rather different. I met Sun Jie in the summer of 2009 when I was conducting interviews with Chinese women in Taiwan who had young children from previous marriages whom they had been forced to leave behind in the mainland. As a result, I knew that the child in the film did not belong to the couple but was borne to Sun's younger sister, who also had married a veteran. Because Sun's sister and brother-in-law suffered from mental illness, Sun decided to relocate to Taiwan to care for her sister and her sister's child. The only avenue available to her to make that move, however, was to marry a Taiwanese (the elderly man portrayed in the film).

This decision required that Sun Jie divorce her Chinese husband and leave her own son behind in China. When subsequent conflicts with her ex-husband resulted in her son's virtual abandonment by his father, Sun, unwilling to leave her sister and nephew but desperate to resolve her son's plight, petitioned MAC officials to relax restrictions on Chinese spouses' ability to sponsor minor birth children in China for residency and citizenship in Taiwan. As I discussed in chapter 3, the efforts of women such as Sun Jie and activist NGOs finally led to policy revisions that enabled Sun to bring her son to Taiwan in July 2009.

The film, however, ignores Sun's more complex family responsibilities and the extent to which her family is not based solely in Taiwan but extends across the Strait. Her sister's marriage to a veteran and subsequent birth of a child, mental illness, and Sun's own divorce and custody dispute in China created a family composed of Sun's natal family members and their descendants, her child from a previous marriage in China, and her current elderly husband in Taiwan. In our conversation, Sun Jie explicitly invoked this expansive family model to explain why Taiwanese spouses should be allowed to adopt mainland children, even if they already had birth or adopted children in Taiwan. "In my view, marriage and family are originally a whole entity (*zhengti*)," Sun explained. "Marriage and a spouse's children are also part of that whole."[17] Although Sun's more expansive vision of the integral family unit justified her own efforts to sponsor her son from China, it deviated considerably from the image of the patrilineal family idealized in the MAC film that identified Sun only as the wife of a Taiwanese man and mother of a Taiwanese child. For Sun Jie, by contrast, equally important were her roles as sister, aunt, mother of a Chinese child, and financial supporter of diverse kin resident across the Strait.

Not all families are as complex as Sun's (and certainly her sister's and brother-in-law's mental illness make her case unusual), but in my discussions with Chinese spouses from diverse walks of life, I was struck by how consistently their family composition and obligations in both Taiwan and China deviated from the ideal model portrayed in the MAC's promotional film. With this complexity in mind, we should view the dependency principles enshrined in traditional family and gender norms as a desired or even romanticized outcome of immigration policies. Although immigration regimes induce concrete regulatory effects, they also reflect aspirational and educational goals on the part of the government—producing these patrilineal families at a time when Taiwan faces historically low rates of marriage and childbirth among its native population *and* educating Chinese women in the gender dispositions necessary to fulfill traditional domestic roles as mothers, wives, and daughters-in-law (roles that native Taiwanese women increasingly are unwilling to perform). Implicitly acknowledging the economic pressures produced by Taiwan's high unemployment rates and stagnant wages, the film also encourages Taiwanese men to comply with the provider role designated for them by these dependency principles, either on their own or in collaboration with their supportive wives.

Despite the gender-neutral language of marital immigration and citizenship policies, both Chinese wives and husbands recognize, implicitly or explicitly, the gendered principles of feminized domesticity and dependency that undergird such policies. They respond to these principles differently, however, with women openly acknowledging their impact on their lives, while men attempt to deny or minimize their status as gendered subjects, although with varying degrees of success. When Chinese men are confronted directly with the ways that immigrant standing undermines their male privilege, as Mr. Liu was, they seek to shift the terms of discussion from gender inequalities and kinship status to national identity, thereby reclaiming their own masculine privilege by erasing gender from the terrain of nation and citizenship.

Contemporary immigration policies share certain features with earlier laws in Taiwan that regulated cross-border movement and national belonging through principles of gendered dependence. Chao-ju Chen has described earlier versions of Taiwan's Nationality Law as a "legal endorsement of married women's dependency" (2009, 301), and she argues that the 2000 revision that made the law gender neutral did not make it gender egalitarian. Use of the term "spouse" in current marital immigration policies reflects similar contradictions, in effect disguising the gendered expectations of dependency, domesticity, and caretaking underlying definitions of "authentic" marriages by framing them in gender-neutral language (see also Toyota 2008). The prominent role of state officials and bureaucrats in adjudicating marital authenticity heightens this sense of erasure by embedding the emphasis on gendered kinship roles and patrilineality in governmental practices ostensibly based on rational interest and the claim to protect immigrant spouses from possible abuse.

Similar accusations could be made of policies regulating foreign spouses in Taiwan or of marital immigration laws in neighboring countries (Faier 2009; Freeman 2011; Hsia 2015; Newendorp 2008; Wang and Bélanger 2008). Certainly, Chinese women partnered with Taiwanese men are not alone among their compatriots who marry transnationally in discovering that their citizen-husbands expect them to fulfill traditional gender roles and perform a domesticated style of femininity (Clark 2001; Constable 2003a; Freeman 2011; Ho 2014; Newendorp 2008). Scholars studying binational marriages in Europe and North America have also illustrated the gendered demands placed on foreign wives who are expected to provide domestic labor and care work while, in some cases, assisting their husbands with family businesses that require forms of labor undesirable to many citizen women (Cole 2014; Constable 2003a; Schaeffer 2013). Cross-border marriages always require negotiations around expected gender roles, and immigrant spouses must maneuver delicately within both their citizen-partner's demands and the legal constraints imposed on them by immigration policies.

However, discourses of gender and sexuality also highlight anxieties about immigrant difference and failed integration. In contexts such as Western Europe, nationalist accusations of gender oppression and repressed sexuality in immigrant communities may stand in for fears of Muslim alterity and shift responsibility for creating conditions of social and economic dislocation away from national elites and onto immigrant men. Because Taiwan does not permit permanent immigration except under a narrow set of family reunification principles, it does not necessarily fear the creation of separate immigrant communities whose values challenge egalitarian principles. Instead, Chinese spouses introduce their different expectations for gender roles into their marriages and family ties with citizens, thereby bringing the threat of socialist values and political commitments into the very heart of Taiwanese families. Most powerfully, their political difference is enacted through the desire to engage in paid work outside the home, a commitment that is seen to come at the expense of primary domestic responsibilities.

Conflicts over gender ideologies and role expectations constitute an important means through which cross-Strait political tensions may legitimately be expressed and, in some cases, potentially neutralized. References to older women's Cultural Revolution experiences and younger women's concern with gender egalitarianism at home and at work reflect deep anxieties among Taiwanese about the lasting imprint of socialist values and socialization processes, especially when Chinese spouses appeal to those values to challenge the dependency principles enforced by immigration policies and some citizen spouses. Defining Chinese wives and husbands as kin-dependents embedded in patrilineal Taiwanese families channels these political tensions into discourses of proper gender roles and authentic marital behaviors. Although these gender discourses potentially neutralize the threat of political difference, they generate their own conflicts in couples' marriages and family life, and they foreshadow the far-reaching obstacles faced by Chinese spouses as they seek to claim belonging in Taiwanese society.

SIX

Home and Belonging

It's as if Taiwan is saying to us, you can come as a guest, but you can't settle down.

YUAN MEI

I want to tell the citizens of the Republic of China: wherever we are, that is home.

DENG LIFANG

THE STATEMENTS ABOVE FROM YUAN MEI AND DENG LIFANG, two Chinese women who have lived in Taiwan for over a decade, convey powerful disjunctures between home and presence, between legal recognition and a sense of belonging. For Chinese marital immigrants (the "us" and "we" in the epigraphs), these terms combine in unpredictable ways, depending on how, where, and when they are invoked and put into practice (Feldman 2006). Practical considerations and the demands of everyday life are balanced against deep attachments to people and places. These potent combinations are also shaped by the legal and emotional effects of documents and policies that legitimate claims to presence and recognition.

Both women's statements, moreover, reflect a particular temporality of migration in their presentist claims to home. Neither speaker employs the hopeful future tense to assert her right to belonging in Taiwan; instead, each uses the present tense to justify the power of physical presence (Deng Lifang) and to underscore the Taiwan government's repeated refusal to recognize presence as a claim to permanence (Yuan Mei). The present tense captures the temporal conflicts engendered by migration as well as the complex ways that migrants' efforts to create a sense of belonging may not follow future-oriented temporal sequences or prescribed life-course trajectories. Precisely because "immigration controls and the relationships that they generate . . . can force people to live in an eternal present" (Anderson et al. 2009, 7), some immigrants struggle to imagine new life possibilities, to take risks to change their present circumstances, or to envision a different kind of future for themselves (Pine 2014).

Creating a sense of belonging as an immigrant requires coming to terms with new configurations of place and time; migration itself, as Frances Pine (2014, S99) notes, "involves the migrant in different temporalities of past, present, and future and different spaces of home and elsewhere." The spatial referents of home may change over time, encompassing new locations, while transforming immigrants' relationships to original sites associated with family and deep roots. For Chinese spouses, temporal associations may also shift as the past, while familiar and comforting, reinforces the indelible imprint of their mainland origins and their assumed connection to an unproductive, authoritarian Maoist era. The present, however, introduces the possibility of being stuck in an endless cycle where claims to recognition and rights are denied by virtue of a seemingly never-ending immigration process. And the future, a source of hope as well as anxiety, demands a particular form of immigrant commitment expressed through both productive and reproductive contributions to a new home. For Chinese spouses in Taiwan, concepts of "settling down" (*chang zhu*), "home" (*jia*), and "belonging" integrate these complex relationships to place and time in often contradictory ways, a consequence of the inequalities and exceptions generated by nonlinear migration trajectories and anomalous legal statuses in Taiwan. Chinese spouses, therefore, strive to forge configurations of emplacement and temporality that promise, albeit without guarantee, to redress the uncertainties of life lived across the Taiwan Strait and the insufficiencies of juridical citizenship.

Chinese spouses may have different investments in creating a sense of belonging and a commitment to a future in Taiwan as a result of their diverse experiences in China. Some see juridical citizenship as necessary to overcome the feeling of being a mere transient (*guoke*) destined to return to China at any moment, while others question whether legal recognition will bestow the sense of belonging they desire in Taiwan. Those marrying for the first time at a young age often have few financial or emotional connections with Chinese society beyond their natal families. However, for older women and men with extensive ties to China—including not only natal family and friends but also children, investments, pensions, and housing—the fear of detachment from their past looms large.

The greatest challenge for many Chinese spouses is maintaining a foothold on both sides of the Strait over time. For those who intend to reside in Taiwan, citizenship is vital: it expands their employment opportunities, allows them to claim certain financial resources and property rights, facilitates greater mobility beyond cross-Strait travel, and grants them a political voice. But Taiwanese citizenship also comes with a heavy price. The Taiwan government now requires mainland Chinese to revoke their official household registration in China within three months of receiving Taiwanese citizenship, a requirement that effectively denationalizes them. When they return to China after that point, they do so as "Taiwan compatriots" (*Tai bao*) and not PRC citizens. As a consequence, Chinese spouses fear they may have to give up rights to pensions, insurance plans, property, and even long-term residence in China. The ideal scenario is to retain citizenship standing in both places, a right many argue is available to Taiwanese who hold "first world" citizenships (in the United States, Canada, or Australia, for instance) but that is foreclosed for those who hail from China and Southeast Asian countries.

The desire for dual citizenship reflects practical concerns about present and future needs that encompass material resources, health care, and political participation. But the fact that a large number of Chinese spouses do claim Taiwanese citizenship also highlights a more amorphous set of personal commitments, affective attachments, and temporal orientations that root marital immigrants in both societies and bespeak a future spent moving back and forth across the Strait. How Chinese spouses create a sense of belonging for themselves given these diverse commitments and spatiotemporal orientations is the focus of this chapter.

Below I describe the experiences of three women to assess the different trajectories of belonging made possible by cross-Strait marital migrations, supplementing their stories with those of other Chinese spouses where relevant. None of these women have followed linear paths, and in this regard they are representative of most of the Chinese women and men I met in Taiwan. Their routes are circuitous, moving between China and Taiwan, among different sites in both countries, and sometimes to third countries—circuits that reflect their status as transmigrants with multiple attachments to times and places (Glick Schiller et al. 1995). Their physical paths mirror marital temporalities that are similarly nonlinear: marriages that take time to acclimate to and achieve mutual understanding, those that end in divorce or death, or tumultuous relationships that persist on paper but entail separations, conflict, and questioning. And yet all three women desire belonging in ways both temporary and permanent; their struggles and anxieties illuminate the diverse resources they deploy to construct a sense of themselves as both grounded in the present and free to imagine new possible futures.

A WOMAN'S GREATEST PROBLEM IS INSECURITY

I still remember the shock I experienced when Xiao Hong entered the side room of a Taipei restaurant where I had joined a group of wives from China during a brief trip I made to Taiwan in February 2010. She was frighteningly pale and thin, her hair pasted flat against her head, her entire persona expressing utter exhaustion. The contrast with her twenty-year-old daughter who was visiting during her winter break from a university in coastal China could not have been starker, but even more striking was the vast gap that separated this Xiao Hong from the one I had seen only the previous summer, tastefully dressed and skillfully made-up. Xiao Hong's appearance in the past had never betrayed her forty-some years, but her elderly husband's death in December and the toll of returning to long shifts as a nursing aide had aged her nearly beyond recognition.

At that point, I had known Xiao Hong for over three years, and during that time I gradually learned more about the routes she had traveled from her previous life as a divorced single mother in a township not far from the booming Zhejiang city of Hangzhou to her experiences in Taiwan as the wife of a wealthy man more than forty years her senior.[1] At first glance, Xiao Hong appeared to have made a marriage of convenience, one that would grant her and her daughter resources otherwise unattainable given Xiao Hong's high school degree and employment in a state-owned tourism unit in her hometown. But I quickly learned that her marital circumstances as an immigrant wife had only intensified her feelings of insecurity. When we first met in 2007, Xiao Hong had already stopped working as a licensed nursing aide in Taiwan because her husband's cancer had advanced to a stage where he required her constant care. For the first time in her life, not only was she unable to earn money to support herself, but she was forced to dip into her existing investments in China because her husband's contributions to her daughter's living and schooling expenses covered merely one-third of the total cost. Her daughter was only nine years old when Xiao Hong remarried in 1999, and the financial burden of supporting her daughter and setting her on a path to a stable future weighed heavily on Xiao Hong, compounded by a strong sense of guilt about having left her daughter behind in her parents' care at such a young age.

As Xiao Hong's husband's health deteriorated over the years, her anxieties about her future only deepened. Her own health began to suffer as a result, and she worried that she had missed her prime years of income generation caring for him and would have little to show for it once he was gone. Despite the fact that they had been married for nearly a decade, her husband doled out spending money to her in small allotments and insisted on buying food and even clothing for her. He had contributed RMB200,000 (roughly US$24,000) to purchase an apartment for her in her hometown in Zhejiang, but she had put in half that amount as well. Her husband did not understand her real financial situation, she claimed, and she knew she would inherit very little upon his death because he had already signed over all of his wealth to his children. He tried to reassure her by suggesting that his children would care for her after he died, but Xiao Hong laughed bitterly at the idea, adding that with the inheritance safely in their names, they would forget her immediately. In short, Xiao Hong had a house to return to in China but few resources to support herself or her daughter there, and she feared that her many years of residence in Taiwan had irrevocably distanced her from the rhythms and strategies of life in China. "I didn't engage in a 'buying and selling' marriage (*maimai hunyin*)," Xiao Hong argued, adopting an earlier socialist term for an instrumental marriage contracted through the exchange of money and goods for a bride, "but you have to give me some sense of security!"

By the summer of 2008, Xiao Hong had begun to consider applying for Taiwan citizenship to counter her looming insecurities. It had been several years since she had reached the final extended residence stage, and her choice now was to retain that status (which she could do even after her husband died) or become a Taiwanese citizen.[2] Xiao Hong's main concern was that naturalization required her to give up her PRC citizenship, and she worried that then she would be unable to reside in China for long periods of time or claim her retirement benefits once she reached the eligible age. She debated her options for several months, and when I left Taiwan at the end of July, she had not yet made up her mind. It was only when I returned the following summer that I learned she had gone ahead with the application process.

As we settled into our seats in the cool air of the tea shop on a hot June day in 2009, Xiao Hong and Yuan Mei began to compare their experiences applying for citizenship (see chapter 2). Unlike Yuan Mei, who resided with her husband and school-age son in Taiwan, Xiao Hong had only her husband, and he was unlikely to live much longer. I asked Xiao Hong what ultimately made her decide to give up her PRC citizenship, and she reiterated how originally she had planned to wait until she reached retirement age to make sure she would have access to her pension from her work unit in China. But her husband discovered that once she became a Taiwanese citizen, she would be eligible to receive a portion of his pension, assuming that his children were willing to relinquish their claim.[3]

Despite his poor health, Xiao Hong's husband was evidently still able to agitate her by treating her abusively. She recounted how when his friends asked him how he planned to take care of her in the future, he replied callously that she was still young and could marry again. His temper had not cooled, and when they fought, he called her "a mainland person" and yelled at her to "go back to China." He didn't treat her as a wife, Xiao Hong complained, as evidenced by his recent decision to buy a house for his oldest daughter but persistent refusal to purchase anything for her.

At times like these, she thought seriously about giving up and returning to China, where she was certain she could reclaim her PRC citizenship. "It feels strange" to be a Taiwanese citizen, she confessed to me and Yuan Mei, "as if I don't know what I'm doing. [I had] that status for several decades [referring to her PRC citizenship]. It's a lonely feeling, [as if] leaving my mother." Although Xiao Hong had opted for citizenship to resolve her deep feelings of insecurity about her future, she discovered that giving up her PRC status had only enhanced her uncertainty about where she belonged, where she could call home, and whether she could preserve her bond with her natal family. Unlike future-oriented immigration policies that presented naturalized citizenship as a source of hope, Xiao Hong's marital experiences taught her to see this future only as a source of anxiety (cf. Pine 2014).

Xiao Hong was not the only one who associated the loss of PRC citizenship with the severing of natal ties and the attendant feelings of unease produced by this sudden detachment from the past. Zeng Limeng, a Chinese husband who lived in southern Taiwan, described his 2005 decision to become a Taiwanese citizen as an act of betrayal against the country that had raised him. Like a bride who severed her natal ties on her wedding day, Zeng felt that by giving up his PRC citizenship, he had "married out" of his family and country. Thirty-something Qu Aili, with two young daughters and a husband in Taiwan, also mused aloud to me about her attenuated ties to her natal family now that she had to revoke her PRC citizenship. Qu had delayed applying for Taiwan citizenship for nearly a year and finally relented in late 2007 under pressure from her husband and in response to her repeated failure to secure a white-collar job in Taiwan. But now she faced a three-month window in which to comply with the denationalization requirement, and the prospect of canceling her PRC household registration evoked a string of memories about her fading connections to her home community.

Both of Qu's parents had died, and her mother had left her and her older brother each an apartment in Qingdao, a former German treaty port city on China's northeast coast. Qu was uncertain about whether she would still be able to claim her inheritance after giving up her PRC household registration, precisely because her registration proved she was her mother's child. Framing her denationalization anxieties in pragmatic and familial terms, Qu feared she might lose claims both to her inheritance and to her very membership in her natal family.

Like Qu and Zeng, Xiao Hong viewed birthright citizenship in the PRC and documentary proof of that citizenship status as vital forces substantiating her ties to her natal family. Her acquisition of Taiwanese citizenship, therefore, did not resolve her concerns about the future but merely intensified them, especially after her husband died in late 2009. She returned to work, desperate to make up for years of lost income, but found the long hours and physical demands of nursing increasingly unbearable. At the 2010 gathering at the restaurant, Xiao Hong quickly broke down in tears as she described how diligently she cared for her husband in his final days, his children unwilling to share the exhausting burden of nursing care. And her fears had been realized when, after his death, they fought with her to claim even his meager pension, acquiescing only when his friends intervened on her behalf. She remained in the apartment she had shared with her husband, but she did not know when his son might turn her out to reclaim it for his mistress, in whose name he had registered the deed. She would willingly work herself to death, Xiao Hong proclaimed, in order to provide a more secure future for her daughter and save her from the bitter fate of immigrant life in an insecure, eternal present.

When I saw Xiao Hong more than a year later in summer 2011, her attention had turned fully to supporting her daughter and parents back in China. She had recently returned from a several-month visit to her hometown to care for her ailing father, timing her trip so that she would be back in Taiwan to qualify for the biannual disbursement of her husband's pension. She continued to work as a nursing aide and had learned to handle the workload better, but she remained plagued by guilt about having abandoned her daughter to marry her elderly husband. All of her savings and investments were now in her daughter's name, she explained, and she planned to use her current earnings to help her daughter purchase an apartment in Hangzhou, where the young woman now resided after graduating from college.

Xiao Hong admitted that she remained in Taiwan to earn the money she needed to secure her daughter's future, not because her citizenship status gave her a sense of belonging or enhanced her commitment to her own future in the country. With her husband's death, she had lost her ties to his family and friends, and her strongest connections were with other Chinese wives or her coworkers. But the poignant irony of the gap between her juridical status and sense of belonging also emerged from experiences "back home" in China. On her last visit to care for her father, she had received a call from the local security police in her hometown shortly after leaving her father's hospital room. They wanted her to "come in for a chat," she recounted, a "request" that she skillfully deflected by mentioning the name of an uncle who had held a prominent police post. But she had no illusions about the compulsory nature of the request, for it signaled her suspect status as a returnee who was now a Taiwan compatriot. This experience merely confirmed Xiao Hong's more inchoate feelings, developed over years of residing in Taiwan and flying back and forth across the Strait, that "home was surely no longer a site of security" (Feldman 2006, 30). Despite her extensive community of family and friends in China, she could no longer claim a juridical status there that protected her from state surveillance as a noncitizen and, implicitly, a potential spy. Her sense of belonging to a community was now detached from her legal citizenship standing, with one unable to resolve the present and future dilemmas created by the other.

I WANT A WARM AND CARING HOME AND A FAMILY

I met Wang Fei a mere ten days after she first arrived in Taiwan in April 2008. A young, slight woman in her early twenties who hailed from a poor family in rural Henan province, Wang had been forced to drop out of school before completing junior middle school. Like many other young people in China's rural interior, she migrated in her teens and found work in a factory in the coastal export center of Shenzhen. Wang had an aunt who had married a Taiwanese many years earlier, and she introduced Wang to a native Taiwanese man ten years Wang's senior, whom she would soon marry. When I met Wang Fei in 2008, she was only recently settled in the home her husband shared with his mother in a southern district of Taipei, but she was already growing dissatisfied with her husband's awkward personality and lack of basic social skills. Chafing at the restrictions her husband and mother-in-law placed on her movements, Wang had convinced them to allow her to attend an acculturation course at CARES.

Wang Fei's marital conflicts might have diminished over time as she gradually adjusted to her new life were it not for two events that happened within a month of her arrival. As Wang's fights with her husband intensified, her mother-in-law asked for Wang's Taiwan-issued reunion pass (claiming that their neighborhood precinct head required a copy), but she only returned a photocopy of the pass to Wang. Wang was unhappy enough that she began to think seriously about leaving her husband and returning to China, but she needed her reunion pass to exit the country. And at just this moment, Wang discovered she was pregnant.

The pregnancy forced Wang to pause and reconsider her plans to return to China. Her aunt cautioned her that if she went back now, she would have nothing to show for her time in Taiwan and would be marked with the stigma of divorce. Wang's thinking grew increasingly confused during this period as she grappled with different possible futures. Did she want to have a child? Could she imagine spending the rest of her life with her husband? Did she want to remain in Taiwan after all? The responses from her husband and mother-in-law made it even harder for Wang to reach a decision. Her husband cried when she asked for a divorce and refused to agree to an abortion, and Wang's mother-in-law promised to care for the child so that Wang and her husband could work.[4] But Wang was not swayed by her mother-in-law's promises. After all, she knew that what the family wanted most was the child; she was merely the means to that end.

One June morning I received a phone call and heard Wang Fei rambling incoherently on the other end of the line. Clearly distraught, she asked me for the phone number of the Straits Exchange Foundation (SEF), the official yet technically nongovernmental body that verified documents from China and acted as a liaison with its PRC counterpart organization. At first I assumed that Wang wanted to contact them for legal advice because her mother-in-law and husband still held her identity document, but gradually I came to understand that her husband had told her that the SEF would send her back to China. When I explained that the SEF did not have that power, she pressed me about what she would have to do to be sent back. "Something illegal," I replied, to which she quickly responded, "Like working without a work permit?" "Yes," I said nervously, but then cautioned her not to do anything rash because deportation would certainly cause more problems than it would resolve. Before I could say more, Wang whispered that she had to get off the phone and abruptly hung up.

I was relieved to see Wang Fei the next day at the CARES office. After several phone calls to the NIA, she finally determined that she could replace her reunion pass, but she needed a copy of the police report documenting that she had notified the police when her mother-in-law took away her identification document. Upon Wang's request, I accompanied her to her neighborhood police station in search of the documentation she required. We arrived at the station during a shift change, and a group of police officers gathered in the front of the station to listen with curiosity to Wang's long-winded request, her use of unfamiliar PRC police terminology only enhancing their confusion. Finally, a heavyset policeman assumed the duty officer seat and, grumbling that this task should be the responsibility of the NIA and not the police, listened again as Wang explained that she needed a statement that the police had responded to her phone call by visiting the house and speaking with her husband and mother-in-law about her reunion pass. The duty officer found the report written up by the officers who had made the visit; it briefly noted that Wang's husband had said he had lost the pass, but the officers had added a notation that succinctly characterized the encounter: "dispute" (*jiufen*).

Wang and I waited at the police station for several hours while the duty officer clarified what kind of document the NIA required.[5] With the police report finally in hand, we headed across town to NIA headquarters, where Wang asked for the bureaucrat to whom she had spoken on the telephone that morning. The woman greeted Wang in a friendly voice and instructed her to fill out an application form and write a brief statement explaining what had happened to her previous reunion pass. A look of relief spread across the bureaucrat's face when Wang Fei took out her PRC-issued travel pass because that document would have been much more difficult and time-consuming to replace. She reminded Wang to call the following week to confirm that the pass had been issued and ended by urging her to remain with her husband in the interim so that the family could not report her as missing. Throughout the interaction, Wang mentioned not a word about her pregnancy, and I could not help but wonder whether the bureaucrat would have been as accommodating had she known. After Wang and I departed, and before we went our separate ways on the metro, I asked her to call me every other day to keep me informed about her situation. I also suggested gently that she not do anything rash in the interim.

When I wrote up my notes from that tumultuous experience a day and a half later, Wang still had not called me. But over the following week I spoke to her on several occasions, the last when she called from the hospital where she had gone to see a doctor because her head hurt so severely. Anxious to escape her current predicament, she urged me to buy her a plane ticket for the following afternoon and said that her new reunion pass would be ready the next morning. But then she had to get off the phone quickly, and although I asked her to call me that evening, she never did.

Wang Fei and I never had an opportunity to discuss her experiences during her final week in Taiwan, our conversations abruptly cut short by various interruptions. A mere twenty-four hours after she called me from the hospital, I received a text message from an unfamiliar number: it was Wang, briefly announcing that she had arrived safely in Shenzhen. Her aunt had purchased her airplane ticket, and Wang had collected her new reunion pass from NIA headquarters that very morning.

A few days after Wang's departure, I picked up my phone to hear the voice of a middle-aged woman who identified herself as Wang Fei's mother-in-law. After inquiring gently whether I knew of Wang's whereabouts, she launched into a series of complaints about Wang's behavior during her two short months in Taiwan: the thousands of dollars she cost them calling long distance to China, hours spent in front of the computer talking to friends back home, and Wang's refusal to listen to the older woman's protective advice, insisting that her mother-in-law was bent on controlling her and keeping her tied to the house. Wang's aunt, the woman continued, kept pressuring Wang to go out to work, but she had refused because it was her son who would suffer the consequences as Wang's official guarantor were Wang to be caught without a work permit. Her refusal seemed only to fuel her daughter-in-law's discontent, however, and the older woman repeated again how much money Wang Fei had cost them. As she continued to press me for more information about Wang's current whereabouts, I heard a man's voice in the background and wondered whether it was Wang's husband. Although clearly unhappy with Wang's flight, the older woman seemed resigned to her son's failed marriage, and she ended the conversation with polite platitudes, inviting me to come for a visit when I had the time.

My conversation with Wang's mother-in-law raised more questions than it answered about how to interpret the struggles Wang experienced during her short marriage. For a working-class family, the cost of cell phone calls to China was not insignificant, and it was easy to see how Wang's efforts to ease her homesickness might exacerbate family conflicts over resources. Whereas Wang interpreted her mother-in-law's efforts to limit her mobility as a form of abusive control, the older woman claimed she sought to protect her new daughter-in-law and help her acclimate to an unfamiliar environment. And then there were the topics that Wang's mother-in-law failed to raise during our short conversation: her own decision to keep Wang's identity document and her son's erratic behavior. Although the former could also be explained as a form of protective care, the latter would be more difficult to justify and perhaps explained the older woman's quiet resignation to her daughter-in-law's departure.

When I casually mentioned this conversation to Wang Fei during one of several chats we had after her return to China, she asked immediately whether I also had spoken with her husband; if I had, she continued, I would have understood immediately that he was not, as she put it, a normal person. She was trying to put him out of her mind, she added, and over time our conversations shifted to her life back in China. After spending a few months in her home village in Henan, she returned to Shenzhen and found work in a factory that manufactured computer parts. It was from Shenzhen that she called me a year later when I was in Beijing.

During our hour-long conversation that July, Wang Fei described how she had been able to process a divorce in China, but she needed her husband's cooperation to divorce legally in Taiwan, and he seemed to have disappeared without even his mother knowing his whereabouts. She mused aloud about where she was most likely to satisfy her desire for a happier marriage and family life, spinning out possible futures tied to specific places: "If I return home, I will suffer a lot of hardship," Wang added. "So perhaps it would be better to be [in Taiwan]." Deeply afraid that she would be unable to find a desirable husband in China because of her divorced status, she complained that everyone she had been introduced to so far had some kind of problem: he might be older, already have children, or still farm in her home region. "In my heart I don't feel that I'm any different," Wang complained. "But I've already been discounted [because I'm divorced]."[6]

The path her life would take in China was already determined, Wang felt, and she knew it would be a simple one. But if she returned to Taiwan, the future bore many more possibilities, as well as greater risks. At present she was still young and had time to consider her options, relying on her aunt to look for prospects in Taiwan while she continued her search at home. Unlike her aunt, who saw Taiwan as the unquestionable better choice, with its work opportunities and potential for economic independence, Wang emphasized again that her priorities were less practical but no less valuable: a warm and loving family.

I did not speak with Wang Fei again until the summer of 2011, when, on a return visit to Taipei, I discovered that she had remarried and was living in a rural community in the central part of the island.[7] A mutual friend gave me her phone number, and when we finally reconnected, Wang's voice cracked with tears as she poured out the story of how she had returned to Taiwan. Her aunt had introduced her to her current husband, whom she described as honest and kind, a never-married man eight years older than she. But he lived in the Chiayi countryside in a place so remote that she was shocked when she arrived that June. There were only old people left in the community, Wang complained, and without the company of a few other Chinese women who had married local men, she would have lost her mind already. Wang seemed mollified by the possibility that she and her husband might move north to open a restaurant, and she talked as if she were trying to convince herself that this time the marriage would work. But she clearly had her doubts and wondered aloud whether she had ended up in a place with as few economic prospects as the interior of China from which she had just fled.

Like Xiao Hong's, Wang Fei's marital journeys have been circular rather than linear. Perhaps it would be more accurate to describe Wang's trajectory as a spiral that loops back and forth across the Taiwan Strait, landing her in new physical and social locations at each turn, not all of them equally desirable. After her first failed marriage, she returned to China and, on the face of it, resumed her life as a young migrant worker in the export sector that dominates China's coastal economy. But her social status was irrevocably altered by her divorce, and, now well into her twenties, she reentered the local marriage market with, as she put it, "discounted" value. She knew what the future held in store for her were she to remain in China. At some point she would age out of the migrant labor force and have no choice but to return to Henan and likely marry a man who had some undesirable feature: a previous marriage, a disability, the burden of children, or simply the stigma of being a poor peasant in the interior.

In contrast to the certainty of her fate in China, Wang saw returning to Taiwan as an opportunity for a different future, albeit one with greater risks. With her aunt's assistance, she was able to finalize her divorce in Taiwan and marry someone new. By her account, he was a decent, kind man who had professional training as a chef, but the marriage landed her in an isolated part of the island that uncomfortably resembled the poor interior of China from which she had worked so hard to escape. Perhaps this was the "discount" she faced in a second marriage in Taiwan: although the relationship promised the warmth and support that she longed for in her first marriage, it came at the cost of economic advancement and the cosmopolitan allure of urban life.

Yet, Wang Fei would surprise me once again with her pluck and ingenuity. On September 4, 2012, I received an email from her with a photo of her newborn son. Her tone was jubilant as she described how she and her husband had relocated north to a township in Hsinchu County, where she now worked as a real estate broker. When we met again the following summer, Wang was eager to display her accomplishments, making a special trip to Taipei to introduce me to her husband and son. As we sat around the table in a crowded dim sum restaurant, Wang showed me pictures of the apartment she and her husband had purchased, all the while fielding phone calls from potential real estate clients. Her husband patiently followed their toddler around the restaurant, and Wang took advantage of his absence to explain how she had convinced him to move away from home and establish a new life as a nuclear family. Taking great pleasure in her business success, she admitted that they had many financial obligations, but she was confident in her ability to meet them. When I asked whether she felt she had attained the kind of home environment she had sought in her previous marriage, she emphasized the pleasure she took in her job and her son. "I now have a clear goal," she continued, one that linked family with financial security to create a stable if ordinary life. Summing up the current state of her life and marriage, Wang Fei proclaimed, "We don't have conflicts, we don't argue. We merely lead a dull, ordinary life (*ping ping dan dan de shenghuo*), and I feel good about it."

WITH A TAIWAN PASSPORT, I CAN TRAVEL ANYWHERE!

The small meeting room on the first floor of the Legislative Yuan office building was crammed full of protesters and members of the press on Father's Day in August 2007.[8] Several NGOs had collaborated to organize the first of several protests against the financial requirement that all immigrant spouses faced at the point of applying for citizenship (see chapter 3). But an imminent typhoon had forced the protest off the street and into the small room, where participants holding placards and posters struggled to make space for speeches and a protest skit, while camera crews and journalists jostled for position. As I maneuvered slowly toward the front of the room, I caught sight of a group of older Chinese women gathered around an elderly man, whom I recognized as one of the leaders of the Cross-Strait Marriage Promotion Association. A stocky woman with graying hair cut in a neck-length bob stood slightly apart from the group, shouting slogans and pumping her fist into the air.

Like the other women, Li Yanhong responded readily to my questions about what had brought her to the protest and willingly gave me her phone number. And when I called her a few weeks later to ask whether she would be willing to talk with me more about her life in Taiwan, she agreed immediately and suggested we meet that Sunday evening at one of the local chain coffee shops not far from my apartment.

Li's initial description of how she came to Taiwan made her seem an unlikely candidate for a caretaking marriage with an elderly veteran. Emphasizing her graduate degree, former position as a college teacher in Shanghai, and Communist Party membership, Li portrayed herself as a fighter who had overcome her father's designation as a rightist in the late 1950s and her subsequent fate as a sent-down youth during the Cultural Revolution. Despite her checkered family background, she was able to join the Communist Party while laboring as a peasant in the Anhui countryside, and her Party membership provided a ticket to college as a member of the last "worker, peasant, soldier" class admitted in 1976. But she always harbored a dream of traveling overseas, she admitted, and although her classmates in graduate school were going abroad to study, her father discouraged her from following in their footsteps because she was already married and had a child. Her father had passed away by the time Li's younger sister introduced her to an elderly veteran from Taiwan, and she began to consider divorcing her first husband to marry this man. By that point in her life, Li was free to determine her own fate.

Marrying a Taiwanese citizen certainly enabled Li to realize her dream of overseas travel, but as our conversation continued, I learned that other pressures had also encouraged her to make this dramatic life change. Her first husband gambled and did little to support the family, and Li's own job had become much less secure than she had first suggested because the Shanghai government had demolished her school's main building in the central part of the city to make way for a new hotel. Many of her fellow teachers had left for other jobs, were demoted, or simply stayed home and took a substantial pay cut. Already in her forties by this point in the mid-1990s, Li faced a competitive job market with few opportunities for women of her generation, even with her education and the connections she had made as a Party member. Moreover, she had high hopes for her daughter to study abroad, but supporting her over the years to reach that goal would require more resources than Li or her husband could provide. To gain access to Taiwan's lucrative job market and escape her unhappy marriage, Li ultimately decided to divorce her first husband and take a temporary leave from her teaching position. In 1996, after knowing her much older husband-to-be for nine months, she married him and moved to Taiwan.

It took Li more than a decade to become a Taiwanese citizen, largely because her elderly husband refused to sponsor her out of fear that she would leave him once she obtained citizenship. He had lied to her about his circumstances in Taiwan, Li confessed, and she was shocked when she first saw the tin-roofed, shack-like structure he called home in a poor neighborhood in Taipei County. Concerns with face and reputation prevented her from giving up and returning to China for good, and on her second trip to Taiwan, she stayed for four years, working as a janitor to support her daughter, who was then attending college, and caring for her husband, whose health had begun to deteriorate with age. Li stressed her conformity to the dictates of a caretaking marriage: she refused to leave her husband's side when he became ill, she "saved" him on several occasions by calling an ambulance when his heart gave out, and, finally, when the doctors told her that he would not survive his last bout of cancer, she managed to send word to his son and daughter from an earlier relationship with an aboriginal woman in southern Taiwan that the end was near and they should come to pay their final respects to their father.

According to Li, it was the doctor who cared for her husband during his final stages of cancer who convinced him to support her citizenship application. Debilitated by disease, her husband traveled by ambulance to the NIA service center to process her application. The clerk came out of the building to confirm her husband's approval as guarantor and Li then went inside to complete the necessary paperwork. But Li's citizenship trials did not end there. At the time there was still a citizenship quota of 6,000 mainland Chinese per year in place, and the quota backlog delayed approval of Li's application for another five months. In the interim, her husband passed away.[9]

Her husband's death threatened Li's chances of receiving citizenship precisely because the NIA had begun to notify Chinese spouses that their application would be denied if they divorced, were widowed, or committed a crime after they submitted their paperwork but before they were granted citizenship. This threat was especially acute for women married to elderly men, who often were in poor health and might not survive for the typical six to twelve months it now took to process a citizenship application due to the quota backlog. The additional quota-imposed waiting period created a powerful sense of temporal limbo and spatial confinement among these women because their unrecognized immigration status during this period prevented them from leaving the country while their citizenship application was pending.[10]

For wives of elderly veterans who had waited anxiously for the day when they would finally be eligible to apply for citizenship, ever fearful that their husbands might die prematurely, the quota delay and the threat of rejection it entailed represented the ultimate confirmation of Taiwan's refusal to accept them into the national body. As a consequence, many of the older women who participated in the 2007 protests against the financial requirement did so precisely because the Marriage Promotion Association added abolition of the quota system to its list of demands. Fifty-year-old Zhang Zhen was outraged when she received a letter from the NIA informing her of the events that could jeopardize her citizenship eligibility after she submitted her application in early 2008:

> Why do they treat us like this just for a national ID? The Vietnamese, the Thais, any other daughter-in-law doesn't suffer as much as [mainland spouses] do. The slightest thing and they order you to get out! Even now they send me this notice: if you divorce, or something happens to your husband, or you have a [criminal] record. I've already entered [the citizenship queue], and they still want to revoke my eligibility. Why do they treat us this way? (Interview with author, May 8, 2008)

Ever alert to her differential treatment as a Chinese spouse, Zhang Zhen read the NIA notice through the lens of repeated experiences of discrimination sparked by her mainland origins, the very "burdens" portrayed so vividly in the Marriage Promotion Association's protest skit during the 2007 demonstrations. Her response to the quota delay, like that of other Chinese women in a similar situation, revealed her astute awareness of how the very temporality imposed by immigration procedures was a strategy of state power: "Being slow," Nancy Munn (1992, 104, 109) affirmed in her now classic review essay, "is not a neutral state" but "a medium of hierarchic power and governance" (see also Lazarus-Black 2003).

Li Yanhong responded to her husband's death by marshaling all the resources at her disposal to guarantee the success of her in-process citizenship application. After seeking advice from different quarters, she decided not to notify the NIA of her husband's death. Irate over what she saw as blatant discrimination on the part of the ruling Democratic Progressive Party in an attempt to prevent more Chinese spouses from voting in the upcoming legislative and presidential elections, Li decided simply to wait it out, confident that she would ultimately obtain citizenship. When her application finally was approved in August 2007, she faced a new obstacle in her path to citizenship: because she had no claim to her husband's rundown house after his death, she had no home address where she could locate her official household registration, a necessary step before she could process her national ID card, passport, and Taiwan compatriot pass. Turning to networks of Taiwanese she had cultivated through a decade of working as a janitor in offices spread across a central district of Taipei city, she convinced the local community head (*linzhang*) to accompany her to the district Household Registration Office to apply for official household registration. When a few months later she took me to visit one of her workplaces, she proudly informed me that this was where her household registration was located, pointing to a side room with a single bed, where she had slept during those first uncertain months following her husband's death.

For Li Yanhong, Taiwanese citizenship did not bring a greater sense of rootedness so much as it facilitated the international mobility she desired. During the first year we knew each other, Li traveled outside of Taiwan every two months or so, and upon each return she proudly recounted to me the details of the trip: to visit her daughter who was attending graduate school in Denmark, to travel with friends to Japan, or to return to Shanghai. In the months leading up to my departure from Taiwan in summer 2008, Li spoke eagerly of her upcoming plan to attend the Beijing Olympics that August. In Taiwan, Li rented a room so small that it held only a bed and a desk, and she ate her meals at the canteen run by one of her workplaces. By contrast, she still owned one apartment in Shanghai, now in her daughter's name, and was considering purchasing another one. Moreover, she had started collecting her pension after formally retiring from her college in 2006.

Returning to China on a Taiwan Compatriot Pass did not cause her any difficulties, Li claimed, a stance that differed radically from Xiao Hong's. Li's age enabled her to initiate her pension disbursement process while she was still a PRC citizen, but younger women forced to make the citizenship decision before they reached the official retirement age faced the very real possibility that they might fail to draw their pensions because they no longer had the identification documents necessary to complete the paperwork. With this particular concern about her future financial security resolved, Li was able to focus on the freedoms she gained with a Taiwan passport and its comparatively unfettered access to international travel.

Other women Li's age, such as Zhang Zhen mentioned above, also emphasized the benefits of greater mobility with a Taiwan passport, but they espoused additional investments in the secure identity conferred by Taiwanese citizenship. Responding with despair to the NIA letter listing the conditions that would derail her citizenship application, Zhang concluded, "If I don't obtain a national ID, then I'm neither a mainland person nor a Taiwanese. I'm not from anywhere, and that's exhausting." Like Li, Zhang Zhen had adult children living abroad, but she also had a husband in Taiwan to whom she felt a sense of commitment and attachment.[11] Perhaps for this reason she expressed a desire for the recognizable identity that she believed would come with citizenship, although she, too, acknowledged that it would do little to mitigate the everyday discrimination she faced from police who stopped her to examine her documents or from Taiwanese who referred to her simply as "that mainland [person]" (*dalu de*). As a result of this pull "back" to inescapable origins imprinted in her speech and physical deportment (Yngvesson and Coutin 2006, 181), Zhang confessed that she would never feel that she belonged in Taiwan and was unlikely to reside there indefinitely.

Li attempted to sidestep the question of identity by linking her future directly to her daughter, with whom she ultimately planned to settle down whether in Europe or China. For the time being, however, Li had created a community for herself in Taiwan and led an active social life. A mere week after our first conversation, she took me to visit a younger Chinese woman whom Li treated as an adopted daughter. Laden with presents for the woman's four-year-old daughter, we arrived at the facial salon the young woman ran on a densely populated street in Taipei County. The two chatted eagerly about the outing they would take to the southern tip of the island the following weekend as part of a trip organized by the woman's husband's workplace. He was employed by one of Taiwan's major banks, and Li later confessed that he also served informally as her investment advisor. Li repeatedly mentioned her strong ties with other Taiwanese she had met through work or political activities as a member of the Nationalist Party, displaying pride in how well she had adjusted to her single life in Taiwan and felt part of a larger community.

For Li, belonging meant having local connections to both Taiwanese and Chinese, while also leaving the country regularly to maintain the family bonds that would sustain her in old age (Greenhouse 2002). Despite acknowledging the "multilayered" quality of citizenship, kinship, and social ties (Long 2004, 88), Li, like Zhang Zhen, nonetheless recognized that she would always face discrimination as an older woman who could not hide her accent or direct style of interaction, and she argued that she would never allow her daughter to marry a Taiwanese. Even voting in Taiwan's presidential election, as Li had done for the first time in March 2008, did not create for her a feeling of substantive citizenship. She was happy to benefit from the privileges of juridical citizenship, especially with regard to cross-border mobility, but she had no illusions that she would ever be accepted by locals as Taiwanese. Ultimately, the lasting benefit of becoming a citizen was the power of the Taiwan passport to ease her routes outward as she continuously reinvigorated ties to far-flung family—her daughter in Denmark, an uncle in Norway, and other kin in Shanghai.

By the time Li and I reconnected in the summer of 2013, Li's daughter had married a Danish man, borne a child, and appeared to have settled in Europe permanently. As a consequence, Li was forced to think anew about her future. Although she visited her daughter several times a year or met her on visits to Shanghai, she no longer envisioned moving to Denmark in her old age. And although she traveled regularly to Shanghai to spend time with her aging mother, her brother and his family, and friends and former colleagues— sometimes even making weekend trips now that direct flights shortened the journey—she described herself as increasingly unaccustomed to life in China and unable to imagine a permanent return. The social welfare resources she enjoyed in Taiwan as the widow of a veteran and the networks she had built up through participating in neighborhood associations and Nationalist Party organizations reassured her that her future lay in Taiwan. Did she feel she belonged in Taiwan, I asked, as we sipped coffee in the noisy McDonald's not far from where she lived? No, she replied. But could she imagine living there and feeling taken care of once she was too old to work? Yes, she answered, especially because she did not want to become a burden to her family.

Over the years, a number of features emerged regularly in my conversations with Chinese spouses from different walks of life about how they defined home and belonging. Thinking of the present, many emphasized access to employment (while recognizing that it might not match their previous qualifications in China), housing, and the location of family members—especially spouses, children, and parents. Looking to the future, they mused about various welfare benefits and old-age support systems, including pensions from Chinese work units, health insurance, and access to quality health care. Juridical citizenship status certainly played a role in these assessments, perhaps more centrally for women who would have to revoke their PRC citizenship before they became eligible to claim retirement benefits from former work units. Notably, however, there was little mention of whether juridical citizenship provided a stronger sense of recognition and integration, in that even Chinese immigrants most deeply entrenched in Taiwanese society through their children, spouse, conjugal family members, and workplaces recognized the indelible imprint of their mainland origins. Even Zeng Limeng, who had skillfully adopted a Taiwanese accent and style of masculinity, admitted that his mainland identity was in his bones, inevitably slipping out when he grew angry or lost control. That imprint blocked many Chinese spouses' sense of full acceptance by native Taiwanese and undermined their efforts to claim a home in Taiwan, regardless of their legal status. As a result, some continued to envision (and even plan for) an old age spent in China once their children reached adulthood.

Zhang Zhen described feeling exhausted by the possibility of a future without Taiwanese citizenship, a future without any identity. For her and other Chinese spouses, the ability to feel "at home" was not merely compromised by patrilocal residence norms and patrilineal kinship ideals, but it also was thwarted by the "insufficiencies" of juridical status, for even those who chose to become Taiwanese citizens were regularly reminded of their difference, as Zhang perceptively noted. Speaking of efforts by displaced Palestinians to define the space of home in the aftermath of their dispersal by Jewish forces in 1948, Ilana Feldman contends that Palestinians developed a sense of security "not from being in/at home, but from claiming the right of home" (2006, 39). Even this claim, however, as Feldman suggests, is rarely sufficient to produce the sense of security encoded in the warm embrace of community and mutual recognition. The experiences of Deng Lifang, whose opening line in the epigraph constitutes a claim for "the right of home," also show how immigrants may construct their notions of home within the scaffolding of permission and denial erected by bureaucratic regulations and state border controls.

"Wherever we are, that is home," proclaimed Deng during a speech she gave at the closing ceremonies of an employment seminar for immigrant spouses run by the Taipei Department of Labor in November 2007. The "we" in her statement referred specifically to Chinese spouses whose claim to belonging in Taiwan is always tenuous, even when their marriages last and produce children who ostensibly demonstrate the integrating effects of juridical citizenship rights. Deng knew that she lacked these desired features, and they dominated her aspirations for the future as she fought to reclaim her eligibility for citizenship in the wake of her husband's suicide.

"Now that I'm a citizen," Deng admitted to me in 2010 a short five months after she finally obtained her national ID card, "I have to confront the important things in life." Deng sighed and added wearily, "With citizenship, new challenges have appeared," referring specifically to finding a husband and purchasing her own apartment in Taiwan. A palpable cloud of sadness and tension hung over Deng that February afternoon; having resolved the juridical obstacle of citizenship, she now felt burdened by the more pressing goals of marriage and home ownership, the life ambitions that had been denied her until she became a Taiwan citizen.[12] With no local community to introduce her to prospective spouses and no time for hobbies through which to meet men on her own, Deng felt increasingly hopeless about her chances of marrying and having children before she grew too old. And without the support of another income, she found it difficult to imagine how she could afford to purchase an apartment in Taipei's expensive real estate market. "I don't know when my luck will turn," she lamented. Facing the upcoming Chinese New Year holiday isolated from her natal kin, Deng seemed weighed down by the need to rely on herself without the support of her family in Fujian or a spouse in Taiwan.

By the summer of 2011, however, Deng's situation had begun to improve. She remained unmarried, although clients and friends now regularly introduced her to eligible bachelors, and her phone rang on numerous occasions during our time together with offers to set up blind dates. None of her dates had led anywhere (there was no "spark," she complained), but at least she had made some inroads into the local marriage market. More important, she had managed to purchase her own apartment on a narrow alley in an older neighborhood in Taipei County, where concrete apartment blocks stood cheek by jowl with car repair shops, traditional markets, stores selling Buddhist worship paraphernalia, and small, home-based factories. Despite her building's unprepossessing exterior, Deng was proud of how she had renovated the three-bedroom interior with a contemporary kitchen and bathroom and sleek, modern furnishings. Her business success was also evident in the exchange of her moped for a van that she could use to make deliveries.

With her citizenship status and own apartment in Taiwan, Deng could now sponsor her family members for extended visits, and her brother was just completing a month-long stay when I first arrived that summer. Although Deng keenly felt the burden of making her monthly mortgage payment, she was proud of the business she had built, even if her profit margins had shrunk over the last year. Now she owned two apartments—one in Taipei and one in Fujian—and she could afford to let the Fujian apartment sit empty, at least for now.

When I returned to Taiwan in July 2013, Deng and I only managed to squeeze in one long lunch, her business pressures forcing her to work long days and most weekends. She dabbed at tears throughout the meal, despondent over her increasingly attenuated ties to her mother and brother ("After all, a daughter ultimately belongs to others") and the lack of meaning in her life. Desperate to have a child and acutely conscious of her age as she neared forty, she was considering moving in with a man with whom she had maintained a tumultuous relationship over the past several years, breaking up and reconciling on several occasions. He was so unreliable and burdened with debt, however, that she refused to marry him. Yet if he gave her a child, she would at least be able to anchor herself in a family of sorts. Although Deng's citizenship status, business, and apartment substantiated her claim to "the right of home" in Taiwan in juridical and material terms, they could not compensate for the absence of family in her life or provide her the security granted by reproducing a Taiwanese child. Hence she had begun to evaluate alternative paths to creating the familial belonging she so desperately desired. Certainly this was not the kind of belonging Deng had envisioned when she married her first husband or in the aftermath of his suicide when she tirelessly petitioned the government to grant her citizenship, but it was a life that she was committed to building, even in the face of great challenges.

Epilogue

2014 WAS A TUMULTUOUS YEAR. In mid-March, a coalition of students and civic groups occupied Taiwan's Legislative Yuan for nearly a month to protest the ruling Nationalist Party's push to ratify the Cross-Strait Service Trade Agreement without subjecting it to the usual clause-by-clause review. Identifying themselves as members of the Sunflower Student Movement, protesters argued that the trade pact would make Taiwan vulnerable to pressure from Beijing, and they called for the passage of a law establishing detailed procedures and oversight mechanisms for all new cross-Strait agreements. As of this writing, the Service Trade Agreement has not been finalized.

September of that year witnessed the beginning of a massive civil disobedience campaign in Hong Kong, with students, scholars, and civic groups occupying major thoroughfares to demand universal suffrage in the election of Hong Kong's chief executive. Originally known as Occupy Central, the movement spread out from Central to other districts and was dubbed the Umbrella Movement (represented by the iconic yellow umbrella) as it incorporated a broader array of constituencies. Demanding electoral reforms that would diminish Beijing's control over the election process, protesters stood firm against the Hong Kong government and pro-Beijing supporters for nearly three months until the last remaining occupied zone was cleared on December 15. The government refused to make official concessions to the protesters.

On the surface, both movements focused on what could be seen as narrow legal and procedural reforms. Yet they also expressed deep anxieties in Taiwan and Hong Kong about future relations with China and Beijing's influence over their political and economic affairs. When Hong Kong was formally incorporated into the PRC in 1997, its new status as a Special Administrative Region (SAR) did little to quell residents' growing concerns about swelling flows of mainland Chinese into the territory (some as wives of Hong Kong men) or the impact on Hong Kong's social, economic, and political futures. In Taiwan, the six years of Ma Ying-jeou's Nationalist presidency witnessed an unprecedented spate of cross-Strait agreements that have intensified fears in some quarters of Taiwanese society about growing economic dependence on the mainland and its potential to undermine Taiwanese sovereignty. Local elections held in Taiwan in November 2014 dealt a major blow to the Nationalist Party, an outcome that some interpreted as a popular response to the events in Hong Kong and a sign of growing opposition to closer ties with China (Kaiman 2014).[1]

At the height of the Hong Kong protests, James Yu, press director for the Taipei Economic and Cultural Office in New York (Taiwan's unofficial consulate in the United States), published a letter to the editor of the *New York Times* in which he proclaimed, "Taiwan will not be tomorrow's Hong Kong" (Yu 2014). What made Taiwan different from Hong Kong? Yu explained, "The Republic of China (Taiwan) is a free democratic country with its own government and military," and its citizens have rejected the governing formula of "one country, two systems" under which Hong Kong people now chafe. Yu called on Beijing's leadership to "honor their promise and listen to the demands of the people of Hong Kong," an expression of support for the protesters echoed by President Ma Ying-jeou just two days later in a televised speech on Taiwan's National Day. Clearly, both state actors and average citizens in Taiwan were watching the events in Hong Kong closely, trying to understand what they might portend for Taiwan's own future.

What do the tumultuous events of 2014 tell us about the fate of Chinese spouses in Taiwan or the future of Taiwan's relations with China? I have no straightforward answers to these questions, other than to underscore the deep disquiet and fraught relationships that all of the events brought to the forefront of public debate. But I believe that it is important to pose these questions even without clear answers, for the very reason that, as I have argued throughout this book, Chinese spouses powerfully influence the form and substance of Taiwan's own sovereignty struggles. When Taiwanese bureaucrats encounter Chinese spouses, they respond in ways that hew closely to existing models for asserting sovereign statehood and making claims to independent rule: issuing documents, regulating border flows, assessing the intimate bonds that bestow rights to residency and citizenship, crafting a robust immigration law and policy regime, and affirming the core principles of that regime when addressing diverse audiences. Might such encounters also offer a different kind of potential precisely because they promise to make more intelligible forms of similarity and difference that otherwise constitute Chinese spouses as unassimilable?

The Taiwan government's regulatory practices and interactions with Chinese immigrants will not suddenly produce the cumulative effect of rendering Chinese spouses nonthreatening or their motives fully comprehensible. Official and everyday encounters, however, gesture simultaneously backward and forward in time, their temporal fluidity reopening histories while also pointing toward diverse future paths (Ahmed 2002, 568). In a provocative article on the temporalities of feminist politics and ethics, Sara Ahmed proposes nearness as a particular form of encounter that "involves getting closer to others in order to occupy or inhabit the distance between us" (2002, 569). For Ahmed, a politics based on these encounters allows for "the promise of the 'not yet'" (2002, 559), a promise that takes shape through new temporal and spatial possibilities that maintain the sharp recognition of difference as opposed to facile assumptions of common identity or shared cause. As differently situated groups of people come together and commit themselves to the hard work required by collective endeavors, they pry open a space for envisioning what Geraldine Pratt suggestively terms "other geographies and histories" (2012, xxxiv).

Ultimately, I hope that this book enables us to begin this process, starting with one small yet significant context in which history and geography have been configured in obdurate, confrontational terms that leave little room for thinking alternatively. Perhaps it is through recognizing both their shared intimacies and enduring differences that people on both sides of the Strait can begin to envision new maps, new borders, that are less likely to exclude the intimate lives of some, while privileging those of others. Chinese spouses clearly recognize how their intimacies are tightly bound up with the political in ways that circumscribe their own desires to belong and to feel at home. But this recognition may also generate other paradigms for conceptualizing political commitments that refuse the dominant binary of reunification versus independence. The protesters in Taiwan and Hong Kong formulated their demands for a different kind of relationship with China through existing democratic frameworks premised on specific legislative and electoral procedures. The challenges of "as if" sovereignty and "not quite" belonging require a more searching critique. To realize the promise of the "not yet," we must begin to rethink our very models of sovereignty and national inclusion.

NOTES

INTRODUCTION

1. The women in the first part of the video are actresses from a Taiwanese theater troupe who recite narratives culled from public responses to a blog, *The Illegal Immigrant*, that Chen established in the aftermath of his humiliating AIT experience. The second section features Chinese women narrating their own experiences.

2. Having fled to Taiwan as members of the Nationalist forces in 1949, these veterans formed a marginalized community largely isolated from local Taiwanese society. A military marriage ban in effect from 1952 to 1974 prohibited low-ranking soldiers from marrying, and only those who demobilized early could seek wives while still young. As a result, many veterans remained single or forged temporary unions with working-class Taiwanese or aboriginal women (Chao 2004a; Lin 2003). By the late 1980s and 1990s, these men were in their fifties, sixties, and seventies, facing old age in Taiwan without family support.

3. As I discuss in chapter 2, young women suspected of using marriage to enter Taiwan's sex industry also inspired the development of a more rigorous regulatory regime both in the country and at the border.

4. Limited premarital interaction meant that couples rarely were well acquainted with each other's personalities or living habits before they married, and this unfamiliarity could produce conflict once they embarked on a new life together. After they had moved to Taiwan and disengaged from their everyday lives in China, however, most Chinese spouses saw divorce and the return to China it typically required as a loss of face so severe that they contemplated it only under the most abusive or untenable of situations.

5. According to Taiwan government statistics, 95 percent of Chinese spouses who applied for entry to Taiwan between 1987 and 2013 were women (Taiwan National Immigration Agency and Department of Household Registration, "Number of Foreign and Mainland Spouses in Each County and City").

6. Nicole Constable (2005) describes these diverse marriage motivations as a form of "marrying up" captured by the term *global hypergamy*. Global hypergamy does not assume that marital immigrants end up in more comfortable economic circumstances by marrying across borders; instead, they may sacrifice material comfort for greater opportunities to develop personally, emotionally, and professionally.

7. From the perspective of China's vast population, by contrast, cross-Strait unions were a drop in the bucket: registered marriages with any non–mainland Chinese have never exceeded more than 1 percent of all annual marriages in China, although cross-Strait unions constituted nearly half of that tiny percentage in the early years of the new millennium (PRC Ministry of Civil Affairs 1989–2008).

8. Foreign spouses may not be able to capitalize on those work rights due to language barriers, domestic responsibilities, or opposition from husbands and in-laws (Wang and Bélanger 2008). And although they are eligible for citizenship in four years, successfully naturalizing in that time frame requires them to reside in Taiwan for the full fourth year, a requirement that many cannot meet due to family obligations in their home countries. At present, foreign spouses must also show proof of economic self-sufficiency and pass a language test as part of the naturalization process.

9. Prior to its reform in 2000, however, the Nationality Law did not treat foreign wives and husbands equally. In accordance with patrilineal and patrilocal principles, the law automatically bestowed ROC citizenship on the foreign wives of male citizens. Foreign husbands, by contrast, had to meet specific requirements and complete complicated procedures before they qualified for naturalization (Chen 2009).

10. Beginning in January 1992, Taiwanese authorities began to accept family reunion applications from mainland Chinese spouses, but the application process was marred by unclear procedures and difficulties verifying PRC documents. The Act was revised four times between 1992 and 1996, in part to address procedural problems related to the entry of mainland spouses (Lu 2011, 120–21). The Act also paved the way for wives who had been "left behind" when the Nationalists fled to Taiwan in 1949 to reunite with their long-separated husbands.

11. As I discuss in greater detail in chapter 3, however, Chinese spouses' ability to produce Taiwanese children could not erase the taint of their mainland origins, providing evidence of how even immigrants who reproduce heteronormatively may be excluded from the nation on other grounds (Oswin 2012).

12. This initial system first granted Chinese spouses a three- to six-month reunion visa that, once it expired, required them to return to China to apply anew. After two years of marriage, spouses were eligible to enter the quota queue for residency status, but the size of the quota failed to keep up with the growing number of cross-Strait marriages, forcing Chinese spouses to wait four to six years for residency status. Two years of residency made them eligible for "permanent residence" (*dingju*), the terminology used in place of naturalization (*gui hua*), which was reserved for foreigners.

13. With this new system, Chinese spouses first entered on a six-month reunion visa that could now be renewed in Taiwan. After two years of marriage or birth of a child, they became eligible for kin-based residency (*yiqin juliu*), and after four years at this stage, they could apply for extended residency (*changqi juliu*). Two years of extended residency made them eligible for permanent residence (*dingju*) or citizenship.

14. The permanent residence quota was set at 6,000 persons per year or 500 per month. By the mid-2000s, the number of Chinese spouses applying for citizenship each month outstripped the quota, imposing an additional waiting period. This quota remained in place until January 2009.

15. Although the Democratic Progressive Party (DPP) and the Nationalists (Kuomintang or KMT) represent the broad divisions in Taiwan's current political spectrum, they are aligned with smaller parties to create, respectively, the "pan-green" and "pan-blue" alliances, the former advocates of greater independence for Taiwan and the latter in favor of closer ties with China.

16. When the Communist regime took over the mainland at the end of China's civil war, the United States supported the Nationalist government in Taiwan as part of its Cold War battle against the spread of communism. But the myth that the ROC would eventually retake the mainland became impossible to sustain over time, leading to the ROC's loss of its UN seat and the subsequent US decision in 1979 to switch its official diplomatic recognition to the PRC. Most states now maintain official ties with the PRC alone, evidence of a pattern of ROC derecognition that has culminated in Taiwan's current status as a de facto sovereign state.

17. Mazzarella's argument is about affect more broadly; he contends that "affect is not in fact external to bureaucratic process . . . but rather a necessary moment of any institutional practice with aspirations to public efficacy" (2010, 298). Geraldine Pratt insightfully shows how affective intensities might become "a resource for politics" (2012, xxix) by calling attention to how affect and emotion "can open up or close down (rather than replace) deliberative public debate" (2012, xxx). My reference here to shared sympathies draws inspiration from Pratt's astute consideration of how affect's motivating force facilitates political engagement and mobilization across communities with otherwise diverse interests and experiences.

18. Native Taiwanese are descended from Chinese who migrated to Taiwan from Fujian and Guangdong provinces beginning in the seventeenth century. In the late 1940s, they numbered approximately six million.

19. Different visions of the nation emphasized Han Chinese origins in the mainland, native features derived from Taiwanese and aboriginal societies, the legacies of Japanese colonial rule, and contemporary values rooted in a constitutional democracy.

20. Foreign spouses may also face home inspections and police harassment, especially because they are often mistaken for migrant workers who have run away from their employers. On the government's different responses to foreign spouses and foreign workers, see Hsia (2015) and Lan (2008).

21. These anxieties, I should add, do not necessarily prevent Taiwanese citizens from marrying mainland Chinese, but they may provoke discord and even abuse in those marriages.

22. This is not to suggest that citizenship status is unimportant. For marginalized groups in particular, it often provides the basis for claims to belonging that are not only political but also social and affective in nature (Hall 1993; Sunder Rajan 2003).

23. Engin Isin (2002) argues that, over time, citizenship produces difference instead of homogenizing it; citizenship literally requires hierarchies of otherness to constitute the national self. Lisa Disch (2003, 381) describes this constitutive function most clearly when she asks what Isin's insights mean for liberatory struggles that aim for inclusion: "How can inclusion emancipate if those groups who imagine themselves to be outsiders are already necessary to and presupposed by the citizen body—but in a degraded status?" (see also Canaday 2009).

24. Put another way, Chinese spouses live the kind of fragmented citizenship that Aihwa Ong (2000) identifies with the differential biopolitical treatment of populations within a national territory under conditions of graduated sovereignty (see also Benhabib 2002).

CHAPTER ONE

1. The sovereignty effect of official stamping is seen in the multitude of examples worldwide where stamps are not made in certain documents or where documents stamped by certain countries are not recognized by others. For instance, travelers entering Israel may choose to have a stamp imprinted on a separate piece of paper instead of the passport, in recognition that such a stamp would bar one from entry into most other Middle Eastern countries. Similarly, Navaro-Yashin (2007) describes how bureaucrats of the Turkish Republic of Northern Cyprus, a state unrecognized by the international community, will also stamp a paper instead of the traveler's passport. In the realm of cross-Strait relations, many third countries refuse to stamp the Taiwan passport out of concern that such an act would connote sovereign recognition and therefore anger Chinese authorities.

2. By including both possible names, Taiwan and the Republic of China, Mr. Lu neatly sidesteps the contested nature of this distinction in Taiwan's domestic political arena.

3. For instance, the identities produced by documents may be taken up by subjects in ways that undermine the very goals of state recognition that motivated the turn to documentary practices in the first place (Coutin 2007; Gordillo 2006; Navaro-Yashin 2007; Yngvesson and Coutin 2006).

4. PRC figures republished by Taiwan's Mainland Affairs Council document over five million annual entries by Taiwanese from 2011 to 2013. Even after accounting for multiple entries by the same individual, the numbers are substantial (www.mac.gov.tw/public/Data/49116553371.pdf).

5. In 2012, nearly two million Chinese tourists visited Taiwan, an increase of 50 percent from the previous year. That figure grew 13 percent in 2013 to 2.3 million. Chinese visiting for medical purposes (including cosmetic procedures) reached approximately 50,000 in 2012 and nearly doubled to some 95,000 in 2013 (www.mac .gov.tw/public/Data/49116553371.pdf).

6. Although Taiwanese travelers never use their ROC passport to enter the mainland, they are required to show it when they reenter Taiwan or when they transit through Hong Kong or Macau on their way to and from the mainland.

7. The full name of the Taiwan compatriot pass is "Travel Pass for Taiwan Residents Coming to the Mainland" (*Taiwan jumin laiwang dalu tongxingzheng*). For mainland Chinese departing for Taiwan, their document is called a "Travel Pass for Mainland Residents Going to Taiwan" (*dalu jumin wanglai Taiwan tongxingzheng*).

8. Direct flights across the Strait began on July 4, 2008, just slightly over a month after President Ma Ying-jeou and his Nationalist party assumed control of the government and initiated more amicable relations with China. It was nearly a year later, however, before Chinese spouses were permitted to fly directly on their first visit to Taiwan. A total of four airports in Taiwan handle direct flights to China: two "international" and two "domestic" (although Taipei's Songshan airport was later upgraded to international status). The existence of direct flights from both categories of airport reaffirms the ambiguous status of cross-Strait borders and the delicate bureaucratic maneuvering necessary to maintain this ambiguity.

9. When asked why the NIA did not mail the original directly to the applicant in China, Mr. Zhu again emphasized practical concerns such as the likelihood that the document might be lost in the mail and the greater cost of cross-Strait as opposed to domestic postage.

10. I am indebted here to Yael Navaro-Yashin's argument that for individuals who are the subjects of these documents (or, I might add, who handle them in their professional capacities), the difference between originals and copies is "experientially very real" even if not substantively significant (Navaro-Yashin 2003, 88). As anthropologists invested in the study of personal experience, we are obligated to show how individuals experience documents and how such experiences might produce very different forms of subjective and affective investment.

11. Meng claimed that she had been duped by this second husband, who absconded with the RMB35,000 (approximately US$4,200) that she had handed over to a marriage broker and never turned up to meet her when she arrived at Taoyuan airport, forcing her to fly back to China without ever having set foot in Taiwan.

12. Just a few weeks earlier in mid-December 2007, I had interviewed the couple in their simple one-room apartment in a working-class Taipei neighborhood where many elderly veterans lived. The local representative of the city Veterans Affairs administration who accompanied me to the interview warned me in advance that Li was likely to dominate the conversation with an account of their legal battles, and he was not mistaken. Over the course of the interview I also learned that Li had been married twice previously as well: first to a local Taiwanese woman who died when their two sons were quite young, and more recently to a much younger woman from

Sichuan Province whom he angrily denounced for swindling him out of several million NT dollars (although, inexplicably, he still kept her photograph in a prominent position atop the television in their apartment).

13. Despite repeated calls to Meng after the hearing, I was unable to reach her and therefore never learned the outcome of her case.

14. These courses were funded by the national government and held in urban districts with substantial populations of Chinese spouses. Course content included job opportunities and training, Taiwanese family culture and kinship norms, social etiquette, health care and emotional well-being, linguistic features of Taiwanese Mandarin, Taiwanese dialect lessons, immigration policies, culinary culture, and child-rearing practices. Separate courses were held for foreign spouses from Southeast Asia who required more language training in Mandarin.

15. At the time of our meeting, Wu Yan only held kin-based residence in Taiwan. Once she returned from Macau, she would be eligible to apply for extended residence, the final residency stage before citizenship.

16. By contrast, Wu Yan's infant son, a Taiwanese citizen, entered Macau on his ROC passport, which enabled him to remain in Macau for thirty days. To extend his stay, he could enter the mainland on his Taiwan compatriot pass and then immediately return to Macau with his passport, granting him another thirty-day stay. Obviously, an adult with similar mobility resources needed to accompany him on this venture.

17. The government later introduced a multiple-entry permit for those at the reunion stage, but this was only available after a Chinese spouse had already entered Taiwan. The system for processing single-entry permits enhanced the power wielded by the guarantor, typically the Taiwanese spouse, who literally controlled his Chinese wife's ability to reenter the country. I heard many tales during my research of husbands who refused to send the required permit to China, in effect preventing his wife from returning to Taiwan and, in some cases, forever separating her from children left behind. A Chinese spouse thus abandoned in the mainland had little recourse to resolve her plight, and many contacted NGOs in Taiwan to see whether they could act on their behalf. This problem was more severe prior to 2004, when Chinese spouses were required to leave the country every six months or annually until they received residency. After August 2009, when reunion status was reduced to the point of first entry only, Chinese spouses no longer faced this specific obstacle, although other opportunities remained for a Taiwanese guarantor to obstruct his wife's progress through the remaining residency stages if he so desired.

18. Jiang needed a Japanese citizen or a foreigner with a work permit in Japan to serve as her guarantor, was required to show bank savings of at least NT$500,000 (roughly US$16,300), and could not remain in Japan for more than fourteen days, a shorter time than the family had allocated for their vacation. Jiang later noted that at the time she was planning her trip, Japan generally only issued visas to mainland Chinese traveling as part of tour groups (Taiwanese, by contrast, did not require visas to Japan). A few months later, however, Jiang applied for and was granted a Canadian tourist visa using her PRC passport. In this case she applied together with

her husband and infant daughter at Canada's unofficial consular office in Taipei, and the family planned to visit her father-in-law, who owned a house in Vancouver. In our subsequent correspondence, Jiang attributed her visa success to the fact that the whole family applied jointly, and she sailed through immigration upon arrival, she argued, because she had traveled with her husband and their small child.

19. At the same time, Chinese spouses do recognize that these documents, flimsy or atypical though they may be, nonetheless enable types of mobility that were previously unavailable to most of them before they married a Taiwanese.

20. For those who first arrived between March 2004 and August 2009, the reunion permit was typically their first identity document issued in Taiwan.

21. The powerful draw of the national ID card was such that under other circumstances, it could supersede its physical form. Antonia Chao recounts the reaction of a Chinese woman who misplaced her recently acquired ID card at the airport en route to the mainland for her first visit home in four years: "Prof. Chao, you know better than anyone how important this ID card is to me. It was so difficult to get that even if it were merely a piece of paper, I still wouldn't want to lose it" (Chao 2006, 130).

22. In fact, Radhika Mongia (1999) argues that in the context of early-twentieth-century intraimperial migration from India to Canada, the passport emerged as a technology for producing the necessary relationship of people to territory that enabled the nation-state to emerge from the contradictions of empire. Moreover, she contends, this technology effectively erased race as the overt basis for regulating legal mobility by disguising it in the ostensibly universal category of nationality.

23. For instance, two Taiwanese business travelers en route from Paris to London in 2007 were strip-searched and detained for two days at Charles de Gaulle International Airport because they held two different versions of the Taiwan passport, arousing suspicion that the documents were fraudulent (Staff Writer 2007).

24. Wang (2004) mentions cases of Taiwanese tourist groups being detained and strip-searched at ports of entry in Australia and Austria by border officials suspicious of their "real" national identity. In March 2010, a middle-aged Taiwanese housewife was detained and questioned at the Vancouver airport, despite the fact that she held a valid passport, visa, and return airplane ticket. Ultimately she was given the choice of signing a document attesting to her "voluntary" immediate departure or facing several days in immigration detention while her case was investigated (Hansen 2010; Qiu 2010). In 2012, Indian police arrested eight Taiwanese visiting a Tibetan monastery near the Indian border with China because of reports that they were Chinese spies (VOA Tibetan 2012).

25. By "loss," officials refer to a range of scenarios. One is that Taiwanese may lose their passports while traveling or have them stolen—at the airport in Taiwan, in transit, and especially in China. Equally plausible, however, is that Taiwanese intentionally "lose" their passports (in short, sell them to black market operators in China), a suspicion that officials convey through voice or gesture by placing inverted commas around the verb "lose." Several immigration officials argued that

the Ministry of Foreign Affairs should impose harsher penalties on lost passports in order to discourage this practice, but they also acknowledged that the government could not refuse to reissue passports to its citizens because owning a passport was a core right of citizenship.

26. US government fears were not completely unfounded, as proven in July 2012 when the NIA cracked a cross-Strait human smuggling ring that used ROC passports to smuggle Fujianese into Australia and Canada (Chung 2012).

27. The United Kingdom and Ireland instituted visa waivers for Taiwanese in 2009. A Schengen visa waiver went into effect for Taiwan passport holders on January 11, 2011, allowing visa-free travel to European Union countries and to Iceland, Norway, and Switzerland. Finally, in November 2012, the United States added Taiwan to its list of visa waiver countries.

28. The result, in effect, is to raise doubts about the presumed correspondence between the document and its bearer or, put another way, to reveal what Caplan and Torpey (2001) term "a central tension in the project of identification." Although Caplan and Torpey are concerned to expose the illusion that we as individuals "fully own or control our identity" (2001, 8), their point also shows how the tension between individuality and shared classification schemes creates the possibility that third parties might manipulate modes of classification in ways that derail a document's ability to capture a unique individuality.

CHAPTER TWO

1. See, for instance, the March 14, 2008, response on the blog for the Coalition Against Financial Requirement for Immigrants (*mei qian mei shenfen lianmeng*), http://nomoneynoid.pixnet.net/blog/post/15392762. Hsieh's campaign sought to rectify his blunder by providing NIA statistics that claimed cross-Strait couples accounted for 70 percent of all sham marriages involving foreign spouses in Taiwan, but such arguments failed to convince activists and immigrants of Hsieh's support for migrant spouses (Hsieh 2008). Hsieh ultimately lost the election to Ma Ying-jeou.

2. For a sample of this literature, see Canaday (2009), Chen (2009), Gardner (2005), Luibhéid (2002, 2013), McKeown (2008), and Yue (2008).

3. When the Entry/Exit Immigration Police Department first initiated interviews in Taiwan in 2002–3, the only legal basis on which they could draw was Article 31 of the Administrative Procedure Law (*xingzheng chengxu fa*), which granted civil servants the right to engage in an administrative investigation. Officials who had participated in the early planning stages admitted to me that this was a rather weak legal basis for the immigration interview, and it made many interviewers uncomfortable with the task due to fear that they were risking their civil servant status should an interview decision be challenged. To address this problem, bureaucrats in the Department drafted a new article requiring immigration interviews

for Chinese spouses prior to entry. They simultaneously pursued two legal channels for putting the requirement into law as both the Immigration Law and the Act were currently being revised. However, the new article was only inserted into the draft Act during last-minute party negotiations in Taiwan's legislature. The absence of full legislative review adds an ironic procedural twist to Mark Salter's point that "every border crosser is at the threshold of law" (2008, 368).

4. And yet on several occasions in 2008, I witnessed interviewers asking female and male spouses when they had first engaged in sexual relations. The question was often phrased in terms of sleeping arrangements ("When did you first spend the night in the same room/bed?"), but the underlying intention clearly was to determine whether the couple had a sexual relationship. Some interviewers also asked whether the woman was using birth control or whether she was pregnant.

5. There was an obviously gendered dimension to this reshuffling. The experienced interviewers who left for better posts were generally men and those promoted to replace them were predominantly women who had performed administrative tasks. Training these women in interviewing techniques also required teaching them how to interact authoritatively with male Taiwanese spouses, who often came from Taiwan's lower socioeconomic strata. The cut in personnel described by airport staff took place across all NIA units and was a great source of discontent among bureaucrats, who regularly expressed anger at their increased workloads and frustration with how personnel shortages made it difficult for them to fulfill their responsibilities effectively.

6. Of the nine or ten personnel on these NIA teams, only four to six have the requisite civil service rank to conduct airport interviews. In addition to interviewing cross-Strait couples, these NIA teams also process landing visas for Hong Kong and Macau residents, and, prior to June 2009, they collected and stored the travel documents of mainland Chinese arriving on short-term, nonspousal visas.

7. Interviewers and officials easily rattle off lists of provinces or regions in China whose residents they suspect of coming to Taiwan for sex work or undocumented labor. Their maps change over time, and senior airport bureaucrats can readily narrate this history. When suspicious about a particular marriage, clerks may download the Taiwan spouse's travel record (to see how often he visited the Chinese spouse). They can also document a Chinese spouse's previous entries into the country to visit relatives or because of a prior marriage. Taiwan's household registration database provides detailed information on citizens and immigrant spouses, including their birthplace, ethnic status, and marital and childbearing histories (if the marriage has been registered in Taiwan).

8. Because the materials are placed in an envelope, interviewers do not know in advance who they will be interviewing, a practice designed to prevent corruption. Interviewers are supposed to select the envelope at the front of the queue, although some intentionally skip "difficult" cases that have been flagged by the desk clerks, preferring to leave them for more experienced colleagues.

9. The rooms are equipped with a computer and video- and audiorecorders. The white walls are unadorned except for a photocopy or two of Taiwanese newspaper

articles documenting the dangers of sex work or domestic violence that potentially await Chinese women in Taiwan.

10. See Lan's discussion of an interview with a Vietnamese spouse at Taiwan's de facto consular office in Hanoi, where the interviewer did request a performance of marital intimacy, even though the official also claimed not to take such expressions seriously (2008, 847).

11. On several occasions, I heard interviewers express surprise when customary practice diverged from their own expectations. When one Chinese wife told an interviewer that she had spent her first night with her husband at the home of her married older sister, the middle-aged Taiwanese woman was so surprised by this contravening of patrilineal principles that she continued questioning on this point to confirm it was true (March 14, 2008).

12. In some cases, these expectations encourage couples to engage in practices they would not otherwise do, out of fear that they will be rejected at the border for failing to meet government standards of marital authenticity. Often this involves behaviors that document the marriage itself, such as posing for formal wedding photographs, a practice popular on both sides of the Strait (Adrian 2003). A Hubei woman in her midthirties grew increasingly quiet and embarrassed over the course of her 2008 interview as she admitted that she and her forty-year-old husband, although marrying for the first time, had not held a wedding banquet in China, nor had he given her a bridewealth payment or jewelry. When asked whether they had taken wedding photos, she pulled a small picture from her purse and added, "We heard that the government requires photographs. My husband doesn't like pictures, and we rarely take them. So we casually took a few."

13. This change in attitude toward arranged marriages was the consequence of pressure from immigrant rights organizations that underscored the ubiquity of such arrangements among older generations in Taiwan. Taiwanese bureaucrats are by no means the only group to apply their own biases to immigration decisions. In the 1980s, the British government discriminated against young South Asian men applying for entry to join their British-born wives on the grounds that the "primary purpose" of the marriage was to facilitate immigration. In succumbing to pressure from advocates, civil society, and the European Court of Justice, the British government "had to concede that immigration decision makers could not unquestioningly apply their stereotypes and biases to assess the motivations of populations they had little understanding of" (Bhabha 2009, 198).

14. On one occasion I observed a middle-aged male interviewer questioning a man from Fujian province who had married an older Taiwanese woman. Afterward, several female interviewers discussed the gendered anomalies of the case during their dinner break, focusing on prevailing expectations that husbands be older than their wives. They asked the male interviewer who had interrogated the couple why he failed to question the man about the couple's age difference, especially because the Chinese spouse hailed from a region known for arranging sham marriages. The male interviewer replied that he couldn't ask the man that question because it would "make him lose face" (March 4, 2008). In this context, sensitivity to male

status expectations placed the male interviewer in the position of supporting the mainland spouse despite marital characteristics that might signal fraud to another interviewer.

15. Some interviewers introduced me as a foreign researcher at the beginning of the interview, while others chose not to explain my presence. So as not to disrupt the interview process, I never spoke during interviews. During these observations, I followed the ethical standards developed by the immigration bureaucracy by not documenting couples' names or identifying information and by not seeking to contact them outside of the formal bureaucratic encounter.

16. These categories are two of six included in Article 10 of the interview guidelines (*Dalu diqu renmin shenqing jinru Taiwan diqu miantan guanli banfa*) issued following the March 2004 revision of the Act. The revised Act contained a new article (10-1) requiring mainland spouses to undergo an interview and be fingerprinted before receiving permission to enter Taiwan. The other four categories for denying admission include refusal to be interviewed, suspicion of collusion, or suspicion that the Chinese spouse will undermine national security or social stability.

17. Here, the officer was referring not to the couple's legal marriage registration in China but to the night of the wedding banquet, which she assumed would take place in Taiwan.

18. Not once in the more than thirty interviews I observed, for instance, did I hear an interviewer or spouse use the term "love."

19. The speaker claimed that this other woman never paid attention to her husband, instead running about all day, engaging in questionable money-making activities. By contrast, the speaker emphasized her own commitment to her caretaking role because she stayed at home to cook for her husband and attend to his illnesses.

20. This categorical ambiguity was also recognized by bureaucrats at the other end of the system, such as those who arrested and investigated Chinese spouses suspected of sham marriages and prepared them for deportation. See Chao (2010, 174–75) for a similar commentary by a mainland affairs police officer about fluidity between categories of sham and authentic marriages.

CHAPTER THREE

1. For one example, see DPP legislator Hsieh Chang-ting's comments (*Legislative Yuan Bulletin* 81 (5) [January 15, 1992]: 34).

2. The primary groups in question were native Taiwanese and Mainlanders (*waishengren*), the latter a term coined in the late 1940s to identify mainland Chinese who fled to Taiwan with Chiang Kaishek and the Nationalist forces. Literally "people from outside provinces," the term labeled this population according to their origins in parts of China other than Taiwan, discursively advancing the Nationalists' claim to be the legitimate government of China. By the time the second wave of cross-Strait immigration began in the early 1990s, Mainlanders and their descendants enjoyed unquestioned citizenship status in Taiwan.

3. These included implementation procedures (*shixing xize*), administrative orders (*xingzheng mingling*), quota tables (*shu'e biao*), management procedures (*guanli banfa*), and permit regulations (*xuke banfa*) that regulated the minute details of documentation, entry procedures, interviews, immigration eligibility, work rights, family reunification, and the like.

4. Taiwan is by no means the only country to rely on administrative policies to govern the sensitive domain of immigration. Constable (2007, 145) notes that Hong Kong's restrictive New Conditions of Stay, otherwise known as the "two-week rule," were formulated in 1987 as an administrative policy that was treated "as though it were law," even though it did not pass through the legislative process. See also Calavita (1992) on the US bracero program.

5. Richard Wilson (2007, 354) describes another context in which appeals to human rights may be a pragmatic strategy: settings where demanding full sovereignty or self-determination might lead to state violence. Although Wilson discusses the mobilization strategies of indigenous groups in Latin America, his insights also help us understand how the Taiwan government advocates human rights as a strategy for sovereign maneuvering in response to China's saber rattling at any overt declaration of Taiwanese independence.

6. Most Chinese spouses who participated in the demonstrations were not formal members of the Marriage Promotion Association because the Act banned a mainland individual, corporation, or organization from serving as a member of a Taiwan organization or assuming a formal position within it. Furthermore, Article 10 of Taiwan's law of assembly and demonstration (*jihui youxing fa*) disqualifies anyone who is not a national from assuming a position of responsibility, acting as a spokesperson, or serving as a disciplinary officer for a public demonstration. Antonia Chao argues that although these exclusionary laws legitimized the efforts of Taiwanese husbands to speak on their wives' behalf during the demonstrations, they did not guarantee that the husbands would accurately represent (or even fully understand) the diverse interests of Chinese spouses (Chao 2006, 97–98).

7. In the draft organizational structure of the NIA, 75 percent of all personnel were drawn from policing units and their tasks focused on border regulation and monitoring immigrants and migrants within the country. Little attention was given to protecting human rights or providing channels to appeal abuses. The Alliance's constituent organizations were dedicated to advancing women's rights, labor rights (for citizens and migrants), and human rights more broadly.

8. The Alliance held public forums to mobilize awareness of the issues facing non-Chinese immigrants and migrants in Taiwan, and they began to draft their own revised Immigration Law to address human rights concerns. The Alliance's draft law was submitted to the Legislative Yuan in March 2005, with support from several legislators. Although not all proposed amendments were included in the final version of the law approved on November 30, 2007, key elements of the Alliance's agenda did make it in, including an antidiscrimination article, domestic violence exceptions for foreign spouses, and the right of assembly and public demonstration.

9. This was precisely the argument made by the Grand Justices of Taiwan's Constitutional Court in 2006 when they ruled to uphold Article 21 of the Act, which banned mainland Chinese from any level of civil service for ten years after becoming a Taiwanese citizen. Naturalized foreigners, by contrast, were eligible for all lower- and midlevel appointed civil service positions immediately upon acquiring citizenship. Despite the defense's argument that the article violated the constitutional right to equality by creating unequal subcategories of Taiwanese citizenship, the Grand Justices sacrificed this constitutional guarantee on the altar of national security concerns (Friedman 2010b; Liao 2007).

10. As Bridget Anderson (2013, 99) points out, "Ways in which noncitizens can become citizens or acquire citizenship are not simply legal details and technicalities, but indicate and shape the foundations of how membership is imagined."

11. The financial requirement was imposed on Chinese spouses as part of revisions to the Act implemented in March 2004. Initially, the revised Act required applicants to show proof of assets of at least five million NT (US$154,000). After public protests, the Ministry of the Interior first delayed implementation of this requirement until June 1, 2004, and then added a new condition that enabled applicants to demonstrate an average monthly household income over the past year of at least two times the minimum wage, or roughly NT$380,000 (US$11,700) at the time. Spouses of elderly veterans, the group most disadvantaged by the financial requirement, were able to meet its demands because the Veterans Affairs Council had struck a deal with the NIA and its predecessor institution to accept as proof a balance in the veteran-husband's savings account that matched his minimum monthly pension (interview at Taipei City Veterans Center, September 27, 2007).

12. Revisions to the Immigration Law approved on November 30, 2007 granted foreign spouses rights of assembly and public demonstration. Because the CAFRI protest preceded the law's formal legislative approval, the foreign spouses who spoke publicly were already naturalized citizens. By contrast, the one Chinese spouse who spoke at the protest risked arrest because she was not a Taiwanese citizen.

13. Several women mentioned that, if needed, they could borrow funds from family members in China to meet the financial requirement demands.

14. Although this article appeared in laws and policies regulating both foreign and Chinese spouses, it reflected the broader array of social anxieties and political fears surrounding Chinese spouses' "purpose" in Taiwan (the ever-present threat of political espionage, for instance), and heightened the stakes of violating the article's wide purview (see Article 10 of the Act). As Peter Nyers (2008, 175–76) suggests, the emphasis on voice as the *sine qua non* of the political act fails to recognize the burden of speaking in public borne by nonstatus migrants or, in this case, by the similar yet intensely troubling Chinese immigrant. Simply showing up may be an equally powerful political act for those whose right to be present is otherwise denied.

15. This English translation does not do justice to the main slogan of the September 9 protest, which utilized rhyming sounds in Mandarin to link the date of the protest to the question of how long immigrant spouses would have to wait for citizenship (*jiu yue jiu, women yao deng duo jiu?*).

16. In its response, the Ministry did express willingness to revise the conditions for meeting the financial requirement to allow for greater flexibility. But only in November 2008, after Ma Ying-jeou became president, were the regulations significantly revised for Chinese spouses, first to allow for a wider range of proof and then, in August 2009, to eliminate the requirement altogether. As of this writing, the financial requirement still stands for foreign spouses.

17. The most important of these administrative regulations was *"Dalu diqu renmin zai Taiwan diqu yiqin juliu changqi juliu huo dingju xuke banfa"* (Permit Regulations for Kin-Based, Extended, or Permanent Residence of People of the Mainland Area in the Taiwan Area).

18. There were seven draft submissions in total, but the Alliance draft was the most detailed, with proposed changes to fourteen articles of the Act.

19. The overall time to citizenship for Chinese spouses was reduced from eight to six years, and they became eligible to apply for kin-based residency immediately upon entry. Residency now also granted full work rights. Impediments to inheritance were removed, as was the financial requirement at the point of applying for citizenship, and an appeal process was introduced for Chinese spouses who faced deportation. But legislators rejected Alliance calls to grant mainland Chinese rights to assembly and public demonstration, to make civil service restrictions conform to those faced by foreigners, or to subject the Act to Taiwan's Administrative Procedure Law, which would have weakened the government's ability to play the national security card.

20. This ban did not apply to children from a country other than mainland China.

21. The child could not be older than twelve when it reached its quota number. Upon acquiring citizenship, Chinese spouses were also eligible to sponsor parents age seventy or older, although there was a quota for this category as well.

22. *"Dalu diqu renmin zai Taiwan diqu yiqin juliu changqi juliu ji dingju shu'e biao cao'an zong shuoming"* (Summary Explanation for the Draft Quota Table for People of the Mainland Area Establishing Kin-Based Residence, Extended Residence, and Permanent Residence in the Taiwan Area). Undated MAC document in possession of author, p. 3. Appended to *"Dalu diqu renmin zai Taiwan diqu yiqin juliu changqi juliu ji dingju shu'e biao dingding liyou shuoming"* (An Explanation of Specific Reasons Behind the Quota Table for People of the Mainland Area Establishing Kin-Based Residence, Extended Residence, and Permanent Residence in the Taiwan Area). Undated MAC policy paper in possession of author.

23. Interview by author, tape recording, Taipei, Taiwan, February 15, 2008.

24. Interview by author, tape recording, Taipei, Taiwan, February 15, 2008.

25. Article 17, section 6 of the Act empowers relevant authorities to establish quotas for temporary and permanent residence for mainland Chinese.

26. *"Dalu diqu renmin zai Taiwan diqu yiqin juliu changqi juliu ji dingju shu'e biao"* (Quota Table for People of the Mainland Area Establishing Kin-Based Residence, Extended Residence, and Permanent Residence in the Taiwan Area), effective January 5, 2009. Available at http://gazette.nat.gov.tw/EG_FileManager /eguploadpub/ego14252/ch02/type1/gov10/num4/Eg.htm.

27. *"Women dalu pei'ou Taiwan xifu zhi qiu zhengfu zhun women quanjia tu-anyuan"* (We, mainland spouses and Taiwanese daughters-in-law, request only that the government allows us to reunite our entire family), April 23, 2008. Available at http://blog.udn.com/NO12/1807397. All subsequent quotations come from this website.

28. Interview by author, tape recording, Taipei, Taiwan, June 5, 2009.

29. *"Pochu 12 sui mozhou, rang lupei ye yongyou qinzi tuanju quan ba!* 'Haizi! mama hao xiang ni'"* (Break the age twelve curse, let mainland spouses have the right to family reunification! Child! Mommy misses you). Press conference statement. In possession of author.

30. Beginning June 9, 2009, Chinese spouses with residency status were permitted to apply for renewable six-month visitor visas for birth children under age twelve. Policy revisions effective August 12, 2009 raised the age limit to fourteen and specified that after four years of residence on a visitor visa, the children were eligible for extended residence and after two years of extended residence, they could apply for citizenship. See *"Dalu diqu renmin jinru Taiwan diqu xuke banfa"* (Permit Regulations for People of the Mainland Area Entering the Taiwan Area), Article 20, June 9, 2009 and August 12, 2009; and "Permit Regulations for People of the Mainland Area Establishing Kin-Based, Extended, or Permanent Residence in the Taiwan Area," Article 22, August 12, 2009.

CHAPTER FOUR

1. This was not the MAC's first attempt to spread information in the mainland. In 2006, it published a printed guide to life in Taiwan for mainland spouses that, despite its colorful pictures, presented information through a rather dry narrative (Taiwan Mainland Affairs Council 2006). When MAC bureaucrats met with their Chinese counterparts under the auspices of an NGO-sponsored exchange, they brought several cartons for distribution at local marriage registration offices in China. Despite the MAC's effort to make the guide accessible to mainland readers through a simplified character printing, China's Ministry of Civil Affairs edited and republished the guide, changing the names of Taiwan government offices and places to fit mainland conventions (that reflected the PRC's refusal to recognize Taiwan's sovereign status) and presenting the material in a more formal and even less entertaining style (PRC Ministry of Civil Affairs 2007). This time the MAC had turned to a DVD format to make the information more accessible. It planned to ask China's Ministry of Civil Affairs to distribute the DVD through its local marriage registration offices.

2. The DVD was not released until May 2011 as a consequence of content changes required by the 2009 policy reforms.

3. None of these women participated in the planning session I attended, but they had frequented CARES in the past.

4. Linguistic differences and religious practices feature prominently in their accounts; unsurprisingly, these two issues were singled out by the MAC representative at the planning session I observed. The women also describe learning to navigate new spaces and praise the ease of public transportation in urban Taiwan, while they also underscore the new life habits required to adapt to urban culture, such as waiting in line.

5. The five forums I attended were held in Taipei County (September 2, 2007) and Taoyuan City (May 17, 2008) in the north; Yunlin (May 31, 2008) and Chiayi (June 7, 2009) in central Taiwan; and Tainan City (June 20, 2009) in the south. I also participated in a law and policy session held as part of an acculturation class sponsored by CARES in Kaohsiung, Taiwan's southernmost city, in March 2008, and attended numerous sessions in Taipei during 2007–8.

6. These typically included the Mainland Affairs Council, the National Immigration Agency, the Straits Exchange Foundation, the Veterans Affairs Council, the local Department of Labor, and representatives from the local government's social services divisions.

7. At the time, however, regulations specified that only under circumstances where there were no other relatives to care for elderly in-laws would a Chinese spouse be permitted to remain in Taiwan. Revisions to the Act in August 2009 extended the right to retain residence status in Taiwan after the death of the citizen-spouse to Chinese spouses who had acquired kin-based residency. But given the husband's poor health, the wife likely would have left Taiwan already by that point if her petition was not granted.

8. Most Chinese spouses believed that they would not receive a fair hearing in a Taiwan court as immigrants from China, a stance that might derive from a pervasive sense among average citizens in China that courts and judges typically sided with the more powerful party in disputes (Diamant, Lubman, and O'Brien 2005).

9. Because a battered spouse had to have children to benefit from this exemption, those who were childless but suffered from domestic violence had no choice but to leave Taiwan should they opt for divorce. For a discussion of the choices women made in this kind of situation, see Friedman (2012, 2015). The exemption for abused spouses with children took effect on August 12, 2009. See Article 32 of the "Permit Regulations for Kin-Based, Extended, or Permanent Residence of People of the Mainland Area in the Taiwan Area."

10. Taiwanese family law does not offer no-fault divorce. Therefore, if both partners do not agree to a consensual divorce, the spouse seeking a divorce must sue on the basis of fault, a time-consuming and potentially costly process (Kuo 2014).

11. This was precisely the point made by the Cross-Strait Marriage Promotion Association's protest skit described in chapter 3.

12. This stance, adopted by other NIA officers as well, reaffirmed the NIA's own institutional self-presentation as a policy *implementation*, not policy-*making* body.

13. Even before her husband's death, Deng had been forced to develop some of these survival skills. Because her husband refused to work and his mother and sisters subsequently evicted them from the family home, Deng had assumed responsibility for the couple's livelihood, even working without a permit in order to support them.

14. Deng described the following requirements: to register her temporary household residence with the local police station every three months, to extend her visa every three months, and to leave the country every six months, only to battle with the PRC bureaucracy to complete the paperwork necessary to return to Taiwan.

15. In other words, figures of failed immigrant intimacy are controversial in part because they underscore how national families have yet to resolve long-standing patriarchal tensions and class-specific models of family reproduction and social citizenship based on the male breadwinner and female caregiver/dependent.

16. Featured prominently in the NIA's press release that day were the revisions to Article 34 of the "Permit Regulations for Kin-Based, Extended, or Permanent Residence of People of the Mainland Area in the Taiwan Area." These revisions allowed childless Chinese spouses who had been widowed after reaching the extended residence stage to apply for citizenship after five years of extended residency if they had met other requirements (such as remaining unmarried).

17. Only after these opening statements did the woman proceed to what appeared to be the heart of her complaint: being denied a job as a building security guard, ostensibly because she was from the mainland.

18. These challenges came from diverse constituencies, including Taiwanese nationalists who promoted independence from China (Lynch 2004) and Taiwanese stem cell scientists in search of uniquely Taiwanese (as opposed to Chinese) genes (Liu 2010).

19. Surprisingly, here he adopts a mainland government slogan for the relationship between Taiwan and China, one that is rarely used or endorsed by Taiwanese officials.

20. Moreover, in contrast to their foreign counterparts, Chinese spouses produced racially Chinese Taiwanese children, assuaging anxieties in some quarters of Taiwanese society about the future dilution of Taiwan's population through the birth of mixed-race children.

21. As I discuss in chapter 5, the policies that granted benefits to Chinese spouses who had children with their Taiwanese partners applied equally to mothers and fathers.

22. Tao's relationship with her husband did improve over time, and, as she hoped, his bond with his daughter also strengthened their marriage. Conflicts continued, nonetheless, and some of their fights ended in violence. When I last saw Tao in the summer of 2013, she recounted for me an incident that had occurred a few months prior, when she fled to a friend's house with her daughter after her husband hit her in a fit of anger.

23. Other policies did a similar kind of work—for instance, by specifying the place and length of residence for a child of divorced cross-Strait parents and by identifying what features authenticated a marriage in the absence of children.

CHAPTER FIVE

1. Policy reforms that took effect in August 2009 granted Chinese spouses residency status and work rights shortly after arrival.

2. By identifying the three women exclusively through their Taiwanese family roles, the film ignores their diverse places of origin in China: Guizhou, Heilongjiang, and Fujian.

3. Through her research with Chinese women engaged in undocumented work, Antonia Chao shows how female immigrants gain entry to and become eligible for citizenship in Taiwan because of their status as wives of Taiwanese (2010, 166–67). As emphasized by NIA interviewers at the border, however, these rights are tied to traditional gender roles and conventional expectations for maternal and wifely behaviors, standards that are contested by many Taiwanese women today, not to mention by their Chinese counterparts.

4. For instance, I had met one of the women featured in the film and knew that her husband's adult daughter from a previous marriage lived with them. The film showed only the woman's young son, her husband, and her mother-in-law, completely erasing the stepdaughter's presence in the household. This erasure also drew attention away from the couple's eleven-year age difference. Moreover, this woman had four sisters and two female cousins who had married Taiwanese men, providing her with a web of natal ties that she maintained across Taiwan.

5. European debates about immigration (and especially immigration from Muslim-majority countries) depict gender equality and sexual freedom as core liberal democratic values essential to Europeaness itself, whether in the form of French secularism (laicité) or German postwar disavowal of Nazi racism (Chin 2010; Cole 2014; Fernando 2013).

6. These gendered etiquette expectations were also reinforced by the training class, which sought to educate Chinese spouses in Taiwanese social norms. During the lecture on communication skills, the instructor emphasized that when speaking with others, women should smile slightly, incline their bodies forward at an angle to demonstrate respect, and speak slowly and softly, with less emphasis on the harsh fourth tone (October 9, 2007).

7. I met many Taiwanese wives in cross-Strait marriages through a website they created called "Taiwanese mothers, mainland fathers" (*Tai ma, lu ba*).

8. Chinese women working in Taiwan's sex industry expressed a similar appreciation for men's affective skills, especially when they led to greater financial support. Chao quotes extensively from an informant who came to Taiwan via a "sham" marriage, having divorced her mainland husband, and entered the sex industry to

support children she had left behind. During a gathering in northern Fujian with her "ex-husband" and several of his male friends, the woman confided in Chao, switching to Taiwanese dialect, "To be honest, big sister, our Taiwanese men [referring to her clients] are more considerate, gentler, and have more appeal [than mainland men]" (2010, 186).

9. The forty-seven women in my interview sample who fit this profile by and large had educational and work experiences outside the home prior to moving to Taiwan, and some boasted of successful professional careers.

10. Prior to August 2009, Chinese spouses had to meet one of seven conditions to qualify for a work permit at the first residency stage (which they were eligible for after two years of marriage or birth of a child). Most of these conditions emphasized the Taiwan spouse's marginalized status (elderly, disabled, low income). In spring 2008, the government added birth of a child (proof, in their eyes, of marital authenticity) as an additional qualifying condition.

11. Lu describes how Chinese spouses themselves recognize that this forceful speaking style might undermine their efforts to demand greater rights. She quotes one activist who justified replacing a forceful speaker at a public hearing with a less confrontational woman as follows: "We don't want to project an image of mainland spouses as strong and hysterical" (2011, 128).

12. As a Veterans Affairs officer explained to me, even when couples live separately because the elderly husband has been hospitalized or moved to a nursing home, the Chinese wife "must show that she has continued to care for her husband. [She must] visit him often, on her own initiative, [to show] definitively that she is caring for this 'uncle' (*beibei*)" (interview with author in Taipei, Taiwan, on September 28, 2007). Similarly, a high-level NIA bureaucrat proclaimed at a December 7, 2007 meeting with social workers, lawyers, and NGO representatives that cases in which the citizen-husband is in a nursing home and the Chinese wife works elsewhere as a health aide are viewed with suspicion because the NIA expects the wife to take care of her own husband. This kind of arrangement, the bureaucrat continued, raises red flags when the Chinese spouse applies for citizenship.

13. Middle-aged Chinese women often justified their choice of an elderly man as a marriage partner by describing such men as safe and uncomplicated, a reference both to their husband's diminished sexual demands and simple daily life needs. See also Chao (2008).

14. In an uxorilocal marriage, a husband married into his wife's family, as symbolized by his taking her surname and/or giving her surname to some or all of their children. In traditional Chinese society, only a man who lacked the resources to "marry in" a wife would agree to such an undesirable arrangement, for it often prevented him from fulfilling his duty to continue his own patriline. See Charsley (2005) for a comparative discussion of how the rhetoric of uxorilocal marriage is used in British-Pakistani communities to describe a migrant husband's disempowerment.

15. Interview with author, Taipei, Taiwan, June 30, 2005.

16. Interview with author, Shanghai, China, July 18, 2009.

17. Tape-recorded interview with the author, Taipei, Taiwan, June 11, 2009.

CHAPTER SIX

1. As our friendship deepened, Xiao Hong and I met for meals or afternoon tea when she could spare the time away from caring for her husband. We attended outings together and socialized at my home and during gatherings with other Chinese spouses. Despite the public nature of these settings, Xiao Hong frequently turned to me to discuss her anxieties about the future, and we often found ourselves conversing in hushed tones as activity swirled around us. I never met Xiao Hong's husband or any of his adult children, although she talked about them often. I did spend time with her daughter when she visited Taiwan.

2. Xiao Hong had only recently become eligible for Taiwanese citizenship because her frequent visits back to China to see her daughter had prevented her from meeting the physical presence standards that required her to spend 183 days per year in Taiwan.

3. As the wife of a retired civil servant, Xiao Hong was entitled to half of her husband's pension upon his death. But because she was not his first wife, she could only claim the benefit if his children approved. In other words, the obstacle was not her former status as a mainland Chinese but rather her standing as his second wife. Xiao Hong's portion was reduced even more because her husband had already taken a lump sum payment from his pension.

4. Taiwanese law requires the husband's signature for a married woman to get an abortion. Her husband's refusal to sign meant that Wang Fei would have to return to China to obtain an abortion.

5. The policeman who completed the paperwork Wang needed happened to be one of the two officers who had responded to Wang's call that day. He questioned Wang gently about her relationship with her husband before turning to me and commenting that the power of the guarantor (in this case, Wang's husband) was even greater than that of the police. But the guarantor system was necessary, he added, because of the growing number of mainland "brides" who ran away if their marriages were not compatible. He clearly meant this statement for Wang's ears, and as we stood to leave, he urged her not to tell her husband what she had done. Wang later interpreted his repeated urgings as a sign that the officer had recognized her husband's abnormal mental state and feared his possible violent response.

6. Despite increasing divorce rates across China (Davis and Friedman 2014), Wang Fei's comment attests to the stigma attached to divorce in some rural communities.

7. On November 11, 2010, I received a one-line email from Wang in which she asked me whether I planned to visit Taiwan anytime soon. "I might go to Taiwan early next year," she added. "Now I'm back home in Henan." Intrigued, I replied im-

mediately, asking Wang how she would return to Taiwan. Although I waited patiently for a reply, none came.

8. In Mandarin, the eighth of August (*ba yue ba hao*) is a homonym for "father" (*baba*). Therefore, Father's Day in Taiwan falls on August 8.

9. The quota at this final stage of permanent residence (the equivalent of citizenship) was not eliminated until January 2009. Li's wait of five months was minor compared to that of other women I knew whose citizenship applications were not approved for upward of a year.

10. This sense of confinement resembles the "territorially and politically referenced feeling of stunted temporality" that Navaro-Yashin (2012, 7) found among residents of northern Cyprus in the aftermath of partition with the south.

11. Zhang Zhen's experiences were unusual in that she first visited Taiwan in the mid-1990s as a member of a performing arts troupe. She was long divorced by this point, with two small children in China. An uncle who had fled to Taiwan with the Nationalists offered to introduce her to prospective husbands. Zhang, therefore, had the luxury of meeting several potential suitors and seeing their family and living environments firsthand before deciding which one to marry. Her husband was twenty years her senior and the poorest of the lot, Zhang admitted, but he had never married and had no children, which greatly reduced her household responsibilities and enhanced his appreciation for her company and care.

12. As I discussed in chapter 4, immigration policies barred from Deng Lifang from remarrying if she wanted to maintain her eligibility for citizenship after her husband's death. Similarly, Chinese spouses could not own property in their own name prior to becoming a citizen.

EPILOGUE

1. The election results were also a sign of growing dissatisfaction with Nationalist Party rule and Taiwan's ongoing economic decline (*The Economist* 2014).

REFERENCES

Adrian, Bonnie. 2003. *Framing the Bride: Globalizing Beauty and Romance in Taiwan's Bridal Industry*. Berkeley: University of California Press.

Agamben, Giorgio. 1998. *Homo Sacer: Sovereign Power and Bare Life*. Translated by Daniel Heller-Roazen. Stanford, CA: Stanford University Press.

———. 2005. *State of Exception*. Translated by Kevin Attell. Chicago: University of Chicago Press.

Ahmed, Sara. 2002. "This Other and Other Others." *Economy and Society* 31 (4): 558–72.

Anderson, Bridget. 2013. *Us and Them? The Dangerous Politics of Immigration Control*. Oxford: Oxford University Press.

Anderson, Bridget, Nandita Sharma, and Cynthia Wright. 2009. "Editorial: Why No Borders?" *Refuge* 26 (2): 5–18.

Arextaga, Begoña. 1997. *Shattering Silence: Women, Nationalism, and Political Subjectivity in Northern Ireland*. Princeton, NJ: Princeton University Press.

Balibar, Etienne. 1991. "Racism and Nationalism." In *Race, Nation, Class: Ambiguous Identities*, edited by Etienne Balibar and Immanuel Wallerstein, 37–67. London: Verso.

Beck-Gernsheim, Elisabeth. 2007. "Transnational Lives, Transnational Marriages: A Review of the Evidence from Migrant Communities in Europe." *Global Networks* 7 (3): 271–88.

Benhabib, Seyla. 2002. "Transformations of Citizenship: The Case of Contemporary Europe." *Government and Opposition* 37 (4): 439–65.

Bhabha, Jacqueline. 2009. "The 'Mere Fortuity of Birth'? Children, Mothers, Borders, and the Meaning of Citizenship." In *Migrations and Mobilities: Citizenship, Borders, and Gender*, edited by Seyla Benhabib and Judith Resnik, 187–227. New York: New York University Press.

Bodin, Jean. 1992. *On Sovereignty*. Edited and translated by Julian H. Franklin. Cambridge: Cambridge University Press.

Brown, Wendy. 2010. *Walled States, Waning Sovereignty*. New York: Zone Books.

Bruner, Jerome. 1986. *Actual Minds, Possible Worlds*. Cambridge, MA: Harvard University Press.

Cai, Hui-zhen. 2008. "Fan Yun zhiyi Xie, shun kou liu cun qishi" (Fan Yun challenges Hsieh, jingle is rife with discrimination). *Zhongguo Shibao* (China Times), March 11, p. A6.

Calavita, Kitty. 1992. *Inside the State: The Bracero Program, Immigration, and the I.N.S.* New York: Routledge.

Canaday, Margot. 2009. *The Straight State: Sexuality and Citizenship in Twentieth-Century America*. Princeton, NJ: Princeton University Press.

Caplan, Jane, and John Torpey. 2001. "Introduction." In *Documenting Individual Identity: The Development of State Practices in the Modern World*, edited by Jane Caplan and John Torpey, 1–12. Princeton, NJ: Princeton University Press.

Chang, Mau-kuei. 2000. "On the Origins and Transformation of Taiwanese National Identity." *China Perspectives* 28 (March–April): 51–70.

Chao, Yen-ning. 2004a. "Gongmin shenfen, xiandai guojia yu qinmi shenghuo: yi lao danshen rongmin yu 'dalu xinniang' de hunyin wei yanjiu anli" (Citizenship status, the modern nation and intimate life: a case study of marriages between veterans and mainland brides). *Taiwan Shehuixue* (Taiwanese Sociology) 8: 1–41.

———. 2004b. "Xiandaixing xiangxiang yu guojing guanli de chongtu: yi Zhongguo hunyin yimin nüxing wei yanjiu anli" (Imagined modernities, transnational migration, and border control: a case study of Taiwan's 'mainland brides'). *Taiwan Shehuixue Kan* (The Taiwanese Journal of Sociology) 32: 59–102.

———. 2006. "Qinggan zhengzhi yu ling lei zhengyi: zai Tai dalu pei'ou de shehui yundong jingyan" (Politics of sentiments and alternative social justice: how mainland spouses have engaged in social movements in Taiwan). *Zhengzhi yu Shehui Zhexue Pinglun* (Societas: A Journal for Philosophical Study of Public Affairs) 16: 87–152.

———. 2008. "Qinmi guanxi zuowei fansi guozu zhuyi de changyu: lao rongmin de liang an hunyin chongtu" (Rethinking nationalism through intimate relationships: conflicts in cross-Strait marriages). *Taiwan Shehuixue* (Taiwanese Sociology) 16: 97–148.

———. 2010. "Kuajing muzhi gongmin shenfen: bianqian zhong de Zhongguo minbei guojing bianqu daode jingji" (Transnational maternal citizenship: changing moral economy on state margins). *Taiwan Shehuixue Kan* (Taiwanese Journal of Sociology) 44:155–212.

Charsley, Katharine. 2005. "Unhappy Husbands: Masculinity and Migration in Transnational Pakistani Marriages." *Journal of the Royal Anthropological Institute* 11 (1): 85–105.

Chen, Chao-ju. 2009. "Gendered Borders: The Historical Formation of Women's Nationality under Law in Taiwan." *Positions* 17 (2): 289–314.

Chen, Chieh-jen. 2008. *Empire's Borders I* (*Diguo bianjie yi*). Video art production. Taipei, Taiwan.

Chen, Yi. 2010. "Zaoshou hunyin baoli nüxing dalu pei'ou de qiuzhu kunjing yu shengcun zhi dao" (Help-seeking predicaments and paths to survival for female mainland spouses who suffer marital violence). (Master's thesis, Department of Social Welfare, National Chung Cheng University, Taiwan.)

Chin, Rita. 2010. "Turkish Women, West German Feminists, and the Gendered Discourse on Muslim Cultural Difference." *Public Culture* 22 (3): 557–81.

Chock, Phyllis Pease. 1991. "'Illegal Aliens' and 'Opportunity': Myth-Making in Congressional Testimony." *American Ethnologist* 18 (2): 279–94.

Chu, Julie Y. 2010. *Cosmologies of Credit: Transnational Mobility and the Politics of Destination in China.* Durham, NC: Duke University Press.

Chun, Allen. 1996. "Fuck Chineseness: On the Ambiguities of Ethnicity as Culture as Identity." *Boundary 2* 23 (2): 111–38.

Chung, Jake. 2012. "NIA Cracks Human Trafficking Group." *Taipei Times*, July 12, p. 3.

Clark, Constance D. 2001. "Foreign Marriage, 'Tradition,' and the Politics of Border Crossings." In *China Urban: Ethnographies of Contemporary Culture*, edited by Nancy N. Chen, Constance D. Clark, Suzanne Z. Gottschang, and Lyn Jeffery, 104–22. Durham, NC: Duke University Press.

Cohen, Elizabeth F. 2009. *Semi-Citizenship in Democratic Politics.* Cambridge: Cambridge University Press.

———. 2010. "*Jus Tempus* in the Magna Carta: The Sovereignty of Time in Modern Politics and Citizenship." *PS: Political Science and Politics* 43 (3): 463–66.

———. 2011. "Reconsidering U.S. Immigration Reform: The Temporal Principle of Citizenship." *Perspectives on Politics* 9 (3): 575–83.

Cole, Jennifer. 2014. "Working Mis/understandings: The Tangled Relationship between Kinship, Franco-Malagasy Binational Marriages, and the French State." *Cultural Anthropology* 29 (3): 527–51.

Constable, Nicole. 2003a. *Romance on a Global Stage: Pen Pals, Virtual Ethnography, and 'Mail Order' Marriages.* Berkeley: University of California Press.

———. 2003b. "A Transnational Perspective on Divorce and Marriage: Filipina Wives and Workers." *Identities: Global Studies in Culture and Power* 10 (2): 163–80.

———. 2005. "Introduction: Cross-Border Marriages, Gendered Mobility, and Global Hypergamy." In *Cross-Border Marriages: Gender and Mobility in Transnational Asia*, edited by Nicole Constable, 1–16. Philadelphia: University of Pennsylvania Press.

———. 2007. *Maid to Order in Hong Kong: Stories of Migrant Workers,* 2nd ed. Ithaca, NY: Cornell University Press.

Coutin, Susan Bibler. 2000. *Legalizing Moves: Salvadoran Immigrants' Struggle for U.S. Residency.* Ann Arbor: University of Michigan Press.

———. 2001. "The Oppressed, the Suspect, and the Citizen: Subjectivity in Competing Accounts of Political Violence." *Law and Social Inquiry* 26 (1): 63–94.

———. 2007. *Nations of Emigrants: Shifting Boundaries of Citizenship in El Salvador and the United States.* Ithaca, NY: Cornell University Press.

Das, Veena. 2004. "The Signature of the State: The Paradox of Illegibility." In *Anthropology in the Margins of the State*, edited by Veena Das and Deborah Poole, 225–52. Santa Fe, NM: School of American Research Press.

Das, Veena, and Deborah Poole. 2004. "State and Its Margins: Comparative Ethnographies." In *Anthropology in the Margins of the State*, edited by Veena Das and Deborah Poole, 3–33. Santa Fe, NM: School of American Research Press.

Dauvergne, Catherine. 2009. "Globalizing Fragmentation: New Pressures on Women Caught in the Immigration Law-Citizenship Law Dichotomy." In *Migrations and Mobilities: Citizenship, Borders, and Gender*, edited by Seyla Benhabib and Judith Resnik, 333–55. New York: New York University Press.

Davis, Deborah S., and Sara L. Friedman. 2014. "Deinstitutionalizing Marriage and Sexuality." In *Wives, Husbands, and Lovers: Marriage and Sexuality in Hong Kong, Taiwan, and Urban China*, edited by Deborah S. Davis and Sara L. Friedman, 1–39. Stanford, CA: Stanford University Press.

Diamant, Neil J., Stanley B. Lubman, and Kevin J. O'Brien. 2005. "Law and Society in the People's Republic of China." In *Engaging the Law in China: State, Society, and Possibilities for Justice*, edited by Neil J. Diamant, Stanley B. Lubman, and Kevin J. O'Brien, 3–27. Stanford, CA: Stanford University Press.

Disch, Lisa. 2003. "Review of *Being Political: Genealogies of Citizenship*." *Environment and Planning D: Society and Space* 21: 380–82.

Dunn, Elizabeth Cullen, and Jason Cons. 2013. "Aleatory Sovereignty and the Rule of Sensitive Spaces." *Antipode*: 1–18.

Economist, The. 2014. "Losing Hearts and Minds: Hong Kong and Taiwan." December 6. www.economist.com/news/china/21635515-dissatisfaction-china-hong-kong-and-taiwan-shows-up-streets-and-polls.

Edelman, Lee. 2004. *No Future: Queer Theory and the Death Drive*. Durham, NC: Duke University Press.

Evans, Harriet. 1997. *Women and Sexuality in China: Female Sexuality and Gender since 1949*. New York: Continuum.

Faier, Lieba. 2009. *Intimate Encounters: Filipina Women and the Remaking of Rural Japan*. Berkeley: University of California Press.

Farrer, James. 2002. *Opening Up: Youth Sex Culture and Market Reform in Shanghai*. Chicago: University of Chicago Press.

Feldman, Ilana. 2006. "Home as a Refrain: Remembering and Living Displacement in Gaza." *History and Memory* 18 (2): 10–47.

Fernando, Mayanthi L. 2013. "Save the Muslim Woman, Save the Republic: Ni Putes Ni Soumises and the Ruse of Neoliberal Sovereignty." *Modern and Contemporary France* 21 (2): 147–65.

Fitzpatrick, Peter. 1992. *The Mythology of Modern Law*. London: Routledge.

Freeman, Caren. 2011. *Making and Faking Kinship: Marriage and Labor Migration between China and South Korea*. Ithaca, NY: Cornell University Press.

Friedman, Sara L. 2006. *Intimate Politics: Marriage, the Market, and State Power in Southeastern China*. Cambridge, MA: Harvard University Asia Center, Harvard University Press.

———. 2010a. "Determining 'Truth' at the Border: Immigration Interviews, Chinese Marital Migrants, and Taiwan's Sovereignty Dilemmas." *Citizenship Studies* 14 (2): 167–83.

———. 2010b. "Marital Immigration and Graduated Citizenship: Post-Naturalization Restrictions on Mainland Chinese Spouses in Taiwan." *Pacific Affairs* 83 (1): 73–93.

———. 2012. "Adjudicating the Intersection of Marital Immigration, Domestic Violence, and Spousal Murder: China-Taiwan Marriages and Competing Legal Domains." *Indiana Journal of Global Legal Studies* 19 (1): 221–55.

———. 2013. "Men Who 'Marry Out': Cross-Strait Marriages and the New Faces of Chinese Patriarchy." Paper presented at the conference, Is Chinese Patriarchy Over? The Decline and Transformation of a System of Social Support. Max Planck Institute for Social Anthropology, Halle, Germany, June 26–29.

———. 2015. "Regulating Cross-Border Intimacy: Authenticity Paradigms and the Specter of Illegality among Chinese Marital Immigrants to Taiwan." In *Migrant Encounters: Intimate Labor, the State, and Mobility across Asia*, edited by Sara L. Friedman and Pardis Mahdavi, 206–29. Philadelphia: University of Pennsylvania Press.

Gao, Xiaoxian. 1994. "China's Modernization and Changes in the Social Status of Rural Women." In *Engendering China: Women, Culture, and the State*, edited by Christina K. Gilmartin, Gail Hershatter, Lisa Rofel, and Tyrene White, 80–97. Cambridge, MA: Harvard University Press.

Gardner, Martha. 2005. *The Qualities of a Citizen: Women, Immigration, and Citizenship, 1870–1965*. Princeton, NJ: Princeton University Press.

Gershon, Ilana. 2011. "Critical Review Essay: Studying Cultural Pluralism in Courts versus Legislatures." *PoLAR: Political and Legal Anthropology Review* 34 (1): 155–74.

Glick Schiller, Nina, Linda Basch, and Cristina Szanton Blanc. 1995. "From Immigrant to Transmigrant: Theorizing Transnational Migration." *Anthropological Quarterly* 68 (1): 48–63.

Gordillo, Gastón. 2006. "The Crucible of Citizenship: ID-paper Fetishism in the Argentinean Chaco." *American Ethnologist* 33 (2): 162–76.

Graham, Mark. 2002. "Emotional Bureaucracies: Emotions, Civil Servants, and Immigrants in the Swedish Welfare State." *Ethnos* 30 (3): 199–226.

Greenhalgh, Susan. 1993. "The Peasantization of the One-Child Policy in Shaanxi." In *Chinese Families in the Post-Mao Era*, edited by Deborah Davis and Stevan Harrell, 219–50. Berkeley: University of California Press.

———. 2012. "Patriarchal Demographics? China's Sex Ratio Reconsidered." *Population and Development Review* 38 (Supplement): 130–49.

Greenhalgh, Susan, and Jiali Li. 1995. "Engendering Reproductive Policy and Practice in Peasant China: For a Feminist Demography of Reproduction." *Signs: Journal of Women in Culture and Society* 20 (3): 601–41.

Greenhalgh, Susan, and Edwin A. Winckler. 2005. *Governing China's Population: From Leninist to Neoliberal Biopolitics*. Stanford, CA: Stanford University Press.

Greenhouse, Carol J. 2002. "Citizenship, Agency, and the Dream of Time." In *Looking Back at Law's Century*, edited by Austin Sarat, Bryant Garth, and Robert A. Kagan, 184–209. Ithaca, NY: Cornell University Press.

Gupta, Akhil. 2012. *Red Tape: Bureaucracy, Structural Violence, and Poverty in India*. Durham, NC: Duke University Press.

Hall, Stuart. 1993. "Culture, Community, Nation." *Cultural Studies* 7 (3): 349–63.

Hansen, Darah. 2010. "Furor in Taiwan after Woman Abruptly Turned Back from YVR: Ottawa, Taipei Officials Wade in to Discuss Incident with Airport Border Security Agents." *Vancouver Sun*, March 19.

Herzfeld, Michael. 1992. *The Social Production of Indifference: Exploring the Symbolic Roots of Western Bureaucracy*. Chicago: University of Chicago Press.

Hetherington, Kregg. 2011. *Guerilla Auditors: The Politics of Transparency in Neoliberal Paraguay*. Durham, NC: Duke University Press.

Heyman, Josiah McC. 2002. "U.S. Immigration Officers of Mexican Ancestry as Mexican Americans, Citizens, and Immigration Police." *Current Anthropology* 43 (3): 479–507.

Ho, Petula Sik Ying. 2014. "An Embarrassment of Riches: Good Men Behaving Badly in Hong Kong." In *Wives, Husbands, and Lovers: Marriage and Sexuality in Hong Kong, Taiwan, and Urban China*, edited by Deborah S. Davis and Sara L. Friedman, 165–88. Stanford, CA: Stanford University Press.

Honig, Emily, and Gail Hershatter. 1988. *Personal Voices: Chinese Women in the 1980's*. Stanford, CA: Stanford University Press.

Hsia, Hsiao-chuan, ed. 2005. *Bu yao jiao wo waiji xinniang* (Don't call me foreign bride). Taipei: Zuo An Wenhua.

———. 2008. "The Development of Immigrant Movement in Taiwan: The Case of Alliance of Human Rights Legislation for Immigrants and Migrants." *Development and Society* 37 (2): 187–217.

———. 2015. "Reproduction Crisis, Illegality, and Migrant Women under Capitalist Globalization: The Case of Taiwan." In *Migrant Encounters: Intimate Labor, the State, and Mobility across Asia*, edited by Sara L. Friedman and Pardis Mahdavi, 160–83. Philadelphia: University of Pennsylvania Press.

Hsieh, Frank C. T. 2008. "Jia jiehun anjian duoshu laizi Zhongguo, bing fei dalu pei'ou you qi cheng shi jia jiehun" (The majority of sham marriage cases come from China, not 70% of mainland spouses are in sham marriages). *Chang Zai Buluo Cheng* (Hsieh's Blog), March 11. http://blog.udn.com/FrankCTHsieh /1686541.

Hull, Matthew S. 2012. "Documents and Bureaucracy." *Annual Review of Anthropology* 41: 251–67.

Hung, Eva P. W., and Stephen W. K. Chiu. 2003. "The Lost Generation: Life Course Dynamics and Xiagang in China." *Modern China* 29 (2): 204–36.

Illouz, Eva. 2007. *Cold Intimacies: The Making of Emotional Capitalism*. Cambridge, UK: Polity Press.

Isin, Engin F. 2002. *Being Political: Genealogies of Citizenship*. Minneapolis: University of Minnesota Press.

Jacka, Tamara. 2006. *Rural Women in Urban China: Gender, Migration, and Social Change*. Armonk, NY: M. E. Sharpe.

Kaiman, Jonathan. 2014. "Taiwan Premier Resigns after Election Deals Blow to Pro-China Party." *The Guardian*, November 30. www.theguardian.com/world/2014/nov/30/china-urges-taiwan-close-ties-pro-beijing-party-routed-polls.

Kim, Hyun Mee. 2007. "The State and Migrant Women: Diverging Hopes in the Making of Multicultural Families in Contemporary Korea." *Korea Journal* 47 (4): 100–22.

Kim, Minjeong. 2010. "Gender and International Marriage Migration." *Sociology Compass* 4 (9): 718–31.

Kuo, Grace Shu-chin. 2014. "The Alternative Futures of Marriage: A Sociolegal Analysis of Family Law Reform in Taiwan." In *Wives, Husbands, and Lovers: Marriage and Sexuality in Hong Kong, Taiwan, and Urban China*, edited by Deborah S. Davis and Sara L. Friedman, 219–38. Stanford, CA: Stanford University Press.

Lan, Pei-Chia. 2006. *Global Cinderellas: Migrant Domestics and Newly Rich Employers in Taiwan*. Durham, NC: Duke University Press.

———. 2008. "Migrant Women's Bodies as Boundary Markers: Reproductive Crisis and Sexual Control in the Ethnic Frontiers of Taiwan." *Signs: Journal of Women in Culture and Society* 33 (4): 833–61.

Lazarus-Black, Mindie. 2003. "The (Heterosexual) Regendering of a Modern State: Criminalizing and Implementing Domestic Violence Law in Trinidad." *Law and Social Inquiry* 28 (4): 980–1008.

Liao, Yuan-hao. 2007. "Shiyongshi de Taiwan ren? Chengren cideng gongmin de shi zi 618 hao jieshi" (Probationary Taiwanese? Judicial ruling 618 acknowledges second-class citizens). *Quanguo Lüshi* (Taiwan Bar Journal) 5: 27–37.

Lin, Sheng-wei. 2003. "Cong 'zhanshi' dao 'rongmin': guojia de zhidu jiangou yu renkou leishu de xingsu, 1949–1970" (From "soldier" to "veteran": state institution-building and the formation of demographic categories in Taiwan, 1949–1970). *Taiwan Shehui Yanjiu Jikan* (Taiwan: A Radical Quarterly in Social Studies) 52 (December): 187–254.

Liu, Jennifer A. 2010. "Making Taiwanese (Stem Cells): Identity, Genetics, and Hybridity." In *Asian Biotech: Ethics and Communities of Fate*, edited by Aihwa Ong and Nancy N. Chen, 239–62. Durham, NC: Duke University Press.

Long, Lynellyn D. 2004. "Viet Kieu on a Fast Track Back?" In *Coming Home? Refugees, Migrants, and Those Who Stayed Behind*, edited by Lynellyn D. Long and Ellen Oxfeld, 65–89. Philadelphia: University of Pennsylvania Press.

Lu, Melody Chia-Wen. 2011. "Strategies of Alliance among Cross-Border Families and Chinese Marriage Immigrants." In *Politics of Difference in Taiwan*, edited by Tak-Wing Ngo and Hong-zen Wang, 116–33. New York: Routledge.

Luibhéid, Eithne. 2002. *Entry Denied: Controlling Sexuality at the Border*. Minneapolis: University of Minnesota Press.

———. 2013. *Pregnant on Arrival: Making the Illegal Immigrant*. Minneapolis: University of Minnesota Press.

Lynch, Daniel C. 2004. "Taiwan's Self-Conscious Nation-Building Project." *Asian Survey* 44 (4): 513–33.

Mazzarella, William. 2010. "Affect: What Is It Good For?" In *Enchantments of Modernity: Empire, Nation, Globalization*, edited by Saurabh Dube, 291–309. London: Routledge.

McKeown, Adam M. 2008. *Melancholy Order: Asian Migration and the Globalization of Borders*. New York: Columbia University Press.

Mongia, Radhika Viyas. 1999. "Race, Nationality, Mobility: A History of the Passport." *Public Culture* 11 (3): 527–56.

Munn, Nancy D. 1992. "The Cultural Anthropology of Time: A Critical Essay." *Annual Review of Anthropology* 21: 93–123.

Navaro-Yashin, Yael. 2003. "Legal/Illegal Counterpoints: Subjecthood and Subjectivity in an Unrecognized State." In *Human Rights in Global Perspective: Anthropological Studies of Rights, Claims and Entitlements*, edited by Richard Ashby Wilson and Jon P. Mitchell, 71–92. London: Routledge.

———. 2006. "Affect in the Civil Service: A Study of a Modern State-System." *Postcolonial Studies* 9 (3): 281–94.

———. 2007. "Make-Believe Papers, Legal Forms and the Counterfeit: Affective Interactions between Documents and People in Britain and Cyprus." *Anthropological Theory* 7 (1): 79–98.

———. 2012. *The Make-Believe Space: Affective Geography in a Postwar Polity*. Durham, NC: Duke University Press.

Neveu Kringelbach, Hélène. 2013. "'Mixed Marriage,' Citizenship and the Policing of Intimacy in Contemporary France." International Migration Institute Working Papers Series, Paper 77. www.imi.ox.ac.uk/publications/wp-77-13.

Newendorp, Nicole DeJong. 2008. *Uneasy Reunions: Immigration, Citizenship, and Family Life in Post-1997 Hong Kong*. Stanford, CA: Stanford University Press.

Nyers, Peter. 2008. "No One Is Illegal between City and Nation." In *Acts of Citizenship*, edited by Engin F. Isin and Greg M. Nielsen, 160–81. London: Zed Books.

Ong, Aihwa. 1999. *Flexible Citizenship: The Cultural Logics of Transnationality*. Durham, NC: Duke University Press.

———. 2000. "Graduated Sovereignty in South-East Asia." *Theory, Culture and Society* 17 (4): 55–75.

———. 2003. *Buddha Is Hiding: Refugees, Citizenship, and the New America*. Berkeley: University of California Press.

———. 2006. *Neoliberalism as Exception: Mutations in Citizenship and Sovereignty*. Durham, NC: Duke University Press.

———. 2009. "A Bio-Cartography: Maids, Neo-Slavery, and NGOs." In *Migrations and Mobilities: Citizenship, Borders, and Gender*, edited by Seyla Benhabib and Judith Resnik, 157–84. New York: New York University Press.

Oswin, Natalie. 2012. "The Queer Time of Creative Urbanism: Family, Futurity, and the Global City Singapore." *Environment and Planning A* 44: 1624–40.

Parreñas, Rhacel Salazar. 2008. *The Force of Domesticity: Filipina Migrants and Globalization*. New York: New York University Press.

Partridge, Damani J. 2012. *Hypersexuality and Headscarves: Race, Sex, and Citizenship in the New Germany*. Bloomington: Indiana University Press.

Pine, Frances. 2014. "Migration as Hope: Space, Time, and Imagining the Future." *Current Anthropology* 55 (S9): S95–S104.

Povinelli, Elizabeth A. 2002. "Notes on Gridlock: Genealogy, Intimacy, Sexuality." *Public Culture* 14 (1): 215–38.

Pratt, Geraldine. 2012. *Families Apart: Migrant Mothers and the Conflicts of Labor and Love.* Minneapolis: University of Minnesota Press.

PRC Ministry of Civil Affairs (Zhonghua Renmin Gongheguo Minzheng Bu), ed. 1989–2008. *Zhongguo minzheng tongji nianjian* (China civil affairs statistical yearbook). Beijing: China Statistics Press.

———, ed. 2007. *Liang an hunyin zhengce zhinan* (A guide to cross-Strait marriage policies). Beijing: Ministry of Civil Affairs.

Qiu, Pei-fen. 2010. "Guanggao zhenshiban: Jia haiguan diaonan Tai fu, waijiaobu tao gongdao" (Reality advertising: Canadian border officials create difficulties for Taiwanese woman, the Ministry of Foreign Affairs demands justice). *Zhongguo Shibao* (China Times), March 17.

Rigger, Shelley. 2002. "Nationalism versus Citizenship in the Republic of China on Taiwan." In *Changing Meanings of Citizenship in Modern China,* edited by Merle Goldman and Elizabeth J. Perry, 353–72. Cambridge, MA: Harvard University Press.

Riles, Annelise. 2006. "Introduction: In Response." In *Documents: Artifacts of Modern Knowledge,* edited by Annelise Riles, 1–38. Ann Arbor: University of Michigan Press.

Rofel, Lisa. 1994. "Liberation Nostalgia and a Yearning for Modernity." In *Engendering China: Women, Culture, and the State,* edited by Christina K. Gilmartin, Gail Hershatter, Lisa Rofel, and Tyrene White, 226–49. Cambridge, MA: Harvard University Press.

Rutherford, Danilyn. 2012. *Laughing at Leviathan: Sovereignty and Audience in West Papua.* Chicago: University of Chicago Press.

Salter, Mark B. 2007. "Governmentalities of an Airport: Heterotopia and Confession." *International Political Sociology* 1 (1): 49–66.

———. 2008. "When the Exception Becomes the Rule: Borders, Sovereignty, and Citizenship." *Citizenship Studies* 12 (4): 365–80.

Schaeffer, Felicity Amaya. 2013. *Love and Empire: Cybermarriage and Citizenship across the Americas.* New York: New York University Press.

Schmitt, Carl. 1985. *Political Theology: Four Chapters on the Concept of Sovereignty.* Translated by George Schwab. Cambridge, MA: MIT Press.

Scott, James C. 1998. *Seeing Like a State: How Certain Schemes to Improve the Human Condition Have Failed.* New Haven, CT: Yale University Press.

Shah, Nayan. 2011. *Stranger Intimacy: Contesting Race, Sexuality, and the Law in the North American West.* Berkeley: University of California Press.

Shih, Shu-mei. 1998. "Gender and a New Geopolitics of Desire: The Seduction of Mainland Women in Taiwan and Hong Kong Media." *Signs: Journal of Women in Culture and Society* 23 (2): 287–319.

Shuman, Amy, and Carol Bohmer. 2004. "Representing Trauma: Political Asylum Narrative." *Journal of American Folklore* 117 (466): 394–414.

Staff Writer. 2007. "Representative Office in France Helps Detained Taiwanese Businesspeople." *Taipei Times*, September 2, p. 3. www.taipeitimes.com/News /taiwan/archives/2007/09/02/2003376882.

Stoler, Ann Laura. 2004. "Affective States." In *A Companion to the Anthropology of Politics*, edited by David Nugent and Joan Vincent, 4–20. Malden, MA: Blackwell Publishers.

Sturm, Circe. 2013. "Race, Sovereignty, and Civil Rights: Understanding the Cherokee Freedmen Controversy." *Cultural Anthropology* 29 (3): 575–98.

Sunder Rajan, Rajeswari. 2003. *The Scandal of the State: Women, Law, and Citizenship in Postcolonial India*. Durham, NC: Duke University Press.

Surkis, Judith. 2010. "Hymenal Politics: Marriage, Secularism, and French Sovereignty." *Public Culture* 22 (3): 531–56.

Suzuki, Nobue. 2000. "Between Two Shores: Transnational Projects and Filipina Wives in/from Japan." *Women's Studies International Forum* 23 (4): 431–44.

Taiwan Department of Household Registration, Ministry of the Interior (Neizhengbu Huzhengsi). 2013. "Statistics on Marriages between Nationals and Foreigners" (Wo guoren yu waiji renshi jiehun tongji). December 31. www .immigration.gov.tw/public/Attachment/412916174468.xls.

Taiwan Mainland Affairs Council (Zhonghua Minguo Xingzhengyuan Dalu Weiyuanhui), ed. 2006. *Dalu pei'ou yiju Taiwan de shenghuo zhinan*, 2nd ed. (A guide for mainland spouses to life in Taiwan). Taipei: Mainland Affairs Council.

———. 2011. *Qian shou Taiwan, xiangyue xingfu* (Hold hands with Taiwan, make a date with happiness). DVD. Taipei: Dong Ji Guandian Advertising Company.

Taiwan Ministry of the Interior (Zhonghua Minguo Neizhengbu). 2007. "Baozhang waiji pei'ou zui di shenghuo tiaojian, jushi jieran" (Guaranteeing a basic living standard for foreign spouses, it's the same around the world). *Ziyou Shibao* (Freedom Times), August 21.

Taiwan National Immigration Agency (Yiminshu) and Department of Household Registration (Huzhengsi). 2014. "Number of Foreign and Mainland Spouses in Each County and City by Documented Status, 1987–2013" (Ge xian shi waiyi, waiji pei'ou renshu yu dalu [han gang'ao] pei'ou renshu an zhengjian fen). January 29. www.immigration.gov.tw/public/Attachment/4102117131688.xls.

Ticktin, Miriam. 2006. "Where Ethics and Politics Meet: The Violence of Humanitarianism in France." *American Ethnologist* 33 (1): 33–49.

Torpey, John. 2000. *The Invention of the Passport: Surveillance, Citizenship and the State*. Cambridge: Cambridge University Press.

Toyota, Mika. 2008. "Editorial Introduction: International Marriage, Rights and the State in East and Southeast Asia." *Citizenship Studies* 12 (1): 1–7.

Tseng, Yen-fen. 2004. "Yin jin waiji lao gong de guozu zhengzhi" (Expressing nationalist politics in guestworker program: Taiwan's recruitment of foreign labor). *Taiwan Shehuixue Kan* (Taiwanese Journal of Sociology) 32: 1–58.

van Walsum, Sarah K., and Thomas Spijkerboer. 2007. "Introduction." In *Women and Immigration Law: New Variations on Classical Feminist Themes*, edited by Sarah K. van Walsum and Thomas Spijkerboer, 1–11. New York: Routledge-Cavendish.

Vincent, Joan. 1994. "On Law and Hegemonic Moments: Looking Behind the Law in Early Modern Uganda." In *Contested States: Law, Hegemony and Resistance*, edited by Mindie Lazarus-Black and Susan F. Hirsch, 118–37. New York: Routledge.

VOA Tibetan. 2012. "Indian State Police Arrests Eight Taiwanese for Visa Violation." Voice of America, June 13. www.voanews.com/tibetan-english/news/Indian -State-Police-Arrests-Eight-Taiwanese-for-Visa-Violation-158897205.html.

Wachman, Alan M. 1994. *Taiwan: National Identity and Democratization*. Armonk, NY: M. E. Sharpe.

Wang, Hong-zen, and Daniéle Bélanger. 2008. "Taiwanizing Female Immigrant Spouses and Materializing Differential Citizenship." *Citizenship Studies* 12 (1): 91–106.

Wang, Horng-luen. 2004. "Regulating Transnational Flows of People: An Institutional Analysis of Passports and Visas as a Regime of Mobility." *Identities: Global Studies in Culture and Power* 11 (3): 351–76.

Wang, Zheng. 2000. "Gender, Employment and Women's Resistance." In *Chinese Society: Change, Conflict and Resistance*, edited by Elizabeth J. Perry and Mark Selden, 62–82. London: Routledge.

Wikan, Unni. 2002. *Generous Betrayal: Politics of Culture in the New Europe*. Chicago: University of Chicago Press.

Willen, Sarah S. 2010. "Citizens, 'Real' Others, and 'Other' Others: Governmentality, Biopolitics, and the Deportation of Undocumented Migrants from Tel Aviv." In *The Deportation Regime: Sovereignty, Space, and the Freedom of Movement*, edited by Nicholas P. De Genova and Nathalie Peutz, 262–94. Durham, NC: Duke University Press.

Williams, Brackette F. 1989. "A Class Act: Anthropology and the Race to Nation across Ethnic Terrain." *Annual Review of Anthropology* 18: 401–44.

Wilson, Richard Ashby. 2007. "Tyrannosaurus Lex: The Anthropology of Human Rights and Transnational Law." In *The Practice of Human Rights: Tracking Law between the Global and the Local*, edited by Mark Goodale and Sally Engle Merry, 342–69. Cambridge: Cambridge University Press.

Yngvesson, Barbara, and Susan Bibler Coutin. 2006. "Backed by Papers: Undoing Persons, Histories, and Return." *American Ethnologist* 33 (2): 177–90.

Yu, James. 2014. "Taiwan's Perspective." *New York Times*, October 8. www.nytimes .com/2014/10/09/opinion/taiwans-perspective.html?nlid=28953414&src =recpb&_r=0.

Yue, Audrey. 2008. "Same-Sex Migration in Australia: From Interdependency to Intimacy." *GLQ* 14 (2–3): 239–62.

INDEX

Note: Page numbers in *italics* refer to illustrations.

abortion, 72, 178, 216n4

abusive situations, 113–14, 125–26, 153–54, 156, 212n9

acculturation courses, 21, 136, 138, 202n14

Act Governing Relations between the People of the Taiwan Area and the Mainland Area (1992): and Administrative Procedure Law, 88; on adoption of children, 102–3, 109–10, 124–25; and border interviews, 207n16; categories of people in, 10–11, 87–88, 92; on civil service, 209n9; on death of citizen spouse, 212n8; footnotes in, 105–6; and inflexibility of policies, 125; and public demonstrations, 208n6; revisions of, 102–3, 198n10, 210n18. *See also* financial requirement imposed on immigrants

Administrative Procedure Law, 88

Agamben, Giorgio, 15–16

age of spouses, 6, 74–75, 206n14

Ahmed, Sara, 195

Alliance for Human Rights Legislation for Immigrants and Migrants: and adoption ban, 109; causes of, 208nn7–8; on footnotes in the Act, 105–6; human rights emphasis of, 90–92, 101; opposition to financial requirement, 93–96, *96*; and proposed revisions to the Act, 102–3, 210n18

Anderson, Bridget, 209n10

appellations for Chinese spouses, 7

authenticity of transnational marriages. *See* marital authenticity

Balibar, Etienne, 20

belonging. *See* home and belonging

bigamy, 36

Bohmer, Carol, 58

border interviews: availability of transcripts from, 56; bureaucratic categories in, 66; deferring judgement in, 62–68; and evaluation of marriage authenticity, 52, 58–68, 206n12; genders of interviewers, 205n5; guidelines for, 66, 67, 76–77; international precedents for, 54; and lack of consular offices in China, 54; legal basis for, 204n3; and marital intentions, 53–58, 60–62; and marriage fraud, 59–68, 77; and motivations for marriage migration, 59; plot gaps in, 67; press coverage of abuses, 55; procedures of, 205–7nn5–20; and protests against immigration policies, 99, 100; regulation of, 55–56, 66; and sex trade concerns, 64–65; therapeutic engagement in, 68–73

borders and border control: ambiguity of, 29, 31; international standards of, 3; role of immigration policies in, 83

bureaucrats and immigration bureaucracy, 112–39; and caretaking marriage trend, 6; and childbearing, 135–38; and

bureaucrats and immigration *(continued)*
children from previous marriages,
123–25, 137–38; and discriminatory
attitudes, 44; educational DVD
produced by, 112–14, 116–18, 119; and
flexibility/inflexibility of policies,
122–27, 129, 134; future orientation of,
126–27, 128, 132, 134–35; and impartial-
ity/heartlessness of policies, 127–31; and
policy-education forums, 119–21, 138;
protectionist justifications for work
bans, 155–56; and sham marriages, 52,
53; and sovereignty claims of Taiwan, 4,
14–18, 28, 133–34, 139; symposium
hosted by, 112–15. *See also* border
interviews; Mainland Affairs Council
(MAC); marital authenticity; National
Immigration Agency (NIA)

Cai, Mr., 81–82, 131
Canada, 49
Caplan, Jane, 204n28
CARES, 112–13, 119, 124–25
caretaking marriages trend, 5–6, 62, 160,
166, 184–85
chain immigration, 102–10
Chao, Antonia, 203n21, 208n6, 214n3, 214n8
Chen Chieh-jen, 2
Chen Shui-bian, 12, 13, 96, 197n1
Chiang Kaishek, 10, 207n2
Chiayi County, Taiwan, *8*
children: adoption of, 102, 107, 108–9,
124–25, 167; and chain immigration,
102–10; childbearing and status of
mothers, 132, 135–38, 192, 198n11; and
custody after divorce, 125–26, 153–55,
162; and death of citizen spouse, 122;
and flexibility/inflexibility of policies,
122–25; and gender ideologies, 155; and
immigration laws and policies, 161; from
intermarriages, 86, 87; left in mainland
China, 102, 108–9, 113–14, 137–38, 166,
173; mixed-race children, 213n20; and
policy-education forums, 122–25; from
previous marriages, 6, 102, 103, 104,
108–9, 144, 166–67; sponsorship of,
102–6, 107, 109–10, 118, 123–24, 166;
visitor visas for, 211n30

Chin, Rita, 146
China. *See* People's Republic of China
Chinese spouses: acculturation courses for,
21, 136, 138, 202n14; ambiguous status
of, 4–5, 10, 17, 81, 133, 191; appellations
for, 7; Chinese husbands, 161–65; and
death of spouse (*see* widowhood); and
direct speech, 19, 157–58; exceptional
status of, 9–14; immigration of (*see*
border interviews; bureaucrats and
immigration bureaucracy); linguistic
differences of, 212n4; and mainlander
status, 22, 23; marriages of (*see* marital
authenticity; Taiwanese spouses);
middle-aged/older women, 156–61;
national allegiances of, 21; nonprocreative spouses, 137; and notions of home,
191; perceptions of, 19; political context
of, 81–82; prevalence of, 7–8; social
anxieties regarding, 7, 8; stereotypes and
assumptions regarding, 7, 91; term, 7;
and threat of similarity, 18–23; travel/
identity documents of (*see* documents,
travel and identity). *See also* gender and
gender ideologies
Chung Hwa Travel Service, 33, 56
citizenship in Taiwan: and childbearing,
135–38; for children (*see* children); and
death of spouse, 14, 129, 185–86;
discrepancies in path to, 9–10; and dual
citizenship, 172; and employment
opportunities, 171; and feelings of
transience, 171; and home and
belonging, 190–92; and inequitable
rights for Chinese spouses, 21; and loss
of Chinese citizenship, 172, 174, 175–76;
and marginalized groups, 200n22; and
quota system, 99, 103–4, 107, 118, 186,
199n13; and threat of similarity, 21–22
citizen spouses. *See* Taiwanese spouses
civil disobedience, 193
civil society, 89, 97
Coalition Against the Financial Requirement for Immigrants (CAFRI), 93–96,
96, 100–101
Cold War legacies, 8, 15, 20
communism, 7, 147
Constable, Nicole, 198n6, 208n4

Council of Labor Affairs, 100
courts, 35–37, 124–26, 212n8
Coutin, Susan, 67
Cross-Strait Marriage Promotion
    Association, 89–90, 94–95, 184, 212n10
Cross-Strait Service Trade Agreement, 193
cultural conventions and heritage, 59–60
Cultural Revolution, 157, 159, 169

Democratic Progressive Party, 89, 187,
    199n14
democratic society and ideals, 129
Deng Lifang: and inflexibility of policies,
    128–31; and notions of home, 170,
    190–91; and potential for remarriage,
    216n12; and pursuit of resident status,
    22, 81–82; survival skills of, 213n13; and
    thumbprints, 57; travel/identity
    documents of, 46–47
dependency model of immigration, 144,
    155, 167, 168
detachment, fears of, 171
Disch, Lisa, 200n23
diversity of cross-Strait marriages, 6
divorces: and child custody, 125–26, 153–55,
    162; and inflexibility of policies, 125–26;
    as last resort, 197n4; and potential for
    policy reforms, 128; social penalty
    following, 181–82; spouse's cooperation
    required for, 35–36, 178, 181; stigma
    attached to, 216n6; suing on basis of
    fault, 212n10
documents, travel and identity, 27–50; and
    ambiguity of border, 29; circulation
    effects of, 29, 40–43; in courtrooms,
    36–37; denial of, 42–43; and emotional
    states, 29; exceptionalism in, 35; and
    forgery concerns, 34, 39, 49; and
    fraudulent use, 49; held by in-laws,
    178–79; and international mobility,
    203n19; material insubstantiality of,
    43–44; and mobility strategies, 37–39;
    multitude of, 35, 39; as opposed to
    passports and visas, 29; and outsider
    status, 47; replacement of, 179; and
    residency permits, 44–46; role of, 30;
    and third-country travel, 41, 202n17;
    and two copies of travel documents,

33–34; and uncertain sovereignty of
    Taiwan, 31, 37, 44, 47–50. See also
    family reunification applications;
    passports
domestic abuse, 113–14, 125–26, 128, 153–54,
    156, 212n9
domestic roles of women, 143–44. See also
    gender and gender ideologies
Dongguan, China, 40
dress, standards of, 61
dual citizenship, 172

East Asia, 3
economy: and employment of Chinese
    spouses, 143–44, 152; and trade
    agreement, 193
educational DVD, 112–14, 116–18, 119
educational institutions, 31, 118
Empire's Borders I (2008–9), 1–2, 4, 5, 9, 10
employment: barriers to, 198n8; and
    Chinese husbands, 164–65; and
    citizenship, 171; delayed access to, 13–14,
    100, 155–56; and foreign migrant worker
    category, 84–86; and gender ideologies,
    143–44, 147–48, 152, 155–56, 158–59,
    165, 169; and marital authenticity, 143;
    policy revisions regarding, 210n19;
    protectionist justifications for bans on,
    155–56; and qualifications for work
    permits, 215n10; and residency status,
    210n19
Employment Services Act, 84, 85, 86
Entry/Exit Immigration Police Depart-
    ment, 54, 204n3
Europe, 146, 168–69, 214n5
European Union, 3
"Exit and Entry Permit," 33. See also
    documents, travel and identity

family reunification applications: and
    Chinese access to Taiwan, 31; and
    discriminatory attitudes, 44; material
    insubstantiality of, 44; as means to
    permanent immigration, 3; and policy
    revisions, 31, 198n10; and travel/identity
    documents, 33
Feldman, Ilana, 190
Fernando, Mayanthi, 146

fiancée visas, 114
financial requirement imposed on
    immigrants: opposition to, 93–96, *96*,
    100, 209n11; as portrayed in protest skit,
    98–99; revisions to, 209n11, 210n16
forgery concerns, 34, 39, 49
France, 18, 146
fraud marriages, 59–68, 77. *See also* marital
    authenticity
Fuzhounese, 48

gender and gender ideologies, 143–69; and
    caretaking marriages, 5–6; and
    childbearing, 155; China's gender
    egalitarianism, 146–47, 149–51; and
    Chinese husbands, 161–65; and
    dependency model of immigration, 144,
    147, 155, 167, 168; and divorce, 153–54;
    and domesticity expectations, 5–6,
    143–44, 147, 148, 149–52, 160, 168,
    215n12; and employment, 144, 147–48,
    152, 155–56, 158–59, 165, 169; and
    femininity models, 145, 157; and gender
    inequalities, 130, 153–55; and male-to-female
    gender ratio, 197n5; and marital
    authenticity, 145, 160, 168; and masculine
    dependence, 161–65; and middle-aged/
    older women, 156–61, 169, 215n13; and
    patriarchal/patrilineal values, 59, 105,
    130, 144–45; and standards of dress, 61
Germany, 146
Gershon, Ilana, 87
global hypergamy, 198n6
Guangdong Province, China, *40*

higher education, 118
*Hold Hands with Taiwan, Make a Date
    with Happiness* (DVD), 116–18
home and belonging, 170–92; and
    citizenship, 190–92; and claiming the
    right of home, 190; and fears of
    detachment, 171; and insecurity, 173–77;
    and international mobility, 184–88, 189;
    and local connections, 188–89; and
    pursuit of caring family and home,
    177–83; and sense of security, 190, 192;
    and temporality, 170–71, 176; and
    tenuous status of Chinese spouses, 191

Hong Kong, 32, 33, *40*, 43, 193–94, 208n4
Household Registration Office, 187
Hsieh Chang-ting, 51, 204n1
Huiling, 157–61
Hull, Matthew, 29
human rights, 89–92, 95–97, 101, 110,
    208n5
human smuggling, 60, 204n26
Hu Ying, 153–56

"ideal" families in Taiwan, 68, 72–73, 116,
    144–45, 165–66, 167
identity documents. *See* documents, travel
    and identity
immigration laws and policies, 81–111; and
    activism by NGOs, 89–93; and
    bureaucrats, 115; and chain immigra-
    tion, 102–10; and dependency model of
    immigration, 144, 155, 167, 168; and
    financial requirement, 93–96, *96*,
    98–99, 100, 209n11, 210n16; flexibility/
    inflexibility of, 120–21, 122–28, 129, 131,
    133, 134–35, 139; and gendered perfor-
    mances, 145; and human rights, 110; and
    ideal families, 68, 72–73, 116, 144–45,
    165–66, 167; Immigration Law (2007),
    9, 81–82, 88, 91, 93, 102; and mainland
    Chinese category, 84–86; as means to
    defining borders, 83; Nationality Law
    compared to, 168; and obtaining
    redress, 127; and "people of the
    mainland area" category, 87, 106, 110;
    and "persons of the Taiwan area"
    category, 103–4, 106, 110; and protests,
    89–90, 97–102, *98*, *99*, *101*, 208n6;
    publicizing human costs of, 106–9; and
    quotas, 99, 105, 106–7, 118, 186; reforms/
    revisions of, 119, 121, 127, 128, 130, 131,
    143, 155, 166; and reproductive care
    work, 161; and sovereignty claims of
    Taiwan, 83, 100–102, 115–18, 120–21,
    127–28; waiting time imposed by, 132,
    186, 198n12, 210n19. *See also* Act
    Governing Relations between the
    People of the Taiwan Area and the
    Mainland Area (1992); policy-education
    forums
Immigration Police, 55

inheritance, 210n19
in-laws, 113, 148, 151, 153–55, 178, 180
insecurity of immigrants, 173–77
intentions of marriage migrants, 53–58,
  60–62
Ireland, 204n27
Isin, Engin, 200n23

Japan, 3, 18–19, 42, 202n18
Jiang Meifeng, 42, 48, 202n18

Keelung, Taiwan, *xxiv*, 7

laborers from mainland China, 86, 207n2
Lai Shin-yuan, 110, 143
laws. *See* immigration laws and policies
Lee Yeou-Chi, 86
legal system in Taiwan. *See* immigration
  laws and policies
Legislative Yuan, 84–87, 109, 193
Liang Xiuyun, 148–50
Liao Lijing, 37–38, 41, 125, 126, 136
linguistic differences, 212n4
Liu, Mr., 162–63, 168
Li Yanhong, 184–89
Li Yuan-ming, 35–37, 201n12
love matches, 6
Lu, Mr., 28, 48, 200n2, 215n11
Luo Jing, 43, 45–46

Macau, *40*; and children of Chinese
  spouses, 124; as point of entry for
  Chinese spouses, 33; and travel/identity
  documents, 32, 38–39, *40*
mail order brides, 52. *See also* marital
  authenticity
Mainland Affairs Council (MAC): and
  children of Chinese spouses, 109;
  educational DVD produced by, 112–14,
  116, 119, 211nn1–2; and flexibility/
  inflexibility of policies, 123; and
  "persons of the Taiwan area" category,
  103; and policy-education forums, 119;
  promotional film of, 143–44, 165–66,
  167, 214n4; quota tables of, 106; and
  revisions to immigration policy, 88; role
  of, 88; special dispensations offered by,
  127, 166; and symposium hosted by

CARES, 114; on travel to/from China,
  200n4
mainland Chinese: and childbearing and
  status of mothers, 198n11; and foreign
  migrant worker category, 84–86;
  mainlander status, 22, 23, 42, 154; and
  "people of the mainland area" category,
  87, 106, 110. *See also* Chinese spouses
Maoism and Maoist era, 7, 91, 147, 157, 171
Mao Zedong, 10
marital authenticity, 51–77; and border
  interviews, 52, 58–68, 206n12;
  bureaucratic evaluation of, 52, 58–62,
  66; categories for distinguishing, 66;
  and characteristics of sham marriages,
  56; and childbearing, 137; and deferral
  of judgement, 62–68; and documentation to support, 55; and emotions, 58;
  and employment of Chinese spouses,
  143; estimated rates of sham marriages,
  51, 55, 76, 204n1; and gendered roles
  and performances, 145, 160, 168; and
  marital intentions, 53–58, 60–62;
  and motivations for marriage migration, 52;
  and norms of conduct, 58; public
  reactions to bureaucratic intrusions,
  73–77; and sexual relations, 55; and
  shared cultural conventions, 59–60;
  and therapeutic engagement of
  bureaucrats, 68–73; and training of
  Immigration Police, 55
marriage brokers and matchmaker-
  mediated courtships, 6, 62
Marriage Promotion Association, 97–98,
  100, 109, 186, 208n6
Ma Ying-jeou: campaign promises of, 102;
  and Chinese access to Taiwan, 31;
  cross-Strait agreements of, 194; and
  financial requirement, 210n16; and
  Hong Kong protests, 194; revisions to
  immigration sequence, 13; and travel to/
  from China, 201n8
Mazzarella, William, 199n17
McKeown, Adam, 47, 68, 72
medical tourism, 31
Meng Hua, 35–37, 201n11, 202n13
middle-aged/older Chinese women, 156–61,
  169, 215n13

Ministry of the Interior: and adoption of children, 124; and financial requirement, 100–101, 209n11, 210n16; and Mainland Affairs Council, 88; as portrayed in protest skit, 98, 100

mobility, international, 184–88, 189, 203n19

Mongia, Radhika, 203n22

motivations for marriage migration, 52, 59, 198n6

Munn, Nancy, 186

Muslim immigrant communities, 146, 169

National Health Insurance, 35

National Immigration Agency (NIA): and ambiguous China–Taiwan relationship, 133–34; Border Affairs Corps of, 28; and border interviews, 55, 56; on character of travel documents, 29; and childbearing's benefits, 136; and children of Chinese spouses, 108, 123–25; and employment of Chinese spouses, 155–56; and flexibility/inflexibility of policies, 120, 122–27, 139; and forgery concerns, 34; and identity documents, 179; and NGO activism, 90; and passport protocols, 27–28; and policy-education forums, 119–21, 123, 124; as portrayed in protest skit, 100; and protests against immigration policies, 100; public response to bureaucratic intrusions, 75–76; quota tables of, 103, 104, 106; and regulation of interviews, 66; and sham marriages, 53, 55; and Taiwanese sovereignty, 15–16; travel documents issued by, 33

Nationalist Party on Taiwan, 193, 194, 199n15, 201n8

Nationality Law of Republic of China, 11, 168, 198n9

National Security Bureau, 100

naturalization, 9, 198n12. See also residence and residency system

Navaro-Yashin, Yael, xiii, 31, 47, 201n10, 216n10

New Age Taiwanese (promotional film), 143

NGOs: activism by, 89–93, 208n6; concessions acquired by, 127; and policy-education forums, 119; and state actors, 114. See also Alliance for Human Rights Legislation for Immigrants and Migrants

norms of conduct, 58, 115

Nyers, Peter, 209n14

Occupy Central, 193

"one country, two systems" model, 133, 194

Ong, Aihwa, xiii, 92, 200n24

Palestinians, 190

Pang Pai-Hsien, 85

passports: loss of, 203n25; and Meng's court appearance, 36–37; misrecognition of, 48; and reentering Taiwan, 201n6; and sovereignty claims, 27, 31–32, 47, 203n22; stamping of, 27–28, 200n1; and states, 47; and travelers detained, 203nn23–24; and travel/identity documents, 29. See also documents, travel and identity

patriarchal/patrilineal values: and aims of immigration policies, 167; and border interviews, 59; and children of Chinese spouses, 105, 144; in China, 147; and Chinese husbands, 162–63; infused in immigration policies, 130; and Nationality Law, 198n9; and sense of home and belonging, 190; and traditional gender roles, 144, 149

"people of the mainland area" category, 87, 106, 110

People's Republic of China (PRC), xxiv; and civil war of China, 10, 15, 20; and gender egalitarianism, 146–47, 149–51; laborers from mainland, 86, 207n2; loss of citizenship in, 172, 174, 175–76; map of, 40; marriage statistics in, 198n7; and "one country, two systems" model, 133, 194; passports from, 27–28, 31; population control policies in, 147; socialist system of, 7, 19, 86, 91, 146–47, 157; and state surveillance of noncitizens, 177; and Taiwanese websites, 118; Taiwanese wives in, 150–51; and threat of similarity, 18–23; travel documents issued by, 32–33, 36; and travel to/from Taiwan, 30–33, 200n4; United Nations seat of, 15 "persons of the Taiwan area" category, 103–4, 106, 110

Pine, Frances, 171

policies. *See* immigration laws and policies

policy-education forums: and bureaucrats' advocacy for the state, 138; emotional narratives heard in, 120; and flexibility/ inflexibility of policies, 120–21, 122–27; format of, 119–20, *120*; and shared-heritage strategy of participants, 132–33. *See also* Taiwanese spouses

population management, international standards of, 3

postsecondary degrees, 118

Pratt, Geraldine, 195, 199n17

presidential campaign of 2008, 51

prostitution: and border interviews, 60–62, 64–65, 205n7; and employment bans, 156; and regulatory regime, 197n3

protests, 89–90, 97–102, *98*, *99*, *101*, 208n6

quotas, 99, 103–4, 107, 118, 186, 199n13

Republic of China (ROC): and civil war of China, 10–11; Constitution of, 10–11, 12. *See also* Taiwan

residence and residency system: and employment, 210n19; and Ma Ying-jeou administration, 13; Nationality Law on establishing, 11; and quotas, 99, 103–4, 107, 118, 186, 199n13; reform of, 12–13; residency permits, 44–46; stages of, 199n13; and Taiwanese spouses' sponsorship, 118–19; and travel/identity documents, 44–46; waiting time imposed by, 198n12

Rutherford, Danilyn, xiii, 117

Salter, Mark, 205n3

Schmitt, Carl, 15

security, sense of, 190

sexual relations in marriages, 55, 205n4

sex work: and border interviews, 60–62, 64–65, 205n7; and employment bans, 156; and regulatory regime, 197n3

sham marriages, 73–77. *See also* marital authenticity

Shanghai, 151

Shenzhen, China, *40*

Shih Shu-mei, 19

Shuman, Amy, 58

Shyu Jong-Shyoung, 102

similarity, threat of, 18–23, 87, 132–33

snakehead organizations, 60, 64

socialist system of China: and assumptions about mainlanders, 7; and gender ideologies, 146–47; and mainland laborers, 86; and progressive NGO activism, 91; and traits of Chinese population, 19, 157

social networking, 6

societal norms, 112

Southeast Asian spouses, 20

South Korea, 3, 18–19, 43

sovereignty (general), 14–18; Agamben on, 15–16; fears of waning, 14; means of affirming sovereign status, 14; Schmitt's scholarship on, 15; and violence, 15

sovereignty of Taiwan, 139; ambiguity in, 5; de facto sovereignty, 13, 14–15, 24, 47–48, 199n16; and evaluation of marriage authenticity, 53–54; and human rights, 89; "as if" sovereignty, 18, 20, 195; and immigration bureaucracy, 4, 14–18, 28, 133–34, 139; and immigration laws and policies, 83, 100–102, 115–18, 120–21, 127–28; and national anxieties, 18; and passports, 27, 31–32, 47, 200n1, 203n22; role of Chinese spouses in producing, 4, 17–18, 22–23, 53–54, 83, 115–16, 139, 194–95

spies, 100, 177

stereotypes, 6

Straits Exchange Foundation (SEF), 178

Sunflower Student Movement, 193

surveillance of noncitizens, 177

Taipei District Criminal Court, 36

Taiwan, *xxiv*; China's contested relationship with, 4, 81–82, 133; economic development of, 86; elections in, 51, 194; evaluation of marriages in (*see* marital authenticity); government websites of, 118; Hong Kong compared to, 194; immigration bureaucracy of (*see* border interviews; bureaucrats and immigration

Taiwan (continued)
  bureaucracy; documents, travel and
    identity); immigration law of (see
    immigration laws and policies);
    international recognition of, 4; and
    Legislative Yuan, 84–87, 109, 193; and
    misrecognition of passports, 48–49;
    national identity of, 7, 8, 21; native
    populations of, 20–21, 199n18, 207n2;
    and passport stamp, 27–28, 200n2;
    significance of cross-Strait marriages to,
    xiv, 2; temporary migrant workers in, 3;
    and threat of similarity, 18–23; and
    tourism, 31, 201n5; and trade agreement,
    193; and travel to/from China, 30–33,
    200n4; and United Nations, 15, 89, 98,
    199n16. See also Republic of China
Taiwan Compatriot Pass, 32, 187, 201n7. See
    also documents, travel and identity
Taiwanese spouses: affective skills of,
    151–52, 214n8; and border interviews,
    64; and caretaking marriages trend, 5–6,
    62, 160, 166, 184–85; death of, 122–23,
    128–29, 132, 176, 185–86; desirability of,
    151–52; gender of, 6; and immigration
    status of wives, 118–19, 185; and marital
    evaluations, 54–55, 56, 57; role of, in
    immigration regime, 161; and sexual
    exploitation, 64–65; state's reinforce-
    ment of power of, 126; stereotypes of, 6
Tao Weihong, 73–74, 125, 136–38, 213n22
Taoyuan Airport Border Affairs Corps, 55
temporality of migration, 170–71, 176, 186
temporary migrant workers, 3, 9
third-country travel, 41, 202n17
time calculations used in immigration
    process, 12–13
Torpey, John, 31, 47, 204n28
tourism, 31, 201n5
transience, feelings of, 171
travel documents. See documents, travel
    and identity
"travel passes," 32. See also documents,
    travel and identity

Umbrella Movement, 193
United Kingdom, 204n27

United Nations, 89, 96, 98, 199n16
United States, 2–3, 42, 49

veterans in Taiwan: and Cross-Strait
    Marriage Promotion Association,
    89–90; and financial requirement,
    209n11; financial situations of, 160; and
    gender expectations, 152; and immigra-
    tion bureaucracy, 5–6, 76; and
    middle-aged/older women, 157, 161; in
    promotional films, 166; and threat of
    widowhood, 95, 186; unmarried status
    of, 197n2
visas, 2, 12, 29, 32, 48. See also documents,
    travel and identity

Wang, Horng-luen, 203n24
Wang Fei, 177–83, 216nn4–6
Weber, Max, 47
Wei Liping, 148–49, 150
widowhood: denial of citizenship
    applications, 14, 129, 185–86; and
    financial insecurity, 176; and
    inflexibility of policies, 122–23; and
    potential for policy reforms, 128–29;
    and revisions to immigration policy,
    212n8, 213n16; waiting time imposed
    by, 132
Wilson, Richard, 208n5
World Health Organization (WHO), 15
Wu Yan, 38–39, 40, 202n16

Xiao Hong, 74–75, 173–77, 216nn1–3
Xiao Lin Beauty Company, 162

Yu, James, 194
Yuan Mei, 74–75, 170, 174
Yu Hua, 108–10

Zeng Limeng, 175, 176, 190
Zhang Zhen, 186, 188, 190–92, 216n11
Zhu, Mr.: on forged documents, 34, 39; on
    identification of sham marriages,
    60–62; on passports, 27–28, 31, 48; on
    visa to Canada, 49
Zhuhai, Guangdong Province, China,
    39, 40